PROACTIVE PROCUREMENT

The Key to Increased Profits, Productivity, and Quality

PROACTIVE PROCUREMENT

The Key to Increased Profits, Productivity, and Quality

DAVID N. BURT
School of Business Administration
University of San Diego

PRENTICE-HALL, INC., Englewood Cliffs, N.J. 07632

Library of Congress Cataloging in Publication Data

Burt, David N.
  Proactive procurement.

  Includes index.
  1. Industrial procurement. 2. Purchasing. I. Title.
HD39.5.B87 1984   658.7′2   83-11239
ISBN 0-13-711465-6

Editorial/production supervision and
  interior design: Barbara Grasso
Cover design: Jeannette Jacobs
Manufacturing buyer: Ed O'Dougherty

This book is available to businesses and organizations at a special discount
when ordered in large quantities. For information, contact Prentice-Hall, Inc.,
General Book Marketing, Special Sales Division, Englewood Cliffs, N.J. 07632.

Printed in the United States of America

10 9 8 7 6 5 4 3

ISBN 0-13-711465-6

Prentice-Hall International, Inc., *London*
Prentice-Hall of Australia Pty. Limited, *Sydney*
Editora Prentice-Hall do Brasil, Ltda., *Rio de Janeiro*
Prentice-Hall Canada Inc., *Toronto*
Prentice-Hall of India Private Limited, *New Delhi*
Prentice-Hall of Japan, Inc., *Tokyo*
Prentice-Hall of Southeast Asia Pte. Ltd., *Singapore*
Whitehall Books Limited, *Wellington, New Zealand*

CONTENTS

12

How To Ensure Timely Delivery of the Right Quality   185

Organizing and Staffing for Subcontract Administration / Planning and Preparing for Subcontract Administration / Managing for Timely Delivery / Ensuring Receipt of the Right Quality / Scope of Warranties / Inspection / The Economics of Inspection and Quality Control / Summary

13

Purchasing and the External Environment   202

Strategic Purchasing / The Advantages of Collaboration / The Development and Management of Vendors / Personal and Organizational Ethics / Trade Relations and Reciprocity / Relations with Vendors During Periods of Shortages / Summary

14

The Procurement Audit   217

Organization, Policies, and Procedures / The Requirements Process / Selecting the Right Source / Getting the Right Price / Subcontract Administration / Other Important Issues / A Few Closing Words

Index   229

PREFACE

The 1980s are the years of the *revitalization of industry*. Managers everywhere recognize the need to increase profits or, in some cases, to become profitable once again. They know that productivity must increase. They know that to compete in the world marketplace, they must improve the quality of their firms' products.

There are abundant solutions to the challenge of industrial revitalization: computer-aided design (CAD), computer-assisted manufacturing (CAM), quality circles, Theory Z; the list seems endless. But the simplest and quickest solution all too frequently is overlooked. It can be exciting, provocative, and challenging. Its impact can exceed all the benefits of CAD, CAM, quality circles, and Theory Z. It is called the *integrated procurement system*.

The procurement of material and services is a process that cuts across organizational boundaries. The process includes activities in marketing, engineering, operations, production planning, quality assurance, inventory control, purchasing, and finance. Integration of the procurement activities performed by these departments results in a synergism, a situation where the whole is greater than the sum of its parts. This type of integration and the resulting synergism takes place in many settings: manufacturing, service firms, not-for-profit organizations, government, and construction firms. The net result for all is greatly increased profitability, productivity, and quality.

Implementation of an integrated procurement system results in proactive procurement, as distinguished from reactive purchasing. With proactive procurement, all members of the procurement system—whether forecasters in marketing, designers and cost estimators in engineering, planners and inventory managers, quality assurance personnel, the purchasing staff, and others—recognize their role in the procurement system. And they cooperate in making the organization more profitable through more effective procurement. With this proactive approach, the purchasing department is involved in the requirements process where it provides input on the commercial implications of alternate materials and services. The purchasing department takes the initiative in *making* savings happen throughout the procurement system. In reactive purchasing, the purchasing department becomes involved in the procurement process only on receipt of a requisition for materials, supplies, or services. Under both approaches, purchasing is responsible for source selection, pricing, and expediting.

An integrated procurement system is *the* key to increased profits and productivity and is the quickest way to improve product quality. The success of the integrated procurement system in improving profits, productivity, and quality is largely determined during three separate yet interdependent activities: (1) the determination of what, when, and how much to buy; (2) the determination of the proper source, contract type, and correct price to pay; and (3) the management of the resulting purchase order to ensure on-time availability at the specified quality level. For these activities to be performed effectively and efficiently, many related tasks must be accomplished.

Successful integration of the system leading to proactive procurement requires dedication, a "can do" attitude, qualified managers and subordinates, and an understanding of sound procurement techniques.

This book outlines and discusses the steps required to develop and implement successfully an integrated procurement system. Forty-five specific problems that frequently block effective procurement are identified together with suggestions for avoiding or overcoming them. The book is written with the objective of aiding busy managers in their efforts to increase the success of their organizations.

This book will aid you in many ways. It

- Creates an awareness of the benefits resulting from implementation of an integrated procurement system
- Shows you how to develop and sell your integrated system, including advice on how to overcome resistance to the required changes
- Provides understanding of the *key* procurement activities so that *all* individuals involved in procurement understand their responsibilities and those of their counterparts
- Identifies and addresses 45 problems or problem areas that result in ineffective procurement

- Identifies 6 points in the engineering design process at which purchasing can make a contribution to the profitability of the firm
- Describes how the procurement system can improve the quality of your firm's products
- Shows how to integrate engineering into the procurement system
- Portrays the cost implications of alternate approaches to describing requirements and shows how to conduct procurement research systematically
- Shows how to improve purchasing lead time and how to live with material requirements planning
- Provides insight into the conflicting forces that should be considered when developing inventory policies
- Tells when make-or-buy analyses should be conducted and discusses the issues that should be considered
- Discusses issues to be considered when dealing with vendors in foreign countries and lists several critical cultural nuances to consider in such dealings
- Describes the keys to successful negotiations in concise and understandable language and discusses the role of nonpurchasing members of the negotiating team
- Tells how to develop and implement a profit contributing value analysis program
- Shows how to ensure timely delivery of the prescribed quality
- Describes the benefits resulting from purchasing's involvement in the corporate planning process
- Tells how to develop a strategic material plan
- Describes the benefits from purchaser-supplier collaboration and long-term relations
- Shows how to develop and manage competent suppliers
- Analyzes the pros and cons of trade relations
- Shows how to minimize the impact of material shortages
- Introduces a comprehensive list of questions to be used when conducting an audit of the procurement system
- And much more!

ACKNOWLEDGMENTS

This book is an outgrowth of more than 25 years of experience as a practitioner, professor, and student of procurement. It is based on the belief that proactive procurement is the key to greatly improved profits, productivity, and product quality.

While written for the purchasing manager, *Proactive Procurement: The Key to Increased Profits, Productivity, and Quality* has considerable relevance for top management. The understanding and support of senior management will greatly facilitate implementation of the recommended improvements.

Many people have contributed directly or indirectly to the development of this book. My first and greatest teachers were two people who "worked for me" in my first two purchasing offices during the 1950s: Dick Curtis and Ed Williams. Many people in academia have played significant roles in the development of my understanding of business activities: George W. Zinke and Ruben A. Zubrow of the University of Colorado; Clyde Johnson and Normal Maier at the University of Michigan; and Bob Davis, Gayton F. Germane, Lamar Lee, Jr., and Steve Wheelwright at Stanford University. Colleagues during my days in Dayton—Joe Boyett, Dean Martin, Frank Stickney, Ted Thompson, and Bob Trimble—played key roles in the development of my philosophy and insight into the procurement process. Steve Achtenhagen, Mel Kline, Bill Little, Jack and Cathy Bergquist, and the late Ed Cochran and Gail Murray all provided guidance and inspiration as the project developed and grew.

Many individuals in industry have provided assistance: Ralph Dixon of Hughes Aircraft provided invaluable input and counsel; Richard Y. Moss II of Hewlett-Packard developed the charts describing the engineering design process depicted in Chapter 2; and Evelyn Szabo of Megateck was the source of great assistance. In addition, others in industry gave freely of their time: Nick Alex of NCR; Richard Baribault and his staff at Alcoa; Tony Derczo of Rohr Industries; Kenneth Gay and Bob Peterson of Rockwell International; James M. Hill of Raytheon; Bill Lambert of Boeing; Gordon Olson, Malcom Smith, Don Taylor, and John Veterren of Hewlett-Packard; Bob Paul of Lockheed; Myron Schwartz of Memorix; Bob Reynolds of McDonnell Douglas; Andrew Scanlon of Hobart; James Walz of General Electric; D. C. Weinstein and Larry Michael of Westinghouse; John Kelsey and Dick West of the Ford Motor Company; Dick Erskine of the Bechtel group; John Zech of Kaiser Engineering; and Harry Wright of FMC.

Deans James Burns and Robert O'Neil of the University of San Diego provided both support and encouragement. And I was truly blessed with a most perceptive, helpful, and diplomatic editor, Ted Jursek. Joanne Cote, Linda Teplitz, and Angie Walters provided both cheerful and professional typing and outstanding graphic support.

My wife, Sharon, provided scholarly advice, counsel, Table 3.1, and much encouragement.

PROACTIVE PROCUREMENT

The Key to Increased Profits, Productivity, and Quality

chapter one

INTEGRATING THE PROCUREMENT SYSTEM

It is Saturday afternoon, September 6. Ted Jones, purchasing manager for the Eagle Manufacturing Company, is in his office reviewing his life at Eagle. Since becoming the head of purchasing, Ted has been struggling with one crisis after another while trying to placate operations, plant maintenance, and seemingly half the management team (and their secretaries). Although only 35, Ted feels like 60. (His wife thinks he's starting to act like 60, too.) Eagle is expecting a great deal for the money it is paying Ted.

In the two years since taking over the department, Ted has put together a great team of buyers, expediters, and support staff. Their work is tops . . . they are all professionals. But morale has started to be a problem. On Friday, Bill Wilson, Ted's senior buyer, submitted his resignation. Bill decided to take a job with a handsome salary increase at Cable Manufacturers of America. He said, "If I'm going to get ulcers, I might as well be paid for them!"

Ted looks at the August performance data for the office: 743 transactions, 98% with delivery dates on or before specified, 87% of supplies and material purchases at or within 5% of target price, 9% late deliveries, and a 5% rejection rate of materials and supplies received. When compared with previous months' activity, the trends look good, but there is still room for improvement. Ted feels that his department can have a much greater impact on the firm's profitability if only he can generate more cooperation with the other departments. He also realizes that a better training program will bring along some of his own people a bit faster.

Ted thought about some of the "big ones" that had happened in August. The maintenance department had submitted a purchase request for a new robot on August 29. The machine, according to the estimates supplied, would cost $2.2 million. The machine was to be delivered and operational in seven months. Only one source of supply had been able to meet the delivery date. Ted wondered how much extra money the lack of lead time had cost on that one.

Tim Raines, vice president of operations, had held Ted's feet to the coals in the weekly staff meeting on August 7. Operations had run out of parts that week. The vice president of marketing, Ron Hankins, had helped to apply the coals on that one. In retrospect, Ted was puzzled over the hop-scotch communication patterns among operations, material control, market-ing, and his own office.

Tim jumped Ted on August 14, again during the staff meeting, saying that quality on the incoming parts was causing major production problems. Ted tried to explain the greater attrition rate inherent in new production processes, but Tim was not convinced.

In fairness, not all his problems were with operations, Ted thought during this Saturday afternoon reverie. The president's secretary had called twice to say that the janitorial services contractor had not washed the win-dows properly. Ted mentioned that poorly described, unenforceable specifi-cations were part of the problem. But the secretary was just trying to do her job in seeing that somebody else's job was done right . . . she didn't know about the "contractual provisions."

Mary Jacobs, head of administration, had been complaining to Ted on a daily basis about the new brand of reproduction paper. It seemed the quality of reproduction was down and the paper was constantly jamming the ma-chine. That downtime was reducing productivity and increasing frustration with her people. Ted pointed out that finance had reduced funds available for supplies by 20% and that this consequently had forced some sacrifice in quality.

Yesterday, John McCauly, an experienced buyer and normally as cool as a cucumber, had exploded when Ted asked how everything was going. John had replied, "Those blankety, blank estimators. This morning, I was negotiating with Fenwick Electronics for that robot. The maintenance depart-ment's estimate was $2.2 million. Fenwick proposed $2.9 million. You know that because of time, they were already in a 'sole-source' position. Imagine my reaction when I learned that our $2.2 million 'estimate' was not an esti-mate at all but merely the amount budgeted for that machine last year! I had no basis for developing a realistic negotiating objective. I literally had to throw myself on the mercy of Fenwick's marketing manager."

Bringing his thoughts back to the present, Ted decided there just had to be a better way.

Extreme? Perhaps. Perhaps not. But all managers have experienced many of these problems. There is a way of avoiding most of them, and, in turn helping the purchasing department contribute a greater input to profitability. That way is the *integrated procurement system (IPS)*. And *you* can and should be responsible for making it happen.

THE INTEGRATED PROCUREMENT SYSTEM

Procurement is the systematic process of deciding what, when, and how much to purchase; the act of purchasing it; and the process of ensuring that what is required is received on time in the quantity and quality specified. Procurement is much broader than purchasing, involving activities that take place in many departments.

The quantity, quality, and price of purchased items affect the quality of the firm's product, the ability to produce it, productivity, and, most important, the firm's profitability. Determination of what to buy does not begin when the purchase requisition is written but, rather, with the decision to produce the product. Early involvement of purchasing can avoid these common situations:

- The manufacture of technically excellent products that are too costly to survive in the marketplace
- The purchase of large volumes of materials at quantity discounts resulting in high inventory carrying costs
- Inventory reductions that result in manufacturing downtime due to stock outages
- Slower modes of transportation used to save transportation dollars but resulting in large inventory carrying costs or manufacturing downtime

Organizations exercise the best control over the cost of purchased goods and services only when the various departments involved in the process operate as an interdependent, integrated system. When this happens, a synergism takes place with the result of the integrated efforts becoming greater than the sum of the individual efforts. On the other hand, uncoordinated action by one department may optimize the success of that department while causing undesirable results in another, to the detriment of the organization as a whole. For example, incorporation of extremely high tolerances may result in a product of great excellence but a product that is too costly to survive in the marketplace. The purchase of large quantities of materials or supplies may result in lower unit prices through quantity discounts. But increased inventory carrying costs will result. Conversely, inventories may be reduced in an effort to lower carrying costs, resulting in downtime in manufacturing due to stock out-

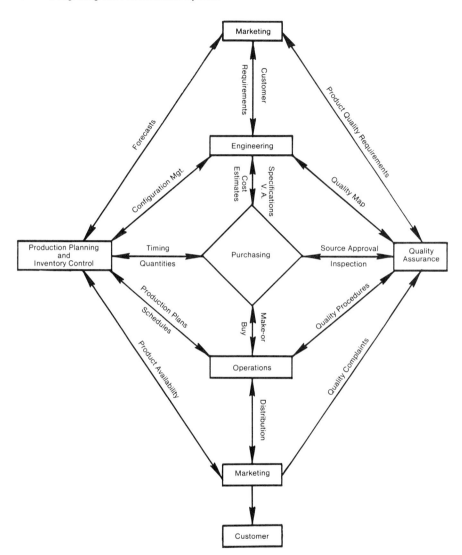

FIGURE 1.1   The Many Interfaces of the Integrated Procurement System

ages, more frequent purchases at higher unit costs, or both. Slower modes of transportation may save shipping dollars but result in larger inventories or downtimes in manufacturing. The many interfaces and interdependencies of the IPS are portrayed in Figure 1.1 and are discussed throughout this book.

Implementation of an IPS results in proactive procurement, as distinguished from reactive purchasing. With proactive procurement, all members of the procurement system—whether forecasters in marketing, designers and cost estimators in engineering, production planners and inventory managers, quality assurance personnel, the purchasing staff, and others—recognize their role in the procurement system. And they cooperate in making the organization more profitable through more effective procurement. With this proactive approach, the purchasing department is involved in the requirements process where it provides input on the commercial implications of alternate materials, equipment, and services. The purchasing department takes the initiative in making savings happen throughout the procurement system. In reactive purchasing, the purchasing department becomes involved in the procurement process only on receipt of a requisition for materials, supplies, or services. Under both approaches, purchasing is responsible for source selection, pricing, and expediting. An integrated procurement system is the key to increased profits and productivity and is the quickest way to quality improvement.

During the design stage in the development of a product, incorporation of the "right" material to be purchased results in a significant reduction in material expenditures. For example, with purchasing's help,

- A manufacturer found that a zinc alloy was an acceptable alternative to a high-leaded tin-bronze casting alloy under consideration. The zinc alloy cost one-half the price of the tin-bronze alternate.
- Another manufacturer found that a synthetic insulation material was far superior to asbestos in the production of high-temperature hose lines. The synthetic material cost one-third as much as the asbestos and avoided the latter's hazards.
- An appliance manufacturer found molded plastic knobs to be suitable alternates to machined metal knobs, at a savings of 85%.

Market share, prices, and profits are all favorably affected by attention to quality. Today, *quality has replaced price as the key to increased market share and profit margins.* Procurement of materials of the right quality frequently is the quickest and easiest way to improve the quality of the final product. Procurement of the right quality of materials is far more likely to occur when a firm operates under an IPS than under the traditional reactive approach. For example,

- An electronics manufacturer was able to reduce rework and warranty expenses by over 50% through consideration of supplier quality capabilities during the design process.
- A T.V. manufacturer reduced field failure and warranty expenses by 45% by specifying a more appropriate level of quality for purchased components during the redesign of a T.V. set.

The use of the right purchase description can have a major impact on quality and costs. An electronics manufacturer converted from use of his own custom-designed specifications to commercial standards, resulting in savings in excess of 10%. The use of performance specifications to describe the anticipated function of capital equipment allows an organization to solicit competitive prices resulting in significant savings. The correct method of specifying construction services has a great impact on reducing expenditures in this unique area.

The make-or-buy analysis is an extremely important component of the IPS and a major profit contributor. The decision to make or to buy is one of the most challenging and critical issues to confront management. Great amounts of money are wasted making goods and services that could be purchased more economically, and great amounts of money are wasted buying those things that properly should be made by the firm.

Expenditures for goods and services bought by the purchasing department can be reduced significantly. For example, the right degree of competition, proper execution of negotiations, and implementation of a

FIGURE 1.2   Effect of Quality of Purchased Material on Productivity and Profits

	Manhours	Standard Materials (in 1,000)	Manhours	High Quality Materials (in 1,000)
Sales (10,000 units)		$325		$325
Cost of Goods Sold:				
Purchased Materials		100		110
Labor (production)	3,000	30	3,000	30
Labor (fault finding and rework)	12,000	120	6,000	60
Fixed		20		20
Total Costs	15,000	$270	9,000	$220
Operating Income		$ 55		$105

Note 1:   Productivity improvement (Productivity is defined as the number of units produced per manhour.)
Standard Materials: 15,000 hours to produce 10,000 units = .67 units per manhour.
High Quality Materials: 9,000 hours to produce 10,000 units = 1.11 units per manhour.
Productivity improvement = change in output per manhour ÷ by original output = $|(.67-1.11)/.67|$ = 65% improvement.

Note 2:   Profit improvement: $|(55-105)/55|$ = 91%.

Note 3:   This is a rather conservative analysis wherein it is assumed that a higher level of quality of purchased material will result in greater material expenditures.   In many instances, this may not be necessary.

sound value analysis program all result in reduced expenditures. Additional savings result from selection and effective management of the right source—one that provides the right level of service, one that is dependable to the point where inventory can be reduced safely, and one that provides the specified level of quality. Unfortunately, *the savings that can be achieved by a reactive purchasing department generally are constrained by activities that have taken place before purchasing becomes responsible for the procurement.*

The very survival of the organization may be affected by the presence or absence of a viable strategic material plan. Under the myopic approach of traditional reactive purchasing, the firm may awaken one day to a world in which sources of supply capable of meeting its requirements are unavailable. *The IPS includes strategic material planning as a key responsibility and helps to avoid such situations.*

The implementation of an integrated proactive approach to procurement can have a significant impact on productivity. For example, all too many of the quality problems encountered in manufacturing are the result of defective purchased material. Their common sources are the inefficiencies of the procurement system: specifications that call for the wrong level of quality, selection of the wrong source, or inadequate quality assurance and inspection. Recently, the plant manager of a leading electronics manufacturer stated that if deficiencies in incoming material could be eliminated, he could increase throughput at his plant by 400% with no increase in equipment or labor.[1] The savings may far offset the incremental cost of materials, as shown in Figure 1.2.

The selection of the right material during design also will have a significant impact directly on productivity and manufacturing costs (and, in turn, on profits). Some materials are much more economical to work than others. For example, selection of bronze rather than lower-priced steel will greatly reduce machining costs. The savings may far offset the incremental cost of materials, as shown in Figure 1.3.

Productivity also is affected by procurement of the "right" supplies, capital equipment, services, and plant. The additional cost for the right item of capital equipment may be offset many times through increased productivity, whether in a manufacturing, service, governmental, or construction setting. As Ted saw, procurement of a low-grade copy paper may reduce purchase expenditures but result in reduced secretarial productivity and additional copier maintenance expense.

---

[1]These defects resulted from the requirement for purchased components whose production processes had not stabilized. Defects in the purchased components could not be detected until the final assembly in which they were incorporated was tested. Specification of more proven components could have had relatively little effect on performance of the end product but would have avoided the vast majority of test and rework, thereby resulting in much greater productivity!

	Manhours	Costs (steel)	Manhours	Costs (bronze)
Sales		$100		$100
Costs of Goods Sold				
Raw material cost		5		10
Direct Labor (machining)	2	30	1	15
Variable overhead		6		3
Fixed overhead		50		50
		$ 91		$ 78
Operating Income		9		22

Note 1: Productivity Improvement: $|(.5-1.0)/.5|$ = 100% improvement

Note 2: Profit Improvement: $|(9-22)/9|$ = 144% improvement

FIGURE 1.3   Effect of Different Materials on Productivity and Costs

- A local hospital formerly used a nonacrylic wax for its floors. The floors were waxed on a daily basis and required frequent labor-intensive stripping to reduce the effect of wax buildup. Conversion to an acrylic wax reduced the requirement for waxing from one to three days. In a sense, janitorial productivity increased threefold!
- Two seemingly similar lathes may have very different actual capacities and maintenance requirements, greatly affecting productivity.
- A typewriter with an easy erase feature greatly increases the productivity of the average secretary.

Service contracts have become a popular way of obtaining janitorial services, security guard services, transportation, and cafeteria services. Emergency rooms and pharmacies are operated under contracts at some hospitals. The quality and enforceability of the provisions and resulting contracts affect both the quality of services received and the personnel required to administer the contracts.

Procurement of the "right" type of construction affects productivity. Several years ago an electronics manufacturer purchased two new manufacturing plants. One building consisted of two stories. The second plant consisted of one story and was cooled by 70 unit air conditioners located on the building's roof. Productivity in the two plants was significantly different! In the first plant, the two-story construction posed material handling and management problems. Further, the central air conditioner became inoperable on several occasions, resulting in the closure of the entire plant. None of these problems existed at the second plant. Needless to say, productivity there was considerably higher as a result of selection of the proper purchase method.

HOW MUCH CAN BE SAVED?

Discussions were held recently with executives responsible for purchasing at 10 major manufacturing organizations. Annual sales at these organizations ranged from $200 million to in excess of $8 billion. The more significant components of an IPS were described. Next, the traditional reactive approach to purchasing was discussed. Several of the executives indicated that they were familiar with firms that operate in this reactive mode. One executive stated that a recently acquired subsidiary had operated in this traditional reactive fashion "before I got my hands on it."

The executives were requested to estimate the savings resulting from the transformation of a reactive orientation into the proactive one that underlies the IPS. Estimates of total potential savings ranged from 6% to 30%. Several executives offered the belief that, while the savings potential was approximately the same for all sizes of firms, implementation of the IPS would be relatively easier in smaller firms. These executives felt that two areas of major savings potential were especially critical: adequate purchasing lead time and incorporation, during the design stage, of the right material to be purchased.

FIVE APPROACHES TO DOUBLING PROFITS

Virtually all managers want to improve the performance of their organizations. For profit-making organizations, profits are a key indicator of performance. For government and other not-for-profit organizations, budgets reflecting successful cost control are common indicators of performance. The principle contained in the following example is easily transferable to any of these organizations. A hypothetical situation with our friends at Eagle Manufacturing emphasizes the profit-making potential of procurement.

Eagle has a product line with a sales volume of $1 million and expenses as shown:

Sales	$1,000,000
Purchased material	500,000
Labor	250,000
Overhead	200,000
Profit	$ 50,000

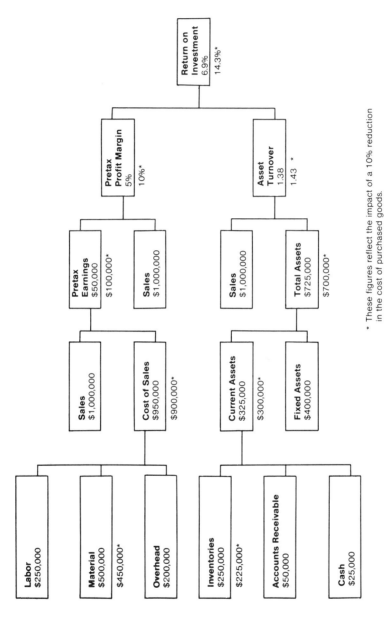

FIGURE 1.4 Effect of Purchasing Savings on Return on Investment

* These figures reflect the impact of a 10% reduction in the cost of purchased goods.

10

Eagle desires to double its profits to $100,000. This may be accomplished in any of the following five ways:

Increase sales	100%
Increase prices	5
Decrease labor costs	20
Decrease overhead	25
Decrease material costs	10

In most organizations, it is far easier to reduce purchasing expenditures for materials and services by 10% than it is to double sales, decrease labor costs 20%, decrease overhead 25%, or increase prices 5% in a competitive market. Thus, we see that an investment in reducing purchasing expenditures will have a great impact on the organization's profitability. If we consider reduced quality, rework, field warranty, and inventory carrying costs resulting from implementation of an IPS, the savings and profit impact will be even greater.

The return on investment (ROI) impact of a 10% reduction in the cost of goods purchased can be even more impressive, since such a savings affects both the pretax profit margin and the asset turnover rate.

Figure 1.4 shows the effect of such a savings on return on investment at Eagle under the following conditions: inventory turnover rate is four times per year, accounts receivable is $50,000, cash on hand is $50,000, and fixed assets are $400,000. Figure 1.4 shows that ROI more than doubles (from 6.9% to 14.3%) as a result of a 10% reduction in purchasing expenditures.

THE INTEGRATED PROCUREMENT SYSTEM IN DIFFERENT SETTINGS

The IPS is truly a broad, pervasive, united effort that involves all major units of a business enterprise. It is a system of great interaction and interdependency. The IPS does not depend on any one organizational structure. It works in organizations such as manufacturing firms, hospitals, and government.

Manufacturing Firms

The IPS begins in design engineering when concepts calling for alternate materials are being considered in response to new product ideas developed by marketing (see Figure 1.5). This is the point at which good procurement commences. It continues as specifications are developed or adopted.

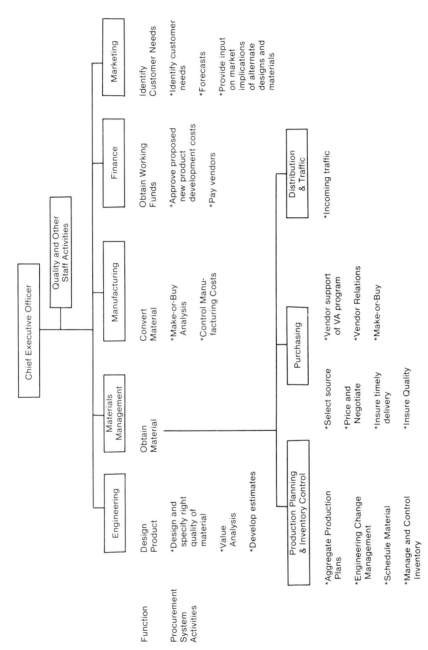

FIGURE 1.5 The Functional Organization and the Integrated Procurement System: Manufacturing

12

Quality assurance should review proposed design specifications and manufacturing plans to ensure that the quality called for by marketing is the quality that will result if engineering's design is followed. During the source selection process, quality assurance is involved in determining a prospective supplier's ability to comply with specifications. Quality assurance also is involved in ensuring that the quality of incoming materials is as specified on the purchase order or contract.

The IPS moves on to a determination of the timing of and quantities on the resulting purchase order. Although make-or-buy analyses should be made periodically throughout the process of manufacture or purchase of an item, the most critical make-or-buy analysis should take place before the first item is manufactured or purchased.

After a decision to purchase an item or service has been made, the purchasing department becomes responsible for selecting the right source, pricing (including negotiation, if appropriate), and issuing the purchase order. Then purchasing must take action to ensure that the item or service is received on time and in the quality specified. To provide its maximum contribution to the well-being of the enterprise, purchasing must actively develop and manage sources of supply to ensure that an adequate number of qualified suppliers is available now, and in the future.

Finance is responsible for timely payment to suppliers after delivery of the material. Finance monitors the firm's investment in inventory. In a well-run organization, finance closely controls working capital and cash flows, based in large part on sales forecasts and accurate purchasing delivery schedules.

In a sense, marketing begins and ends the IPS activities. Marketing identifies the need for the item to be developed by engineering that leads to a requirement for purchased material. Marketing is responsible for the sale and delivery to the customer of the item that incorporates the purchased material. Purchasing must maintain a good dialogue with marketing on changes in material prices and availability to allow marketing to update sales quotations and current selling prices. Purchasing may have information that will influence marketing's plans for future changes in its product lines.

Service Organizations

As with manufacturing firms, no one organizational chart can represent all service activities. However, the organization for a hospital in Figure 1.6 provides a vehicle for the discussion of the IPS in a service setting.

Purchasing normally is responsible for 30% to 50% of the expenditures of a service organization. For hospitals, the expenditure for capital

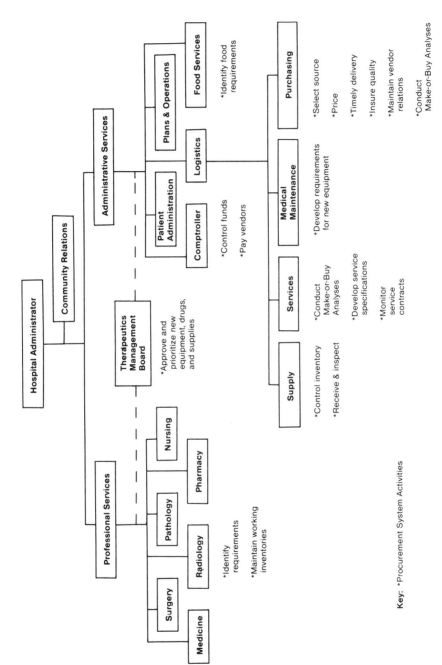

FIGURE 1.6 The Functional Organization and the Integrated Procurement System: Hospitals

equipment, drugs, utilities, and supplies approximates 33% of the annual budget. If food services, janitorial services, operation of the pharmacy, and similar services are obtained through contracts, this figure may increase to 50% of the hospital's budget.

The vast majority of a hospital's expenditures are of a repetitive nature. In most instances, standards, descriptions, and stock levels for drugs, medical supplies, and administrative supplies already have been established.

Requirements for new equipment, new drugs, or new supplies need to be controlled. Hospitals are confronted by funding limitations and have the same need to standardize as do other organizations. The Therapeutics Management Board (TMB) shown in Figure 1.6 is responsible for the review, approval, and ordering of priorities of all requests for capital equipment, drugs, and supplies not previously approved. The TMB consists of representatives of both Professional Services and Administrative Services (including purchasing). Once an item has been approved by the TMB and funds are made available, purchasing becomes responsible for the procurement.

Many hospitals frequently purchase some of their services such as food services, janitorial services, radiology services, the operation of the pharmacy, and similar services. Decisions to purchase services are the result of one or both of two forces: the nonavailability of qualified personnel or the cost savings resulting in purchasing from an efficient specialist. When cost savings are used to justify a request to contract for services, a make-or-buy analysis, as described in Chapter 7, should be conducted.

The development of specifications for such a service is the responsibility of the services branch of the logistics division shown in Figure 1.6. The development of such specifications and the monitoring of the resulting contract are extremely challenging responsibilities. These functions are discussed in Chapter 4.

Government

There are over 80,000 government bodies in the United States with the power to spend public funds. For a number of historic and political reasons, no single approach to organizing the agencies and departments charged with providing government services has evolved. Figure 1.7 depicts an organizational approach that results in grouping the many departments and agencies into six "systems," each accomplishing similar activities. Under each system are listed representative departments or agencies. In most governments, any of these departments or agencies may initiate requirements (within budgetary constraints) that will be acted on by purchasing. Each department or agency develops specifica-

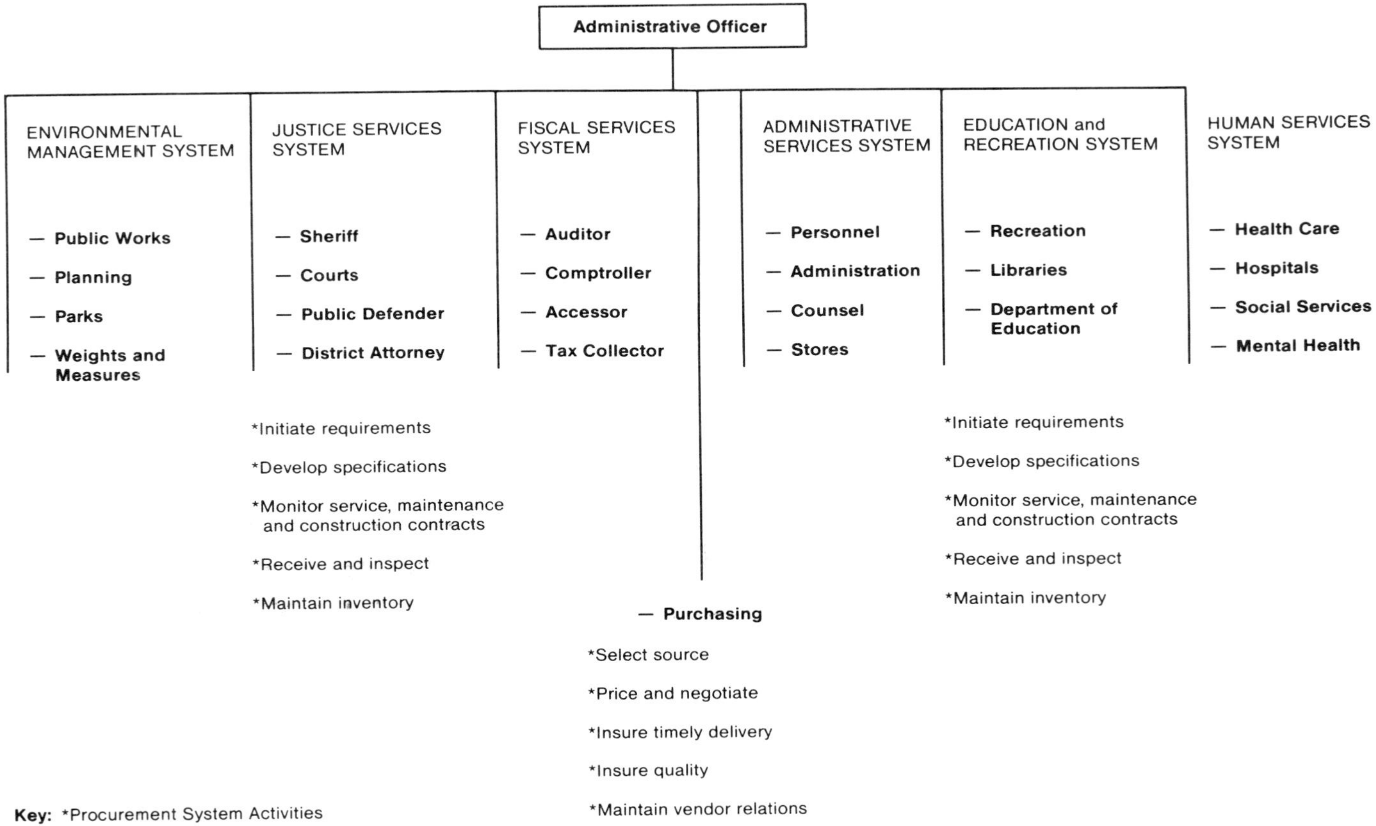

Administrative Officer

ENVIRONMENTAL MANAGEMENT SYSTEM	JUSTICE SERVICES SYSTEM	FISCAL SERVICES SYSTEM	ADMINISTRATIVE SERVICES SYSTEM	EDUCATION and RECREATION SYSTEM	HUMAN SERVICES SYSTEM
— Public Works	— Sheriff	— Auditor	— Personnel	— Recreation	— Health Care
— Planning	— Courts	— Comptroller	— Administration	— Libraries	— Hospitals
— Parks	— Public Defender	— Accessor	— Counsel	— Department of Education	— Social Services
— Weights and Measures	— District Attorney	— Tax Collector	— Stores		— Mental Health

*Initiate requirements

*Develop specifications

*Monitor service, maintenance and construction contracts

*Receive and inspect

*Maintain inventory

— **Purchasing**

*Select source

*Price and negotiate

*Insure timely delivery

*Insure quality

*Maintain vendor relations

*Initiate requirements

*Develop specifications

*Monitor service, maintenance and construction contracts

*Receive and inspect

*Maintain inventory

Key: *Procurement System Activities

FIGURE 1.7 The Functional Organization and the Integrated Procurement System: Government

tions for services required to be performed under contract. Each department monitors the supplier's performance under the order or contract issued by purchasing. Each department inspects, receives, and inventories supplies, materials, and equipment purchased for its particular needs. (The stores department of the Administrative Services System performs these functions for items common to two or more departments.)

Purchasing is charged with the responsibility of selecting the source of supply, obtaining a reasonable price for the supply or service, ensuring timely delivery of the specified quality, and maintaining good vendor relations.

The comptroller is responsible for the control of funds and for paying vendors. This organization also is responsible for monitoring the investment in inventory.

Construction

In many ways, the IPS for a construction firm is very similar to that described for a manufacturer.

As shown in Figure 1.8, sales initiates the IPS in a construction firm as it represents the firm in discussions with the client on the cost and quality implications of various approaches to satisfying the requirement. Each design approach has procurement implications. Purchasing must keep sales informed of changes in material prices and availability. This information is essential for accurate quotations and bids.

The engineering department in the construction firm, or an independent architect-engineering (A-E) firm, designs a project to meet a client's requirements. The design calls for work to be performed either by the construction firm's own employees or by subcontractors. The engineering department (or A-E) performs several IPS functions. Engineering specifies the right equipment and materials. It is involved in any value analysis-value engineering activities. Engineering develops specifications for work to be performed under subcontracts. It develops its own estimates of equipment, material, and subcontract costs. These estimates will be used by purchasing as a basis of comparison in negotiations. The importance of their accuracy was illustrated in the Eagle Manufacturing case at the beginning of the chapter.

The material division consists of two branches: the yard (stores) and the purchasing and subcontracts branch. The yard is responsible for inventory control of capital equipment and expendable supplies that are common to several jobs. The purchasing and subcontracts branch is responsible for selection of sources, pricing, and negotiation of purchase orders and subcontracts. Purchasing also is responsible for ensuring that the firm receives purchased material on time and in the quality specified. The yard and the construction division provide inspection and monitoring

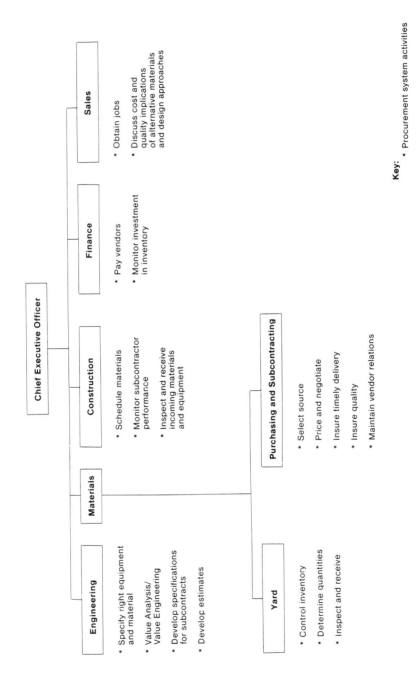

Chief Executive Officer

Engineering

* Specify right equipment and material
* Value Analysis/ Value Engineering
* Develop specifications for subcontracts
* Develop estimates

Materials

Construction

* Schedule materials
* Monitor subcontractor performance
* Inspect and receive incoming materials and equipment

Finance

* Pay vendors
* Monitor investment in inventory

Sales

* Obtain jobs
* Discuss cost and quality implications of alternative materials and design approaches

Purchasing and Subcontracting

* Select source
* Price and negotiate
* Insure timely delivery
* Insure quality
* Maintain vendor relations

Yard

* Control inventory
* Determine quantities
* Inspect and receive

Key: * Procurement system activities

FIGURE 1.8 The Functional Organization and the Integrated Procurement System: Construction

services to assist in these activities. To obtain the "right" supplies, services, and equipment at the "right" time and the "right" quality, purchasing must maintain viable sources of supplies, services, and equipment.

The construction division frequently is organized along project lines. Each actual or potential job is assigned to a project manager (superintendent) who becomes responsible for the project's successful completion. The project manager's responsibilities include the following IPS activities: scheduling materials and equipment, monitoring subcontractor performance, and inspection and acceptance of material shipped directly to the job site.

Finance makes timely payment to vendors and monitors the firm's investment in inventory. Finance closely controls working capital and cash flows. This activity is based largely on information contained in the progress payment schedules and purchasing schedules. Purchasing must appraise finance of any changes in delivery schedules that would affect working capital or cash flows.

STEPS TO SUCCESSFUL IMPLEMENTATION

Several successful proactive purchasing managers have stated that top management is ready and waiting for the purchasing manager to take the initiative to reduce purchase expenditures systematically. As we have seen, such action also will result in improved product quality and greater productivity. If you share these objectives, you should

- Study and understand the wants and needs of the other activities (departments) involved in the procurement process. Begin from an informed position. (The next five chapters discuss the general principles.)
- Make sure that your own house is in order. (Chapters 8 through 13 describe the major shortcomings found in purchasing activities and tell you how to do a better job.)
- Adapting the figures in this chapter, portray the IPS for your organization. Demonstrate the savings potential, using examples of previous "good" and "bad" procurements. Developing understanding and rapport with your fellow managers, offer to present the concepts and principles of a systematic approach to procurement and show the benefits to their activities. (Selected sections of this book may make useful reading for your colleagues.)
- Inform and sell top management on the plan to reduce procurement expenditures. Consider the desirability of a procurement audit, as

described in Chapter 14. Set up a task force to implement the integrated system. Include the heads of all involved activities.

- Publicize the resulting benefits to all levels of management, ensuring that all individuals involved in the program receive proper recognition for their cooperation and participation.

SUMMARY

Procurement is the systematic process of deciding what, when, and how much to purchase; the art of purchasing it; and the process of ensuring that what is required is received in the quality specified on time. The IPS cuts across traditional department lines to include activities that take place in marketing, engineering, material (or purchasing), operations, quality assurance, and finance.

The quantity, quality, and price of purchased items affect the quality of the firm's product, the ability to produce it, productivity, and, most important, the firm's profitability. Determination of what to buy does not begin when the purchase requisition is written but, rather, with the decision to produce the product.

An organization exercises the best control over the cost of purchased goods and services only when the various departments involved in the process operate as an interdependent, integrated system. On the other hand, uncoordinated action by one department may optimize the success of that department while causing undesirable results in another, to the detriment of the organization as a whole.

Implementation of an IPS results in proactive procurement, as distinguished from reactive purchasing. With proactive procurement, all members of the procurement system recognize their role in the procurement system. They cooperate in making the organization more profitable through more effective procurement. With this proactive approach, the purchasing department is involved in the requirements process where it provides input on the commercial implications of alternate materials, equipment, and services. The purchasing department takes the initiative in making savings happen throughout the procurement system. In contrast, with reactive purchasing, the purchasing department becomes involved in the procurement process only on receipt of a requisition.

The significant cost savings and increased productivity resulting from introduction of an IPS can be enjoyed in many settings: manufacturing, service, and construction firms; not-for-profit organizations; and government.

In most organizations, it is easier to increase profits and return on investment through a reduction in purchasing expenditures than through any other endeavor. If we consider the increased quality of finished goods (and the resulting market implications) and the savings in rework, field warranty, and inventory carrying costs resulting from implementation of an integrated procurement system, then the savings and profit impact is even greater.

In Chapter 2 we will look at the most critical component of the procurement process: the determination of what material to purchase for operations.

chapter two

DETERMINING WHAT TO PURCHASE: THE DESIGN PROCESS

It is Friday, March 7. A design review is being conducted at the All American Test Equipment Company.

Heinrich Holt, chief engineer, chairs the meeting. "Gentlemen, three months ago, marketing indicated a likely market of 70 Digital Waveform Recorders a month at a selling price of $16,000, provided that we can begin deliveries by October 1. When I first looked at this requirement, I said, 'No way!' But two months ago a sales engineer from Duo Diodes described her firm's new analog-to-digital converter (ADC). Duo has been working on the development of this ADC for two years. They have developed a revolutionary new process that will allow them to produce 350 units a month at a selling price of $1,450. We have tested their ADC and have developed 4 prototype Digital Waveform Recorders incorporating it. The prototypes meet our every desire."

Dick James, director of purchasing, interrupts to ask, "Heinrich, can anyone other than Duo produce this ADC?"

Holt answers, "Obviously not. It's their new process. We will be lucky to get in on their initial sales allocation. Don't get in a lather, Duo can be trusted."

Tom Ham, vice president of operations, interrupts: "Heinrich, the last time we incorporated some newly developed material, we had nothing but problems. We would go along fine for a while; then for no apparent reason, defects would jump so high that we'd be 200% to 300% over budget due to test and rework requirements. Those state-of-the-art materials you guys like so well are going to bankrupt us."

Steve Achtenhagen, vice president marketing, joins the fray: "Gentlemen, not only is this new Digital Wave Recorder potentially very profitable, but it will help our sales representatives to gain access to new customers. We expect this increased exposure to enhance our entire sales program. In fact, it's likely that our sales of test equipment could increase by 10% through the early availability of this Digital Wave Recorder."

Perhaps the biggest failure of purchasing executives is that of not becoming involved at the appropriate points in the requirements development process. It is likely that this is a carryover from the days when purchasing was a reactive clerical function that issued orders based on the decisions and actions of others. But if purchasing is to make its full profit contribution, it *must* be involved early in the requirements determination process.

A second major problem is the failure to integrate engineering constructively into the procurement system.

Determining what materials and services to purchase is the first and one of the most crucial steps in the procurement process. Responsibility for this determination varies with the type of requirement. In many cases, the using department is responsible. For example, plant engineering is responsible for developing equipment requirements. Plant operations develops requirements for operating supplies such as drill bits, lubricating oils, and related items. Administrative services initiates requirements for office supplies, equipment, and services.

The responsibility for determining which component materials to specify for newly designed products is a complex issue, complicated by the frequently conflicting interests, orientations, and biases of the many departments that have an interest in the end item or service. For example, engineering may desire design excellence. Marketing may demand nonstandard and unique features. Operations prefers long production runs utilizing existing equipment, requiring few operators, and using high-quality, easy-to-work materials. Purchasing prefers to buy readily available materials from several dependable sources at reasonable prices.

Historically, purchasing's contributions to the organization's success have been seen as being in two basic areas: ensuring the timely availability of required supplies and services and obtaining them at economic prices. However, these contributions are greatly expanded when purchasing is included at the beginning of the design process. For instance, as material requirements are developed, purchasing should ensure that only essential needs are incorporated in the requirement. The description of the requirement (usually a specification) should not contain features that unduly limit competition among qualified suppliers.[1] Further, purchasing can help the designer to be sensitive to the relative availability of the alternate materials that may satisfy product requirements. Timely availability of required materials and services usually is enhanced by the availability of two or more qualified sources.

THE DESIGN PROCESS
AND PROCUREMENT

Design is an iterative process that results from the progression of an abstract notion to something concrete that has function and a fixed form. This form can be described so that it can be produced at a designated quality. (The process of describing requirements is discussed in the next chapter.) The design stage is frequently the only point at which a major portion of the cost of producing an item can be reduced or controlled. If costs are not controlled at this time, they may be built into the item permanently, resulting in an expensive noncompetitive product.

The design stage is the point at which the desired levels of quality and reliability must be engineered into the item. Quality is the basic nature or degree of excellence that an item possesses. Reliability is the degree of confidence or probability that an item will perform a specified number of times under prescribed conditions. J. M. Juran, a widely published authority in the field of quality control, indicates that 20% to 40% of field failures experienced by durable goods manufactured in America originate during development and design.[2] The incident used to open this chapter showed how faulty purchased material drove manufacturing costs up on one of the firm's previous production items. Had All American Test Equipment not had excellent test procedures in its manufacturing process, products containing faulty purchased components would have been sold to customers. Eventually, field failures would have occurred, resulting in postsales costs and customer dissatisfaction. Profitability

---

[1]Two studies conducted by the author emphasize the importance of competition in achieving purchasing's economic objectives. The first study, entitled "Effect of the Number of Competitors on Costs," was published in the November 1971 issue of the *Journal of Purchasing.* The article indicated that over the range of one to five competitors, prices tended to decrease by 4% each time one additional qualified supplier submitted a price. Thus, an item costing $100 when only one bid had been obtained would tend to cost $92 if three bids were available.

The second study, entitled "Reduction in Selling Price After Introduction of Competition," was co-authored with Dr. Joe Boyett. It was published in the May 1979 issue of the *Journal of Marketing Research.* This study found that an average savings of 12.5% resulted when material that previously had been purchased on a sole-source basis was purchased under competitive conditions.

[2]J. M. Juran, "Japanese and Western Quality: A Contrast in Methods and Results," *Management Review,* November 1978, p. 28.

and even a firm's survival require increased attention to the quality and reliability of its products from the earliest phase of the design stage.

The Investigation Phase

The design process, as portrayed in Figures 2.1(a), (b), (c), begins with the investigation phase. The first major activity is the development of a statement of needs, desires, and objectives. Needs are based on marketing's perception or knowledge of what customers want, balanced against the organization's objectives and resources. Identified needs that are potentially compatible with the firm's objectives (profit potential, sales volume, payback period, etc.) and resources (men, machines, and

FIGURE 2.1 (a)   The Design Process—Investigative Phase

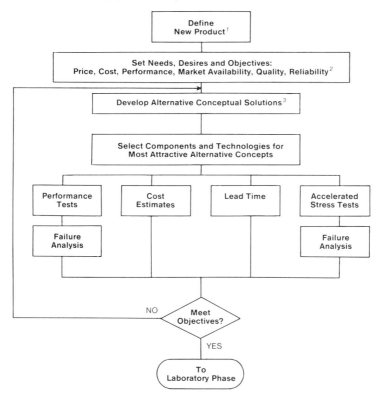

[1] Purchasing should provide a window to new supplier-developed components, knowledge of which may allow marketing and engineering to identify new product possibilities.

[2] Purchasing is the key source of information on the cost, performance, market availability, quality, and reliability of supplier furnished components which may be incorporated in the new product.

[3] Purchasing provides input on the economy and availability of the materials and subassemblies to be purchased under each approach.

management) are then considered for product or engineering development. Product objectives, including performance, price, quality, and market availability, are developed. These needs, desires, and objectives then are transformed into criteria that guide the subsequent design, planning, and decision-making activities.

Alternate approaches to satisfying the needs and objectives will be evaluated against these criteria. In Figure 2.1(a), these are referred to as alternative conceptual solutions. Sound discipline by both design engineering and management is required to ensure the development of alternate approaches.

There is an unfortunate tendency to accept and proceed with the first approach that appears to meet the need. In many instances, less obvious alternatives may yield more profitable solutions. These alternate approaches should be evaluated on the basis of suitability, producibility, component availability and economy, and customer acceptability.[3]

The Laboratory Phase

The next stage of the design process is referred to as the laboratory phase in Figure 2.1(b). During this phase, approaches are subjected to detailed review for feasibility and likely risk. During this phase, efforts are taken to reduce risk to acceptable levels in all areas through the development and testing of prototypes for high-risk items. After tests demonstrate that risk has been reduced to an acceptable level, the most attractive alternative is selected.

When quality is a critical factor in designing a product for the marketplace, engineering should develop a quality map that describes the detailed design logic required to achieve the desired quality. This design logic starts with each desired end-product characteristic. It then identifies the characteristics of purchased materials and process steps that collectively contribute to building the desired attribute into the product. The quality map shows engineering, manufacturing, and purchasing specialists how the customer's expectations will be fulfilled. It details key

---

[3]Suitability is concerned with technical considerations such as strength, size, power consumption, capability, maintainability, and adaptability. Engineering has primary responsibility for suitability.

Producibility refers to the ease with which a firm may manufacture an item. Frequently, an item's design must be constrained or revised to accommodate the firm's ability to produce it economically. Producibility is primarily a responsibility of manufacturing.

Component availability is a function of assured dependable sources of supply. Component economy refers to the cost of the item or service. Component availability and economy are primarily purchasing's responsibility.

Customer acceptability considers likely acceptance of an item by potential customers. This is primarily a marketing responsibility.

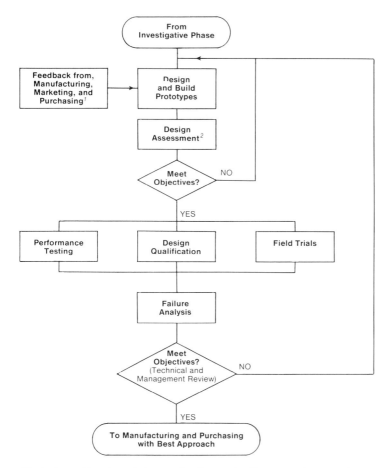

[1] Purchasing provides value analysis suggestions from vendors. These suggestions may reduce cost, enhance performance, or both.

[2] Purchasing participates in the design reviews and provides information on the impact of specifications and availability of items that are standard production for—and/or are inventoried by—suppliers.

FIGURE 2.1 (b)   The Design Process—Laboratory Phase

relationships among (1) customer expectations; (2) raw materials, parts, and assemblies; and (3) relevant steps in the production process.

There is an understandable tendency on the part of many design engineers to develop truly advanced products that incorporate the latest developments or that push the state of the art forward. While this tendency may advance the development and implementation of technology, it is frequently needlessly expensive. Not only does such an approach result in a proliferation of components to be purchased and stocked, but it frequently results in the incorporation of items whose production processes have not stabilized. Quality problems, production disruptions, and delays frequently result.

The process of putting the product designer's logic into the form of a quality map serves several purposes. One is to invite purchasing specialists to comment on the probability of obtaining the desired level of quality in purchased materials. Another is to allow quality assurance to review the design logic. This review ensures that the quality specified by marketing will result if purchasing and manufacturing each complies with the design criteria.

Consideration should be given to the desirability of using standard items during the laboratory phase and carrying them over into the manufacturing phase. Many hidden costs are associated with an unnecessary variety of production items or purchased components: excess paperwork; short, needlessly expensive production runs; higher inventory costs; higher unit costs of small quantities of purchased materials; additional order processing costs; higher inspection and materials handling costs; additional quality problems; and an increased probability of stock outages. The use of standard materials, production processes, and methods resulting from standardization programs can greatly reduce the cost of designing and producing an item.

The Manufacturing Phase

In the manufacturing phase, detailed specifications, the manufacturing plan, and the procurement plan (frequently in the form of a bill of materials) are developed. As shown in Figure 2.1(c), numerous tests take place throughout the manufacturing phase. Anytime that there is an unacceptable degree of risk or uncertainty about the performance of a component, subassembly, or the item itself, appropriate tests are conducted. These tests pinpoint failures in one or more of the following areas: the design, the supplier, the assembly and handling procedures, or the test equipment and test procedures.

Engineering Change Management

Any changes in components required to manufacture a product or the product itself may have profound effects on its cost, performance, appearance, and acceptability in the marketplace. Changes, especially at the component or subassembly level, can have a major impact on the manufacturing process. Thus, unless changes to the configuration of an item or its components are controlled, manufacturers may find themselves in one of several undesirable states. They may possess useless inventories of unusable raw materials or subassemblies resulting in excessive material expenditures. They may possess materials that require

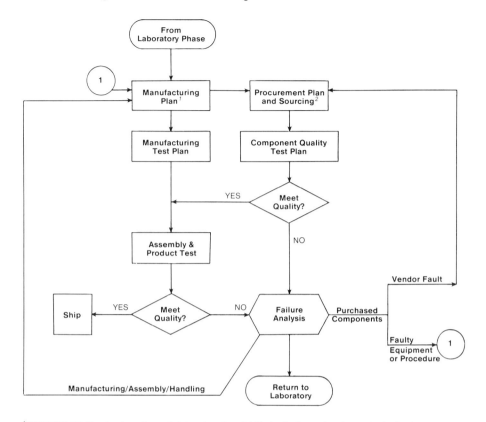

[1] Purchasing provides input on the material cost and availability implications of a change in the item's configuration.

[2] As a result of its early involvement in the design process, purchasing has developed contingency plans. These plans allow purchasing to satisfy the firm's requirements for selected purchased components. Purchasing has worked with design engineering to select the appropriate type of purchase description (Ch. 3). The appropriate plans are now formalized and implemented.

FIGURE 2.1 (c)   The Design Process—Manufacturing/Procurement Phase

needlessly expensive rework to be adapted to a new configuration. Or they may produce an end item that will not meet the customer's needs or that may otherwise be unacceptable in the marketplace.

Engineering change management, a discipline that controls engineering changes, has been developed to avoid such problems.[4] The need for and degree of application of engineering change management to an item will depend on many factors and will be a matter of managerial judgment. But, for most modern technical items, engineering change

[4] Engineering change management is the management of change to a product's design, specifically, its form, fit, and function.

management is a necessity. In some cases, it will be imposed on the manufacturer by the customer.

Under engineering change management, the functional and physical characteristics of an item and its components are identified. Any changes to these characteristics must be controlled and recorded. Marketing and all activities involved in the purchase, control, and use of purchased materials are informed of any proposed changes to the item's characteristics. These organizations then comment on the impact of the proposed change. Such control and coordination is especially important when production scheduling and the release of purchase orders are controlled by a material requirements planning system.

Many organizational approaches to the responsibility for engineering change management exist. Ideally, an engineering change management board should be established with engineering, manufacturing, marketing, production planning and inventory control, and purchasing represented. When a materials management organization exists in the firm, it is recommended that production planning and inventory control chair the engineering change board.[5] The crucial issue is that purchasing and the function responsible for material control must be involved in proposed engineering changes.

Adherence to this or a similar design process is key to the firm's success. Product quality, cost, and availability all receive proper attention. And, as seen previously, engineering, manufacturing, marketing, quality assurance, and purchasing all have vital roles to play in the design process.

KEY POINTS FOR
PURCHASING INPUT DURING
THE DESIGN PROCESS

There are several points in the design process where purchasing can or should provide input on the material to be purchased.

In the investigation phase, purchasing has a major contribution to make during establishment of price, performance, timeliness, quality, and reliability objectives.

Later in this phase, purchasing is the source of information on the

---

[5]This recommendation is supported by Robert W. Holland and Thomas E. Vollman in an article appearing in the September–October 1978 issue of the *Harvard Business Review*. The article, entitled "Planning Your Materials Requirement," reports on various forms of manufacturing organizations. One finding was that a significant loss of effectiveness occurs when engineering change control does not rest with those using the information (purchasing and production planning and inventory control).

abilities of suppliers to meet the objectives being considered. Also, it can provide input on the likely costs (in rough terms) of purchased material and subassemblies. Such early involvement has the benefit of allowing purchasing to initiate long-range plans to ensure that an economic purchase results.

After engineering has developed several alternate conceptual solutions to these objectives, purchasing should provide input on the economy and availability of the materials and subassemblies to be purchased under each approach.

Design reviews are held at several points in the laboratory phase. This is the third point at which purchasing should be involved. At these reviews, particular emphasis should be placed on the use of standard items in the firm's inventory.

The design process results in a manufacturing plan that, in turn, leads to a procurement plan and, in turn, a purchase requisition; see Figure 2.1(c). If purchasing has *not* been involved in the earlier phases of the design process, this may be the first opportunity for purchasing to provide input. At this point, purchasing has the right and the responsibility to challenge requirements that do not appear to be economical or otherwise in the firm's best interest. (Obviously, purchasing should not change the requirement. It can only challenge it!)

After several months' experience in supplying an item, a supplier may be requested to offer cost reduction suggestions under the firm's value analysis/value engineering (VA/VE) program. (This topic is discussed in Chapter 11.) This is the next point at which purchasing may have input on material being purchased.

Finally, changes in an item's design configuration may appear to be desirable or essential during manufacturing. But such changes may have significant cost implications. Purchasing, together with manufacturing, marketing, and inventory control, should provide essential input when such changes are being considered.

HOW TO INTEGRATE ENGINEERING SUCCESSFULLY INTO THE PROCUREMENT SYSTEM

It has been demonstrated that requirements should be balanced between technical and functional considerations, manufacturing considerations, marketing implications of customer acceptance, and the procurement consideration of economy and availability. All too frequently, the design engineer attempts to address all these issues without obtaining the input and assistance of representatives of marketing, manufacturing, quality assurance, and purchasing. Many engineers enjoy interacting with vendors both on technical and *commercial* issues. These engineers are convinced that they are serving their employer's best interest—even while specifying materials that are in short supply or obtainable only from one source.

Professional purchasing managers have their work cut out for them. Their objective should be the development and maintenance of cooperative relations with engineering *that protect the profitability of the firm.* Once this objective has been embraced, the purchasing manager has two basic options: to sell management on the need for a procurement audit (as described in Chapter 14) or to assume total responsibility independently to achieve the objective.

When purchasing managers assume total responsibility for the integration of engineering into the procurement system, they must devise and implement a well-developed strategy. It is essential that the purchasing manager understand the orientation and dedication of the typical design engineer. Obviously, an ability to speak "engineering" is very helpful. A review of the principles of negotiation (see Chapter 10) is very desirable: after all, the purchasing manager is about to undertake a most crucial negotiation. In many situations, it will be possible to enlist the aid of an ally such as the director of finance or operations. Under most circumstances, the purchasing manager's supervisor should be made aware of the objective and the planned strategy.

The present chapter identifies several key points at which purchasing's involvement in the design process has the potential for making the organization more profitable. Several managers of proactive purchasing organizations indicate that they achieved success in the desired engineering-purchasing integration in the following manner. Whenever feasible, they provided advice on the commercial implications of designs under consideration in a positive and constructive manner. When the advice had been accepted, the resulting savings were publicized in a manner to bring credit and recognition to engineering . . . and even to the specific engineer involved. Eventually, these purchasing managers and their buyers were able to establish—through a history of accomplished savings—that the purchasing staff is a valuable resource to engineering. Purchasing, then, is seen as a partner that takes care of business problems, thereby allowing engineers to concentrate on engineering.

Several successful approaches to obtaining the desired level of purchasing input during the design process are described next. One or a combination of these may be right for you.

Material Engineers (Liaison Engineers)

One of the quickest and most successful ways of gaining the cooperation of engineers is to speak their language. Several successful material organizations consider only individuals with an engineering background as candidates for buying positions *when the responsibilities require involvement with design engineering.* Other purchasing organizations divide buying responsibilities into two specialties: material engineering and buying (sourcing, pricing, and negotiating). The material/liaison engineer is responsible for coordination with design engineering, for prequalifying potential sources (usually with the assistance of quality assurance), and participating in value engineering and value analysis.

Engineers Temporarily Assigned to Purchasing

Several organizations have greatly improved working relations and the cooperation between engineering and purchasing by temporarily assigning engineering personnel to purchasing. The assignment usually lasts for 6 to 12 months. While working in the purchasing department, the engineer provides invaluable assistance to purchasing. On returning to engineering, the engineer has a far better understanding of the role and responsibilities of purchasing. Usually, such individuals greatly facilitate the integration process.

No Dead End Streets, If You Please!

Purchasing is an ideal point of transition for an engineer who desires to advance into general management. Several forward-looking organizations do *not* look at purchasing as an end assignment. Carefully selected employees are promoted from other functional areas into purchasing. And carefully selected purchasing employees are promoted to other departments.

Co-location

This approach calls for the placement of members of the purchasing staff in locations where design engineering is accomplished. Frequently, these individuals have technical backgrounds. They are available to assist design engineers by advising them on the procurement implications of different materials under consideration. They obtain required information from prospective suppliers. In some organizations, these members of the purchasing staff have the authority to purchase. In other organizations, they act in a liaison capacity only. This approach is especially effective when a company is bidding on a large project with a short bid time.

Design Review Committee

With this approach, a design review committee consisting (as required) of representatives of engineering, marketing, manufacturing, quality, and purchasing is established to review all designs prior to manufacture or purchase.

Project Teams

Project teams with members from the foregoing departments are established to develop and introduce the desired item into production. Membership on the project team may be either full time or on an "as required" basis, preferably managed through the use of a matrix control system.

Approved Parts List

This procedure minimizes the interface between engineering and the other organizations involved in the procurement system. A parts list or catalog is developed by purchasing in close coordination with the organization's standards engineer and quality engineer. Parts in use are classified into three groups: recommended, acceptable, or not recommended. Engineers are free to select from the recommended group. The use of "acceptable" items or incorporation of new items not on the list requires approval by higher management. Purchasing, standards engineers, and quality engineers constantly monitor and update the lists to ensure currency.

Recently, discussions were held with several proactive executives responsible for purchasing. One of the topics discussed was the integration of engineering into the procurement system. Several of the approaches just cited are based on suggestions offered by these pros. In addition, one or more of the following slightly paraphrased quotations from these discussions may be of interest.

MAJOR PRIMARY PRODUCER:	Hire engineers. Give them field experience. Put purchasing and engineering under the same boss. Rotate future top managers through purchasing. Purchasing is not a dead end street.
ELECTRONICS MANUFACTURER:	Co-locate buyers in engineering. Motivate engineering to accept commercial advice from purchasing by making cost reduction a factor in determining their bonuses.
APPLIANCE MANUFACTURER:	Have the good fortune to have a C.E.O. with purchasing experience. Make sure that the purchasing manager has experience in operations. As buyers, we have much to offer . . . this must be our self-image.
AEROSPACE:	The purchasing manager must earn the respect and cooperation of other mem-

bers of the procurement system. Hire engineers with floor experience to be material engineers. Expect one to two years to orientate them on commercial activities. Have material engineers work with design engineers to adapt textbook solutions to the realities of the supply marketplace.

ELECTRONICS MANUFACTURER: Make engineers dependent on purchasing. Provide an invaluable service. Make engineers use catalog items. If not in the catalog, require approval of engineering and purchasing managers.

COMPUTER MANUFACTURER: Raise field reliability objectives. This puts pressure on all members of the procurement system to increase coordination and cooperation. Make key managers' bonuses a function of profits and cost control. This makes other members of the procurement team receptive to cost-saving suggestions. Management has told engineering that 50% of its efforts should be allocated to design and 50% to cost control.

CONGLOMERATE: We are really hot on value analysis—not only does it save big bucks, but it really helps to break down organizational barriers!

TWO DEFENSE CONTRACTORS: Co-locate!

AEROSPACE: Hire engineers.

HIGH-TECH FIRM: Co-locate. Use project teams when appropriate.

PUBLIC UTILITY: Get a good procurement audit.

SUMMARY

Determining what to purchase is one of the most critical steps in the procurement process. This determination is complicated by the frequently conflicting objectives of engineering, marketing, manufacturing, and purchasing.

The design stage is the only point at which many costs can most effectively be reduced or controlled. The design process begins with a statement of needs, desires, and objectives. It then proceeds through several iterations, starting with the development of alternate approaches and ending with the development of a set of requirements suitable for manufacturing and purchasing's use. Many iterations and reviews take place from the start to the end of the design process. Throughout this process, consideration must be given to technical, manufacturing, procurement, and marketing issues. The key output, from the point of view of the integrated procurement system, is the procurement plan. This plan frequently is in the form of a bill of materials, along with required delivery dates, and becomes the basis of subsequent purchasing actions.

Standardization of materials and manufacturing processes and methods can greatly reduce the cost of designing and manufacturing an item. An effectively implemented standardization program avoids short, expensive production runs, higher inventory costs, higher costs of purchased materials, additional order processing costs, quality problems, higher inspection and materials handling costs, and the costs associated with stock outages.

Engineering change management, a discipline that controls engineering changes, is the final step in the design process. Under engineering change management, the functional and physical characteristics of an item are identified. Changes to these characteristics are controlled and recorded. Engineering change management helps a firm to avoid material waste, excessive manufacturing effort and expense, and the possibility of producing an item that will not be compatible with customers' needs.

Efforts to increase profitability and productivity may be blocked if engineering does not see and understand its role in the integrated procurement system. By understanding engineers' wants and needs and their reasonable requirements, purchasing can help to bring them on side . . . to the benefit of all departments in the firm and the firm itself.

Seven approaches to bringing engineering into the integrated procurement system are (1) material/liaison engineers, (2) engineers temporarily assigned to purchasing, (3) promotional opportunities into and out of purchasing, (4) co-location of purchasing personnel in engineering, (5) formal design reviews in which purchasing participates, (6) a project team approach to development, and (7) use of an approved parts list. No one approach is appropriate for all firms.

Once a decision has been made on what to purchase, it is necessary to select the most appropriate means of communicating this information to the buyer, potential suppliers, and inspectors. This process is discussed in the next chapter.

chapter three

SELECTION OF THE RIGHT TYPE OF PURCHASE DESCRIPTION WILL SAVE YOU TIME AND MONEY

Joyce Firstenberger, city manager of Great White Way, N.Y., is faced with a major decision. Great White Way's rapid growth has resulted in a shortage of classrooms. Revenue has not kept pace with the need for additional school physical plant. To accommodate the growth in student population, it has been necessary to adopt the use of shifts at the high school. Parents and students alike are unhappy with the situation. The school board is demanding a new high school.

This morning, Joyce met with the city comptroller, engineer, and purchasing agent. Hal Eyring, city engineer, indicated that preliminary engineering estimates for a new high school were $5 million. John Pasgrove, the comptroller, stated that, at the very highest, the city could not afford a building costing in excess of $4 million. Hal responded that his estimates were for an austere structure and that $5 million seemed optimistic. Judy Hardy, the purchasing agent, then said that she had recently learned of an approach to purchasing construction through the use of a performance specification.

The performance specification describes the size and function of the building in explicit terms. Qualified builders are then invited to propose their design approaches and prices. Manufacturing plants, when purchased in this manner, tended to be 30% less expensive than when purchased through the use of detailed plans and specifications. Further, the use of performance specifications reduced the time required to complete such projects by one-fourth.

After a spirited discussion, Hal Eyring summarized his position: "Every organization I've ever been with has purchased building construction through the use of detailed plans and specifications. I won't be party to Judy's new-fangled performance specification."

John Pasgrove commented, "If this performance specification approach is any good, the savings would allow Great White Way to get on with the needed school project. With building costs escalating at 10% to 15% a year, if the project does not go forward now, it will be many years—if ever."

Use of the right type of specification will significantly reduce procurement costs. And, as we saw at Great White Way, the right type of specification also can reduce the amount of time required to fill requirements. In an integrated procurement system, purchasing is in a position to influence the development or selection of the right type of specification. This is a critical activity! One of the most efficient manufacturers in America has assigned the development of specifications to the appropriate commodity buying team in its purchasing department. Purchasing should be involved in this critical, but frequently overlooked, activity.

Two problems are common in the area of purchase descriptions:

- Requiring activities frequently fail to consider the cost implications of alternate approaches to describing their requirements.
- Purchasing departments often fail to conduct systematic procurement research and analysis on alternate materials when appropriate.

THE IMPORTANCE OF THE PURCHASE DESCRIPTION

The purchase description forms the heart of any procurement. Whether or not a purchase order or contract will be performed to the satisfaction of the buying organization frequently is determined at the time the purchase description is selected or written. In no other form of communication is there a need for greater clarity and precision of expression. The extent of this precision has major bearing on the successful completion of the procurement.

Purchase descriptions serve a number of purposes. Some of these are to

- Communicate to the buyer in the purchasing department what to buy
- Communicate to prospective suppliers what is required
- Serve as the heart of the resulting purchase order

• Establish the standard against which inspections, tests, and quality checks are made

The purchase description can greatly influence the amount of competition. As seen in Chapter 2, the amount of competition has a major impact on the purchase price. The type of purchase description also may have an effect on the "depth" of competition. This depth of competition may have an even more pronounced effect on the purchase price.

In the situation that opened this chapter, two very different approaches to describing a requirement for a new high school were under consideration. The approach endorsed by the city engineer calls for the development of a very explicit set of plans and specifications that tell in great detail how the successful builder is to construct the required building. Competition then is solicited on this *one* approach.

The alternate approach advanced by the purchasing agent calls for the use of an explicit performance specification that would describe the intended use of the building. Under this approach, solicited vendors are free to bid on alternate approaches to satisfying the requirement. For example, one approach may call for a built-up wood truss roof. Another approach may call for the use of prestressed concrete for the roof. One approach to meeting a requirement for comfort control might employ the use of one central air conditioner. An alternate approach might call for the use of several unit air conditioners mounted on the walls or roof. The level of comfort obtained would be the same, but the cost of the two approaches is substantially different.

The use of performance specifications, then, can result in a "competition of concepts," with great savings enjoyed by the purchaser.

FIVE APPROACHES TO DESCRIBING WHAT TO PURCHASE

Brand or Trade Name

The use of a brand or trade name is the simplest way to describe what to purchase. A brand name is used by a manufacturer to distinguish a product and to aid in its promotion. Brand names ensure that the goodwill developed in satisfied customers is credited to the product. Such goodwill requires that the manufacturer provide consistent quality. The use of a brand name description implies a reliance on the integrity and the reputation of the manufacturer. When purchasing by brand name, the purchaser has every right to expect that follow-on purchases of the brand name will possess the same quality as the original.

Normally, the expression "or equal" should be used immediately following a brand name to facilitate competition. When using an "or equal" after a brand name, it is desirable to set forth those salient physical, functional, or other characteristics of the referenced products that are essential to the purchaser's needs. The term "or equal" means that any proposed item should be able to perform the function to the same level of satisfaction as does the specified brand.

The use of brand names, while simplifying the procurement process, tends to be expensive. Even when competition is introduced through the use of the "or equal" provision, higher prices tend to result than when several of the alternate approaches to describing the item are employed. Brand-name products generally are sold at higher prices than unbranded products of similar quality. There are several advantages and disadvantages in the use of brand names.

Advantages

- It is simple for the requiring department to describe the desired item.
- Purchasing by brand name is relatively simple.
- The product tends to be more readily available than are unbranded items.
- The use of a brand-name purchase description may be the most efficient method of obtaining a desired level of quality or skill when this level of quality cannot be defined easily.
- The branded item may be advertised so widely and successfully as to aid in promotion of the product in which it will be incorporated.
- Inspection of brand-name items is relatively simple.
- Testing of an item may be impractical. The purchaser may avoid such testing by relying on the brand-name manufacturer's quality standards.
- The purchaser is assured that the manufacturer will stand behind his or her brand-name product.

Disadvantages

- Higher prices usually result when purchasing through the use of brand names.
- The use of brand names may result in the purchaser not availing himself or herself of improvements introduced by competitors of the brand-name manufacturer.
- The use of the "or equal" provision may result in items being purchased from a variety of manufacturers. Since each manufacturer exercises his or her own quality control, it is likely that the quality

variation will be larger than if the item were purchased from one source only or purchased through the use of detailed specifications. When commonality of items from purchase to purchase is essential, the use of "or equal" is not desirable.

Samples

The need to develop a purchase description sometimes is avoided through the use of samples. Prospective suppliers are invited to match or duplicate the buyer's sample. Such an approach may be appropriate when special, nonrepetitive items are to be purchased and quality requirements are not a significant factor.

Advantage

- This is a very simple method of communicating what is required.

Disadvantages

- Detailed tests and inspections may be required to determine that the furnished item does meet the sample.
- No definite standards are established either for record-keeping purposes or as the basis of future purchases.

Standard Specifications

Recurring needs for a consistent level of quality have led industry and government to develop standard specifications for many items. Standard specifications include commercial standards, federal specifications, and international specifications. Such standard specifications contain descriptions of the quality of materials and the quality of workmanship to be used in manufacturing the item. Testing procedures are included to ensure that those quality standards are met.

Advantages

- The use of standard specifications greatly facilitates communications. The requirer, purchaser, and supplier all know what is needed.
- The cost of developing a design specification (described shortly) is avoided.
- The use of standard specifications results in wider competition and lower prices.
- The use of standard specifications facilitates the firm's standardization program. Savings in purchase price, inspection, materials handling, and inventory carrying costs result.

- Standardized items tend to be more readily available.

Disadvantages

- Standard specifications may be dated. Accordingly, the buying firm may not take advantage of the latest technology.
- The specification may call for inputs or processes that are difficult or expensive to achieve.
- Testing costs will be higher than with brand-name products.
- Responsibility for the suitability of the purchased item rests with the purchaser. Normally, the supplier who produces under a specification cited in a purchase order is not responsible for ensuring that the item will satisfy the customer's need. (With a performance specification, this responsibility is shifted to the supplier.)
- The use of standard specifications results in the purchase of standardized items. The incorporation of such standardized items in the purchaser's end product may conflict with marketing's desire to sell a unique product.

Design Specifications

Design specifications[1] spell out in detail the materials to be used, their sizes, shapes, and tolerances, exact physical and chemical characteristics, and how the item is to be fabricated. They provide a completely defined item capable of manufacture by a competent manufacturer. They also describe test procedures to be used to verify that all stated requirements have been met. The specification must meet the requirements of many departments in the firm: engineering's concern for technical adequacy, marketing's concern with consumer acceptance, manufacturing's concern for ease of production, and purchasing's concern for availability and economy. As would be expected, design specifications make use of commercial standards and other standard specifications.

Since design specifications frequently are the basis of competitive bidding procedures, it is essential that they communicate what is needed without need for further clarification. Thus, critical dimensions must be spelled out in detail, and all necessary quality requirements must be fully described. At the same time, the specification must avoid imposing unnecessary conditions that would result in disqualifying an otherwise acceptable product because it fails to meet an unessential condition. It is important that the design specification convey a complete and accurate understanding of what is required. The same word or expression is sub-

---

[1]For ease of discussion, blueprints and engineering drawings are included under the heading of design specifications.

ject to varying interpretations by different people. The supplier will interpret the specification to his or her own advantage.

A specification essentially is the means of transferring knowledge between minds. Each mind will test the words of a specification against its own experience. If the design specification is ambiguous, the ambiguity will be construed against the drafter (i.e., the firm using the specification to purchase the item). When design specifications control performance under a purchase order or a contract, there is a presumption that the specifications are adequate for the purposes intended and that, if followed, the desired result will be obtained. There is an implied warranty that the specifications are adequate. Thus, the supplier who produces under the customer's specification is not responsible for the suitability or acceptability of the resulting product. However, if the supplier knows (or perhaps from experience should know) that the desired result cannot be obtained, he or she cannot make a useless thing and expect to be paid for it. Where the supplier knows (or should have known) that the specification is defective, he or she is under a duty to notify the customer of the defect. The supplier discharges this obligation by making the defect known to the customer.

As might be expected, design specifications must be reviewed periodically and updated. Unfortunately, the use of design specifications tends to complicate purchase order administration (expediting) and may increase costs, delay delivery, result in delivery of obsolete items, and sharply increase inventory carrying costs. The use of design specifications may result in the creation of a costly storage and distribution system for items that are not generally commercially available.

There are several advantages and disadvantages in the use of design specifications.

Advantages

- The purchasing organization avoids having to purchase on a sole-source basis. As was seen in Chapter 2, a savings in the neighborhood of 12% is enjoyed by avoiding sole-source situations.
- The purchasing organization avoids paying premium prices on branded goods.
- Design specifications facilitate the corporate standardization program. As we saw in Chapter 2, many savings are enjoyed through such a program.

Disadvantages

- Design specifications are expensive to develop. Both time and human resources are required.

- The purchaser is responsible for the adequacy of the specification.
- The use of design specifications may deny the purchaser the latest advances in both technical development and manufacturing processes.
- The use of a design specification to purchase material that is very similar to an item covered by a commercial standard may result in higher unit prices. Further, the item covered by the design specification will tend to be less readily available.
- The use of design specifications restricts competition to one approach or concept. As we have seen, competition of concepts resulting from use of a performance specification may lead to significant financial and time savings.
- Purchase through the use of design specifications tends to complicate the purchase order administration function. Late delivery of unique items is much more common than it is for standard ones.
- The purchaser usually will have to assume the inventory responsibility for such unique items.

Performance Specifications

Performance specifications generally describe a product by its capacity, function, or operation instead of by its physical, chemical, or quality characteristics. The supplier need only demonstrate performance to achieve acceptance of his or her product.

A performance specification provides a description of the intended use of an item (whether component, plant, or equipment). A performance specification may include a statement of the qualitative nature of the item required. When necessary, it may set forth those minimum essential characteristics and standards to which such item must conform if it is to satisfy its intended use. Performance specifications describe in words what the item is to do instead of describing the item in terms of its physical and chemical properties.

Although a performance specification is much shorter and easier to develop than is a design specification, caution must be exercised in its development. Once again, engineering, marketing, manufacturing, and purchasing requirements must be considered.

The following general principles apply to the development of performance specifications:

- The performance specification must not be so narrow that it stifles creativity.
- While unnecessarily restrictive performance specifications are un-

desirable, the performance specification must be sufficiently specific to obtain desired objectives. If it is written in too broad a manner, potential suppliers may choose not to respond because of the risk involved, their inability to relate work requirements to their talents and capabilities, or difficulties in estimating costs.

- The performance specification serves as the nucleus of the purchase order or contract. The resulting performance is a direct function of the quality, clarity, and completeness of the specification.

- The element of risk to the supplier inherent in producing under the performance specification should affect the type of pricing on the resulting purchase order (e.g., firm fixed price, fixed price incentive). In the appendix to Chapter 9, we will examine the relationship between the degree of risk and uncertainty and selection of the right type of pricing.

As with other approaches to defining and communicating the requirement, the use of performance specifications has inherent advantages and disadvantages:

Advantages

- Performance specifications are relatively easy to prepare.
- Their use tends to avail the purchaser of the latest technology.
- The use of performance specifications assures that the purchaser obtains the specified (desired) level of quality.
- When several already designed, developed, and produced items can meet the performance specification, the depth of competition will be enhanced and purchase costs reduced.
- Performance specifications allow a greater degree of innovation by suppliers. Under performance specifications, the supplier assumes the responsibility of providing a product that is suitable to the purchaser's need.

Disadvantages

- Marginal suppliers look for loopholes in specifications. Care and effort must be taken to screen potential suppliers to ensure that only reputable ones are asked to submit proposals. The use of performance specifications is restricted by purchasing's ability to select capable and honest suppliers.
- Competition tends to be reduced when the performance specification requires potential suppliers to perform considerable engineering in

preparation for submitting a bid or proposal. As we have seen, a reduction in competition may result in higher prices.

While the use of a performance specification may appear to be very attractive, its use is constrained by the ability of the purchasing department to select capable and honest suppliers. The supplier assumes the entire responsibility for providing a product that meets the purchaser's need.

The advantages and disadvantages of these five approaches are summarized in Table 3.1.

TABLE 3.1   Advantages and Disadvantages of Five Approaches to Describing What to Purchase

Approach	Advantages	Disadvantages
Brand or Trade Name	Easily described Easily purchased Readily available Facilitate obtaining special workmanship Promotional pull of incorporated brand name Easy inspection Avoid testing Assurance of quality	Limited competition Higher prices Miss competitors' improvements
Samples	Easy communication of requirements	May require detailed test/inspection No definite standards
Standard specification	Facilitate communication Avoid cost of developing design specification Wide competition Facilitates standardization program Readily available materials	Specifications may be dated May require expensive manufacturing processes High test costs Purchaser has responsibility for suitability of purchased item Standardized material may conflict with marketing's desires for unique products
Design Specification	Avoid sole source Avoid premium prices Facilitates standardization program	Expensive to prepare Purchaser responsible for adequacy of specification Miss latest technology Higher cost than standard item Less readily available More expediting problems Late deliveries Larger inventories
Performance Specification	Easily prepared Gain latest technology Obtain specified level of performance Increased depth of competition	Possible loopholes in specifications Decrease breadth of competition

HOW TO SELECT THE RIGHT APPROACH TO DESCRIBING REQUIREMENTS

While the decision on what type of purchase description to use may appear to be simple, there are many factors that complicate the issue. For small, noncritical procurements, brand names or samples frequently best describe requirements. The use of a brand name as a purchase description is appropriate (1) to obtain the desired level of quality or skill when these are not described easily, (2) to gain the benefits of wide advertising of the brand-named item that would aid in promotion of the purchaser's end product, or (3) to accommodate users who have a bias or prejudice (whether founded or unfounded) in favor of the brand. Such prejudices can be virtually impossible to overcome.

When brand names or samples are inappropriate methods of describing our requirements, some type of specification will be employed. When selecting or developing the specification, consideration must be given to the importance of competition and the desirability of avoiding unnecessarily restrictive criteria.

Once a need has been identified and functionally described, and when the size of the contemplated purchase warrants, procurement research and analysis should be conducted to investigate the availability of commercial products able to meet the firm's need. Normally, these commercial products will be described by one of the standard specifications. This research and analysis also should provide information to aid in selecting a procurement strategy appropriate to the situation. Procurement research and analysis involves obtaining the following information as appropriate:

- The availability of products suitable to meet the need (with or without modification)
- The terms, conditions, and prices under which such products are sold
- Any applicable trade provisions or restrictions or controlling laws
- The performance characteristics and quality of available products, including quality control and test procedures followed by the manufacturers
- Information on the satisfaction of other users having similar needs
- Any costs or problems associated with integration of the item with those currently used
- Industry production practices, such as continuous, periodic, or batch production

- The distribution and support capabilities of potential suppliers

If a suitable commercial product is unavailable at a reasonable price, a determination should be made on whether to use a design or a performance specification.

SUMMARY

The purchase description forms the heart of any procurement. The organization's satisfaction with the purchased item frequently is determined at the time the purchase description is selected or developed. Purchase descriptions communicate to the buyer what to purchase, communicate to prospective suppliers what is required, serve as the principal element of the resulting purchase order or contract, and establish standards for inspection.

Five types of purchase descriptions have been described: brand or trade names, samples, standard specifications, design specifications, and performance specifications. Each has inherent advantages and disadvantages; no one approach is right or best in all circumstances. When the size of the contemplated purchase warrants, procurement research and analysis should be conducted to learn the availability and price of commercial products able to meet the firm's requirement. The availability of commercial products will affect the selection of the appropriate type of specification and the procurement strategy.

The procurement of services is a little understood, yet increasingly important, activity. We will look at this frequently overlooked issue in the next chapter.

chapter four

SIX PROBLEMS TO AVOID WHEN PURCHASING SERVICES

Gerald Brown, purchasing manager at Brandywine Products, has just had an uncomfortable discussion with Silas Eaton, owner-manager of Brandywine. Not even during his days as a pledge in a well-known national fraternity some 20 years ago had Gerald experienced such humiliation. Silas Eaton was livid. Accounts receivable show that $500,000 is being held up by Brandywine customers. It seems that these customers will not pay for their new vibration sensing equipment until they receive the technical manual that marketing promised to provide with the instruments. Further, marketing indicates that it is losing sure sales due to the nonavailability of the manual. (The manual is to contain technical data, installation and operating instructions, and troubleshooting and maintenance information. It also is to be used as a sales aid.) Eaton holds Gerald Brown personally responsible for the snafu. Eaton claims that every day of delay in the availability of the manual is costing Brandywine thousands of dollars in lost sales and interest expense.

The vibration sensing equipment had been under development for three years. The equipment was designed to detect potential malfunctions on expensive heavy equipment. In this way, corrective action could be taken before a catastrophic failure destroyed the equipment monitored by the vibration sensing device.

Eight months ago, the program manager for the vibration sensing equipment had forwarded a memo to technical publications at Brandywine requesting the development of a technical manual. This manual would supply the required technical data, installation and operating instructions, and troubleshooting and maintenance information. A month after receiving this request, the head of technical publications told the program manager that it would be more cost effective to purchase the completed manual than to do the work in house. The technical publications manager said that if her section were to do the work, she would have to hire two artists and several technical writers.

The program manager then contacted Gerald Brown in purchasing. After a few minutes' discussion, the program manager agreed to develop a statement of work describing his requirements. A one-page statement together with four glossy prints of the new equipment arrived in purchasing three days later. The statement of work stated that Brandywine's engineering department would provide requested technical advice to the supplier of the technical manual on request. The estimated cost of 500 finished manuals was $300,000. The manual was to consist of not less than 400 pages. The specified completion date was six and one-half months.

Recognizing the sensitivity of this procurement, Gerald assumed personal responsibility for its satisfactory completion. He contacted three technical writing consulting companies, described Brandywine's requirements, and requested a price from each firm. Only two of the companies were willing to meet the tight delivery schedule.

One of these firms, the C. Y. Hadley Company, employed 23 individuals. Of these, 20 were artists, draftspersons, or technical writers. The firm had been in business for 17 years. Samples of recent Hadley work showed it to be satisfactory. Gerald's efforts to lower its price of $290,000 were unsuccessful. Carole Hadley, owner of the firm, stated that she was operating at near capacity and would have to use considerable overtime to meet Brandywine's schedule. But she guaranteed to meet the required date if her firm received the purchase order within two days.

Brown had better luck with the A-B Commercial Art Company. Discussions with Messrs. Angst and Biddle, co-owners of A-B, revealed that they fully understood the requirement. They stated that they would have no difficulty in meeting the schedule. An examination of A-B's work showed excellent artistic and technical competence. The quality of A-B's work appeared to be superior to C. Y. Hadley's. The partners explained that it was their practice to do the artwork themselves and subcontract the technical writing to any of six local technical writers. Angst and Biddle both had been employed by C. Y. Hadley prior to establishing their own firm 10 months ago. A-B's initial price was $260,000. Through an examination of the firm's estimated costs and subsequent discussions, Brown was able to negotiate a price of $240,000 with a guaranteed delivery of six months.

Gerald Brown awarded a purchase order to A-B Commercial Art Company incorporating the statement of work he had received from the program manager. The purchase order stipulated that the finished technical manual would contain not less than 400 pages. Progress payments at the rate of $500 per page would be made on a monthly basis. All work was to be done to the satisfaction of the program manager.

At the end of the second month, the first 10 pages arrived with a request for a progress payment of $5,000. Gerald Brown visited A-B and was assured that the firm had the project under control and would be able to meet the stated completion date if Brandywine engineers would be more responsive to A-B's requirements. Gerald contacted the program manager and received a commitment for improved engineering support.

Two weeks later, only 20 more pages had arrived. Gerald visited the firm's loft office to find things in a state of total disarray. Messrs. Angst and Biddle were involved in a bitter argument. It soon became obvious that they would never meet the required delivery date.

Gerald then contacted Carole Hadley to see if she would be willing to "pick up the pieces." Carole stated that her firm simply did not have the capacity. Gerald tried, without success, to locate another supplier willing to meet the required delivery date. He then reported his findings to the program manager who immediately went to see Silas Eaton, the owner-manager of Brandywine. Silas, in turn, had had a very heated discussion with Gerald.

The procurement of services is a little understood, yet increasingly important, activity. We often hear that America is becoming a service-oriented society. Expenditures on services by commercial firms, not-for-profit organizations, and government increase each year. The criticality of services to the successful operation of these organizations frequently is more important than the amount of money spent. *The well-run procurement system must be as efficient at obtaining services as it is at obtaining materials, equipment, and supplies.*

Six of the major problems encountered in the procurement of services are as follows:

- *As was true at Brandywine, many organizations treat service requirements with indifference.* The procurement of such requirements frequently represents a sizable expenditure. Of greater importance, such procurements influence the efficiency, productivity, profitability, and morale of the organization.

  In Chapter 1, we saw another example of how critical the procurement of services can be. Ted Jones, the purchasing manager at the Eagle Manufacturing Company, had been called twice in one month by the president's secretary who had complained that the janitorial services supplier had not washed the president's windows properly. This may not be Ted's most critical contract from the point of view of Eagle's profitability and success. But it may be a most important one from the point of view of Ted's success—and even his employment!

- *Many organizations fail to identify their primary objective when purchasing services.* In Brandywine's case, the primary objective was to obtain an adequate technical manual on time. Timeliness was far more critical than was the artistic excellence of the manual or its price.

- *Another common problem is failure to develop an adequate statement of work with appropriate inspection procedures.* In no other area of procurement is there a more complex interdependency between the statement of work (SOW), the method of compensation, source selection, inspection procedures, and a satisfied customer. Standard specifications are unavailable for many service requirements. Thus, unique, *enforceable* SOWs must be developed. Purchasing's early and detailed involvement frequently is the key to a successful service procurement.

- *The type of pricing frequently is not tailored to motivate the supplier to satisfy the organization's principal objective.* Once we know what the primary requirement is (whether timely completion, artistic or design excellence, low cost, etc.), we must structure the purchase order to motivate the supplier to meet our needs. We also should reward good service and penalize poor service.

- *Make-or-buy analyses do not underlie most decisions to accomplish services either in house or by contract.* The services area is a dynamic one. Changes occur in the availability of suppliers and the cost of obtaining services under contract. The cost of performing work with the firm's own employees also may fluctuate. Periodic reviews of these costs can lead to a make-or-buy decision and significant savings. As is true in other make-or-buy analyses, consideration of control, availability, and technical excellence also must be weighed.

- *The process of selecting service contractors is done in an unprofessional manner.* Source selection is much more of an art when purchasing service requirements than when purchasing material. Due to the many problems involved in services procurement, it is essential that established, reputable suppliers be selected. Normally, competitive procedures should be employed.

We now look at the procurement of three classes of services.

PROFESSIONAL SERVICES

Lawyers, consultants, and architect-engineering (A-E) firms are representative of the individuals and organizations whose services are obtained through professional service purchase orders and contracts. To obtain a satisfactory procurement when purchasing professional services, it is essential that the individuals involved in the development of the statement of work know what is *really* required. For example, the vast majority of industrial, not-for-profit organizations and government agencies lose sight of their true objective when purchasing professional services. Many of these organizations enter into what can best be described as a contract designed to reward inefficiency.

The purchase of A-E services is typical of inept procurement of professional services. Frequently, the purchasing organization and the A-E agree that the fee will be a stated percentage of the cost of the building to be designed. (In many cases, a fee ceiling is established.) Under the logic of basing the fee on the cost of the building, the A-E's income increases as the building cost increases. *This is truly a reward for inefficiency.* Fortunately, most A-E firms are ethical and do serve their clients' best interests, even though their financial rewards would be greater if they complied with the incentive provision in the contract. Of equal madness is the approach of compensating A-Es with a firm fixed price contract. As we will see in greater detail in the appendix to Chapter 9, the firm fixed price type of pricing rewards suppliers for their cost control. Every dollar that costs are reduced results in a dollar of additional profit to the supplier. A fixed price contract places the A-E in a most awkward position. If cost is tightly controlled, the A-E's profits increase. But such frugality may result in the design of a building that costs the client considerably more than if the building had been designed for economic construction. Again, the vast majority of A-Es will not slight their professional responsibility and loyalty to their clients. But why take chances? It would make far greater sense to reward the A-E with a reasonable fee through the use of a cost plus fixed fee or cost plus incentive fee contract. To this fee should be added an incentive for designing the building whose cost is less than the previously established target cost. (For a more extensive discussion of this issue, the interested reader is referred to the author's article, "Selecting and Compensating Your Next Architect-Engineer," which appeared in the January 1972 issue of the *Michigan Business Review*.)

Once management in the procuring organization has established exactly what professional service is required (e.g., the design of a low-cost functional building), it is relatively simple to develop a SOW and proceed with the procurement. Unless the professional or professional firm possesses some truly unique skills or reputation, competition *should be* solicited. Provisions providing for review and approval of work in progress should be established. Since the resultant supplier (contractor) is a professional and since his or her reputation is of critical importance, inspection ordinarily is not a major problem.

A variety of compensation schemes is appropriate for professional services: hourly, daily, or weekly rates; firm fixed price when the supplier's reputation has been established; cost plus incentive or fixed fee; and cost plus award fee. The most effective compensation scheme when purchasing A-E services calls for the use of a cost plus fixed fee contract with a cost ceiling *and* an incentive fee that is based on how well the A-E controls construction cost. Such a compensation scheme is identical to a cost plus award fee contract. The various types of contract pricing are discussed in the appendix to Chapter 9.

TECHNICAL SERVICES

Technical services include research and development (R & D) work; the development and installation of management information systems (MIS) and materials requirement planning (MRP) systems; and the development of technical manuals, printing services, and repair services. In virtually all cases, competition should be based on both the quality of the services offered and the prices. As with professional services, it is essential that those responsible for the procurement focus on what *really* is required.

The completeness of the SOW and required inspection procedures is a function of the size and urgency of the requirement and the availability of reputable suppliers. For example, if an item of production equipment requires immediate repairs, time does not permit the development of an extensive SOW. If, on the other hand, a requirement exists for the development and subsequent fabrication of a new robot for manufacturing, then a carefully worded performance specification or SOW can be developed to describe what the machine is to do. Again, the key to a satisfactory and successful procurement is the identification of the firm's real requirement. Once this has been established, the development of a SOW, with appropriate inspection provisions, is relatively straightforward.

Research and development services frequently are purchased on a fixed price basis. When large expenses are likely to be incurred by the supplier, a cost plus fixed fee or cost plus award fee contract generally is more appropriate. Another approach to purchasing R & D services is to allow the supplier to amortize the R & D expenses over a stated production run. This approach is acceptable when no proprietary or patentable processes or equipment would result. If it appears likely that additional orders for the item being designed will occur, then title to and possession of the development data should be obtained. These data will allow the purchasing firm to solicit competition on all reprocurements. This, in turn, will result in significant savings during follow-on procurements.

The procurement of the development and/or adaptation of standard computer software systems such as management information systems and materials requirement planning systems is a most challenging one.

There are far more examples of faulty procurements of software than of efficient ones. The first prerequisite to a successful procurement of computer software is the realization that a team effort must take place both within the procuring organization and between the customer and supplier. Appropriate levels of management within the procuring organization must participate in the development of the SOW. Care must be taken in the development of the SOW to ensure that the resulting purchase order or contract does not become a bottomless pit. Identifiable milestones should be established to serve as the basis of progress payments. Termination provisions must be established to allow the purchaser to disengage from a hopeless situation. A small working project team with representation from all interested activities should be appointed. This project team will assist purchasing in selecting the best qualified supplier.

Such software development services are costly. Pricing approaches range from firm fixed price to labor hour to cost plus award fee. *If* the scope of work is very specific and relatively little uncertainty is present, the firm fixed price approach usually is appropriate. When these conditions are not present, other approaches must be adopted. The labor-hour purchase order is simple to negotiate and administer but has the disadvantage of rewarding inefficiency. Under a labor-hour purchase order, overhead and profit are built into the hourly rate. The supplier's contributions to overhead and profit increase as the number of hours worked increase. The cost plus award fee contract rewards excellent performance, punishes poor performance, yet ensures that the supplier's costs are reimbursed. Unfortunately, the cost plus award fee contract requires considerable administrative effort on the part of the procuring organization. Obviously, judgment and skill are required to tailor a contract to the specific situation. The responsible purchasing manager, as part of the preparation for the purchase, should talk with colleagues from other organizations who have had experience with such procurements. By openly discussing lessons learned, many previously made errors can be avoided.

The purchase of services such as the development of technical manuals and printing is relatively straightforward, once a determination has been made as to what is *really* required. Competition usually is readily available. The keys to a successful procurement are a sound statement of work; selection of an established, reputable supplier; and good purchase order administration. Fixed price contracts usually are appropriate. Due to the nature of these service industries, progress payments may be required. When progress payments are necessary, the purchaser needs to develop a list of identifiable progress milestones against which payments can be made.

The purchase of repair services varies from emergency situations to periodic maintenance. The best way to cope with emergencies is to anticipate them. Equipment does break-down. Sewer lines do get clogged. In many cases, the source (and even price) of such repairs can be established before the emergency occurs. Purchasing personnel recognize that when an emergency occurs, getting the repair done is usually more important than its cost. The vast majority of tradespeople are ethical and will not take advantage of an emergency situation. Thus, if the procuring organization has not anticipated such emergencies, time and materials contracts serve the best interests of both parties.

Requirements for periodic plant and equipment maintenance should allow reasonable time to develop a realistic SOW that includes inspection provisions. When the cost of such services warrants and when competition exists, purchasing then can solicit competitive bids. Warranty provisions on equipment items may require that maintenance service be purchased through the manufacturer's service organization. But as soon as this warranty period expires, the feasibility of obtaining competition should be explored. As we will discuss in the next chapter, the time to establish maintenance prices for new equipment is *during* the competitive stage of source selection of the equipment. This is the time when the most attractive price and service arrangements can be obtained.

OPERATING SERVICES

Operating services are those services that could be performed by the organization itself but that, for any of several reasons, are performed under contract. Examples include janitorial and guard service, food service, and the staffing and operation of hospital pharmacies. Private industry, not-for-profit organizations, and government have found that it frequently is more cost effective to purchase such services than it is to hire and supervise the required personnel.

The operating services area is a fast-changing one. The availability and cost of suppliers can vary dramatically in the course of a year or two. The cost pattern of performing the services in house also can fluctuate over a short period of time. Labor laws, practices, and costs may change. Based on the dynamic nature of this area, it is recommended that a make-or-buy analysis be conducted on any significant service requirement on a semiannual basis.

Again, the key to the successful procurement of such services is a well-developed SOW that includes detailed inspection procedures. In most instances, the SOW describes what is to be done rather than how it is to be done. Identifiable, measurable tasks must be established for both pricing and subcontract administration purposes. A second requirement for success is the selection of a supplier who has the experience and resources to provide the specified level of services. The third key to success is the development of a compensation scheme that rewards the supplier for good service with appropriate penalties for poor service. And of equal importance is the establishment and continued operation of a monitoring (inspection) system that protects the procuring organization's interests.

Selection of suppliers for such services is a rather straightforward matter. Once a good SOW is available, purchasing can solicit competition on a regional or national basis. Widespread competition is desirable and appropriate. Nationwide competition may be possible. For example, janitorial services for a hospital in New York State are provided efficiently and cost effectively by a supplier whose home office is located in a small town in California.

Selecting the method of compensation normally is routine. In most cases, a firm fixed price purchase order should be used. Such a purchase order must contain detailed provisions for price reductions, should any portion of the work not meet established criteria during any period of the contract. When considerable uncertainty exists on the expenses likely to be involved and when the size of the procurement warrants, a cost plus award fee contract is generally more appropriate.

SUMMARY

Many organizations treat service requirements with indifference. Yet such procurements frequently affect the efficiency, productivity, profitability, and morale of the organization. In addition to indifference, five other major problems frequently are encountered in the procurement of professional, technical, and operating services.

The most critical problem encountered in the procurement of services is the failure to identify the *primary* objective. Design, artistic, or technical excellence; timeliness; and low cost are three common objectives. Frequently, these objectives are in conflict. It therefore is crucial that the primary objective be identified and that this be the focus of the procurement.

Many organizations fail to develop an adequate SOW that contains appropriate inspection procedures. Enforceable SOWs are an essential prerequisite for successful service procurements.

The method of compensation frequently is *not* tailored to motivate the supplier to satisfy the customer's primary objective. Once this objective is known, purchasing should structure the compensation scheme in such a way that the supplier will maximize his or her income by fulfilling the customer's needs.

The services area is a dynamic one. Changes occur in the availability and cost of services furnished under contracts and in the cost of performing the work with the firm's own employees. Periodic make-or-buy analysis on the cost, control, availability, and technical implications of "making" versus "buying" will lead to significant savings.

The last problem discussed deals with the source selection process. Source selection is much more of an art when purchasing services than when purchasing materials. Due to the many problems involved in services procurement, it is essential that established, reputable suppliers be selected. Prospective suppliers should be screened with extreme caution. In most cases, it is possible and desirable to use competitive procedures as a tool in source selection.

An organization normally lives with procurement decisions on plant and equipment for many years. Such procurements are complex and costly and have a major impact on organizational productivity. We will look at these two areas in the next chapter.

chapter five

HOW TO STRETCH YOUR EQUIPMENT AND BUILDING DOLLAR

Wilbur Segerson, purchasing manager for the Fairburn Manufacturing Company, is involved in a spirited discussion with Harry Worell, the plant engineer at Fairburn.

HARRY: Wil, as you know, I have authorization and $70,000 to purchase two new lathes. Yesterday, I had a visit from Paul Jacobs, sales manager for Wellbuilt and Sleezy. We have four other Wellbuilt and Sleezy machines and they're tops. Jacobs said that demand is really heavy for the lathes we want but that, as a personal favor to me, he will guarantee delivery within six months if he gets an order this week . . . and at an installed price $1,000 below my budget. What sort of paperwork do you need to wrap this up?

WIL: Wait a minute, Harry. How do we know that Wellbuilt and Sleezy has the best suited equipment? How do we know that they will give us the best service, cooperation, and price?

HARRY: Wil, you simply don't understand industry conditions. These are good prices. And Wellbuilt and Sleezy is the only make that Tom Jones in production and I would let on our floor. If we don't grab this offer of 6 months' delivery, we will have to wait 12 to 18 months. Production needs those machines and as soon as humanly possible!

The procurement of new plant and equipment has a profound impact on the capacity, profitability, and productivity of the organization. Such procurements are complex. They require considerable planning, coordination, and cooperation on the part of all personnel. Substantial dollar amounts are involved. These expenditures have a significant effect on fixed overhead costs and break-even levels.

The productivity of individual workers and the organization is a function of the capacity, precision, and labor requirements of the equipment purchased. Downtime and maintenance expenses can be a significant contributor to costs.

The availability of new plant facilities has a major impact on the firm's ability to introduce new products or to enter new markets in a timely manner. The productivity of the entire organization is affected by the physical layout and flexibility of the plant.

In most organizations, procurement decisions on plant construction and equipment are made infrequently. But once such a decision is made, the organization normally lives with it for many years.

Three problems commonly exist in the procurement of capital equipment:

- Purchase descriptions tend to be either too precise or too broad.
- The requisite purchasing skills frequently are absent.
- Emphasis is placed on the cost of acquiring an item rather than on the total cost of owning and operating it.

When obtaining new plant construction, selection of the wrong method of purchasing construction results in the needless waste of millions of dollars.

Purchasing has a vital role to play in the procurement of the right equipment and facilities at the right price. We will look first at the procurement of capital equipment and then at the procurement of new plant facilities.

PURCHASING CAPITAL EQUIPMENT

The purchase of an item of capital equipment involves personnel from many areas of the firm. Production and manufacturing engineering are vitally concerned with the operating characteristics of the equipment. Plant engineering is concerned with the equipment's physical size and mounting dimensions, power and maintenance requirements, safety features, and pollution characteristics. Design engineering is concerned with the equipment's ability to produce items meeting standards. Engineering also may be concerned with the equipment's ability to meet likely future requirements. Finance is concerned with the initial cost and prospects for payback. On large expenditures, finance is concerned with credit arrangements and other sources of funds. Due to the importance of the procurement, top management frequently is involved throughout the process and generally makes the final decision on timing, sourcing, and the method of financing, based on recommendations from purchasing and the organizations just noted.

Purchasing has the responsibility for obtaining necessary information as the procurement process moves from preliminary analysis, through technical and economic analysis, to a commitment to make the purchase. Purchasing should ensure that the specification is adequate to meet the organization's performance, quality, and cost needs without being unduly restrictive. Purchasing also is responsible for negotiations, the consummation of an adequate legal document, and management of the resulting purchase order.

The typical procurement of capital equipment begins with the identification of a need. Next, initial feasibility studies are made. Production or plant engineering initiates and forwards to purchasing a request for general information about equipment that might satisfy the need. Purchasing *must* be responsive to such requests and obtain the requested preliminary technical, delivery, and pricing data. The least lack of cooperation at this point will cause the customer to start dealing directly with potential suppliers.

Next, engineering studies are undertaken. In many instances, the customer will want to meet with one or more equipment manufacturers' technical representatives. These individuals can provide invaluable information. A question may arise on how much presale engineering work the purchasing firm can receive without incurring a legal or moral obligation to the technical representative's organization.

This issue must be addressed before any possible problem arises. Caution is the key word. The responsible buyer needs to determine the amount of "free" sales engineering work that is common in the particular industry. (This so-called "free" work is a selling expense that must be absorbed by purchasers of the supplier's products if the supplier is to remain in business.) If the cost of an engineering study that appears to be especially desirable exceeds normal industry practice, the purchasing firm should pay for the study. If a "free" study is offered, the wise buyer ensures that neither he or she nor the firm will be under any obligation to purchase the proposed equipment.

Engineering now should be in a position to develop or adopt a specification. The key in developing the specification is an explicit statement of what the item is to do without unduly restricting competition. The specification should indicate whether the equipment is to be used for a particular specified purpose or to be adaptable to satisfy a variety of purposes. The machine's ability to meet and hold tolerances (precision); the size of the parts that are to be machined; the capacity per unit of operating time; the derived power requirements and consumption; the desired operator requirements; a description of desired motions; the desired range of feeds and speeds; the desired or required safety objectives, maximum size, and special features; the equipment's ability to be moved without difficulty; its pollution characteristics; and similar requirements should be specified. To encourage a desirable level of competition, minimum standards or requirements should be established. Normally, a performance guarantee should be included in the specification. This provision guarantees that the equipment supplied under the purchase order or contract will be capable of the performance set forth in the specification. If any adjustments, changes, or replacements are required, they will be accomplished at no additional cost to the purchaser.

Equipment falls into one of the three following classifications: (1) equipment standard to an industry, (2) standard equipment that is customized to meet special requirements, and (3) unique equipment.

Normally, an adequate level of competition can be obtained by specifying an item that is standard to an industry and that is produced by three or more vendors. This competition results in the right quality of equipment and service at attractive delivery and price terms.

When standard equipment must be customized to meet the purchaser's unique needs, the required unique feature must be clearly defined so that it can be completely understood by all potential suppliers. The potential suppliers should be required to indicate in their bids exactly what the additional feature will consist of, how it will affect the machine's operation, and what it will cost.

Two approaches commonly are employed to meet unique equipment requirements. When the procuring organization is concerned with what the machine will do and some freedom exists in how the machine will accomplish the task, the use of a performance specification is appropriate. The previously developed statement of what the item is to do and the identified technical characteristics will serve as the basis of such a specification. Competition can and should be solicited. Source selection utilizing the principle of life-cycle cost (discussed shortly) is relatively simple and straightforward.

In some process industries, it may be desirable to purchase unique equipment through the use of detailed technical specifications. The firm may develop these specifications with its own engineering staff or through a professional services contract. Either approach allows the firm to solicit competition for the fabrication of the required unique equipment. A less preferred approach is to invite two or three carefully prequalified engineering firms to submit proposals for the development of the required specifications under a cost plus fixed fee basis. The firms invited to submit proposals should indicate their planned technical approach, rates, overhead, fee structure, and ceiling costs for design and development. Separate overhead rates, fee structure, and ceiling costs also should be obtained for the fabrication of the required equipment. The procuring organization should specify that it retains the right to award the follow-on fabrication work to the selected engineering firm or such other supplier as it may choose.

On receipt of an adequate specification and when competition is present, the purchasing department prepares a request for quotations. This request should set forth the terms and conditions that will be incorporated into the resulting contract. Many equipment suppliers will attempt to have the purchase order drawn up on their standard sales agreement form. The purchasing firm should establish that its terms and conditions will govern and that any deviations or exceptions will result in the bid being rejected as nonresponsive.

Several benefits are gained by adopting this approach: (1) it is easier to analyze and compare proposals since they are all submitted under the same terms and conditions, (2) the buyer gains a better negotiating position, and (3) the time and effort required for negotiations are reduced. In most instances, the request for quotations should require vendors to bid on the equipment specified and, in addition, allow them to propose alternate equipment that they recommend.

Many standard and several nonstandard issues must be addressed in the terms and conditions. These include payment terms, performance standards, inspection procedures, warranties against defects, a performance warranty, supplier responsibility for postsale services, indemnity for patent infringement, operator training responsibility, installation responsibility, the extent of liability for employee accident, compliance with state and OSHA safety requirements, and the supplier's responsibility for maintaining an inventory of spare parts. The request for quotations should request prices for periodic and emergency maintenance and repairs. The time to get such prices is when competition exists.

On receipt of bids, purchasing should discuss the proposed procurement with finance. This will allow finance to update its economic analysis with current ceiling price information. If the analysis indicates that the procurement will be financially attractive and feasible, finance will give purchasing instructions to proceed. The buyer then should properly prepare for and conduct negotiations on price and any other issues that are not satisfactory.

It is essential that the buyer weigh several considerations during the source selection process. The seller's reliability, willingness and ability to provide required technical assistance, ability to provide spare parts quickly, service history, and an acceptable price all must be considered.

Frequently, two or more items of equipment will satisfy the firm's needs. These items will have different prices and other characteristics such as operator requirements, fuel consumption, expected life, and likely salvage values. The total cost of ownership approach to pricing allows the purchaser to determine the most likely cost of owning and operating an item over its anticipated productive life. This is the only rational approach to determining a true basis for comparing the costs of owning and operating equipment. Further, by considering all the significant costs over the life of the item instead of merely the initial acquisition cost, the firm gains an increase in competition. Firms whose products have higher initial prices but lower subsequent ownership costs may be able to compete.

The cost of ownership includes the initial cost of the item together with installation and start-up costs, the likely cost of operating it (fuel or power consumption, salaries for operators required, etc.), finance costs, training costs, maintenance costs (a function of the reliability and the maintainability of the equipment), insurance costs, tax considerations, and the likely salvage value of the item. The present value of the expected stream of expenditures less expected salvage value should be employed to accommodate for the time utility of money.

This concept is expressed as follows for a simplified example where initial (acquisition) cost, training costs, operating costs, maintenance costs, and salvage value are the only variables under consideration:

$$TCO = A + P.V. \sum_{i=1}^{n} T_i + O_i + M_i - S_n$$

where

TCO = total cost of ownership
A = acquisition cost
$P.V.$ = present value
T_i = training costs in year i
O_i = operating cost in year i
M_i = maintenance cost in year i
S_n = salvage value in year n

When the buyer is conducting price analysis on items of capital equipment, the price to use is the item's total cost of ownership as determined by the appropriate life cycle cost model.

Once a decision has been made on which item to purchase, two other issues should be addressed. Many equipment suppliers now provide excellent financing packages. The cost of such financing should be compared with the cost of alternate sources of funds. If supplier financing appears to be of interest, the buyer should recognize that the rates and duration may be as negotiable as are price and delivery terms.

Leasing frequently is a viable alternative to purchasing the desired item. Leasing is a popular method of acquiring industrial equipment. There are many arguments in favor of and in opposition to leasing. In the final analysis, the acquiring firm must look at the actual effect of leasing on its profit and loss statement.

Having looked at some of the major issues involved in the procurement of capital equipment, we now turn our attention to the purchase of new facilities.

PURCHASING PLANT FACILITIES

It was not long ago that expanding demand and a low cost of capital (by today's standards) allowed many firms to acquire new facilities with little regard to minimizing costs. The president of one large manufacturing company summarized this attitude by saying, "When you need more physical plant, what's $500,000 extra?" But conditions have changed. Building costs have continued to inflate while the cost of capital has soared. Changing market conditions, new product developments, and obsolete plants continue to make new plant facilities attractive to many organizations. But now, increased attention is, or should be, focused on minimizing expenditures for such facilities.

The purchase of new facilities is a commitment for the future. Quality, productivity of the new plant, the time required to effect the purchase, and cost all must be considered. Aesthetic requirements, time requirements, and the availability of highly qualified designers and builders all will tend to influence the selection of a purchase method. However, even before the purchase method can be selected, long-range planning is required.

Top Management Functions

Members of top management must be involved in the planning phase of the acquisition of new plant facilities.

- Facility requirements should be reviewed by top management when corporate plans and long-range goals are reviewed.
- If at all possible, additional facility requirements should be identified at least two years in advance of their actual requirement. Within reason, the more lead time available to those charged with the responsibility of purchasing the new facilities, the better will be the resulting procurement.
- The general location for the new facilities should be agreed on by top management.
- Space requirements at the time of building completion should be

established. Requirements for five years later should be estimated. A preliminary budget should be established. Present and future space requirements and the size of the budget are vital items of information that must be discussed with the designer-builder or architect-engineer.

• Top management must determine whether to lease or buy the proposed facilities.

Task Group Functions

A task group should be formed to take steps necessary for accomplishing the required facility procurement. This group should establish detailed requirements for the facility and should recommend the appropriate purchasing method to be employed. Purchasing, plant engineering, and plant maintenance should be represented in the group. The inclusion of representatives of these three functions will ensure that cost, plant layout, and maintenance implications are all considered.

Alternate Methods of Purchasing Construction

There are five methods for implementing the purchase of construction; however, it is unlikely that any one of the five methods will consistently be the proper choice for all building requirements. Figure 5.1 provides a graphic presentation of the various steps involved in each method from start to completion of a construction project.

Conventional method. This is the most frequently employed approach to buying building construction in the United States. With this approach, design of the required facility is performed by architects and/or engineers (frequently referred to as A-Es) without the involvement of a builder. Design of the facility is completed before potential contractors are requested to submit bids. Two separate organizations are responsible for the design and then the construction phases of the work.

Design and build firm-agreed-price method. This approach could be described as construction with gratuitous design. The owner determines the basic facility requirements, such as size, temperature, electrical, mechanical, and so on. These requirements became the basis of a performance specification. This specification is furnished to carefully prequalified builders who, with their prospective subcontractors, prepare a bid package consisting of a design and price proposal. The purchasing firm awards a firm-agreed-price contract for construction to the builder whose bid, consisting of a design and price proposal, is most attractive.

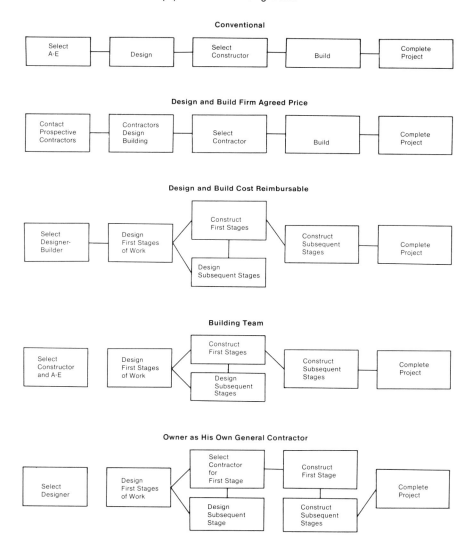

FIGURE 5.1   Sequence of Steps Involved with Alternative Methods

Design and build cost-reimbursable method.   With this method only one contract is awarded for both design and construction. Design is accomplished by architects and engineers employed by the general contractor. Thus, the builder has ample opportunity to influence the design of the required facility. With this approach, construction of a work element (excavation, structural work, and so on) proceeds when the design of the *element* has been completed. It is not necessary to await design of the total project since one firm is responsible for both the design and the construction phases. This approach is particularly useful when a structure is required within a very short time period.

Building team.   With this approach, the owner retains both a designer and a builder concurrently. In contrast to the conventional method, the builder is retained during the design phase and is expected to contribute information on costs, procedures, and time requirements to the designer. As the A-E completes the plans and specifications for a work element, the builder either accomplishes the work with his or her own forces or obtains prices from several qualified specialists in the work (subcontractors) and awards the work to the qualified subcontractor making the best offer (price, time, and quality considered). As with the other methods, the general contractor oversees and integrates the efforts of the subcontractors.

The owner as contractor.   With this method, the owner contracts directly for the various work elements and performs the functions of integrating and controlling that would otherwise be accomplished by a general contractor. Since purchase orders and contracts are awarded on a work element basis, it is possible for construction to proceed prior to completion of the total design phase.

Research on these five methods and the resulting cost of purchasing building construction shows that the conventional method is, by far, the most costly approach to obtaining construction.[1] Savings of approximately 30% are likely to result when the design and build firm-agreed-price method is used in lieu of the conventional method. Savings of 9% are likely when either the design and build cost-reimbursement or the building team method is used in lieu of the conventional method. A savings of 5% is likely when the owner acts as the general contractor.

The amount of time from first contacting the designer or builder until completion of the facility varies significantly with the methods used. On a typical 130,000-square-foot manufacturing plant, 16 months are required with the conventional method, 11.5 months with the design and build firm-agreed-price method, 12 months with both the design and build cost-reimbursable method and the building team methods, and 15.5 months when the owner acts as contractor.

We see that selection of the most appropriate method of purchasing plant facilities can significantly reduce the cost and time required to purchase new facilities.

---

[1]David N. Burt, "Stretching Your Building Dollar," *California Management Review,* Vol. 15, No. 4, Summer 1973, pp. 54–60.

Procurement of Construction by Government

Most governments require the use of formal advertising (competitive bidding) for purchases above a stated threshold (e.g., $10,000). As a result, the vast majority of construction for governments has been purchased using the conventional approach described earlier in this chapter.

Several years ago, an approach that has come to be known as two-step procurement was developed. This approach allows government to avail itself of the benefit of the competition of concepts resulting from use of the design and build firm-agreed-price method of purchasing construction. Use this method only when the following conditions can be satisfied:

- Definite criteria exist for evaluating the technical proposal
- More than one potentially qualified source is available
- Sufficient time is available

In step 1, the engineering department prepares a technical package consisting of

- A general description of the required building, including location, areas of required facilities, comfort requirements, electrical loads, and so on
- A list of available drawings and specifications
- A list of the criteria to be used for evaluating the resulting technical proposals
- The desired completion date

Purchasing then prepares an invitation to qualified builders to submit unpriced technical proposals. This invitation includes, as appropriate,

- The technical package developed by engineering
- A statement that builders may (or may not) submit more than one technical proposal
- The location and closing time for submittal of technical proposals
- A statement that no information on prices shall accompany the technical proposal
- A provision granting the government the right to request further information after the closing date
- An indication that the resulting contract will be fixed price or fixed price plus escalation
- A provision stating that the successful contractor will maintain the

resulting facility for a stated period. (Five years is the recommended period. Such a procedure will tend to ensure that a satisfactory level of quality results.)

- A statement that the second step will include only those firms whose technical proposals are acceptable
- A statement that each builder submitting an unacceptable technical proposal will be notified upon completion of the evaluation process. Such rejection will be final.

After the closing date for receipt of technical proposals, purchasing turns over all proposals to engineering for a technical review. It is recommended that proposals be identified by a code prior to evaluation to preclude any possibility of favoritism or fraud. Engineering carefully reviews the technical proposals and approves those that it feels would satisfy the requirement. Engineering then informs purchasing of the names of the firms whose technical proposals are acceptable.

Purchasing now begins step 2. Purchasing prepares a restricted invitation for bids that is sent only to those firms whose technical proposals have been approved by engineering. The solicited firms are to bid on their respective technical approaches. The cost of maintenance should be shown as a separate item in the price proposal. Award is made to the firm submitting the lowest bid. While a bit more cumbersome than the design and build firm-agreed-price method, two-step procurement does allow government to avail itself of the savings associated with the design and build firm-agreed-price method of purchasing construction.

SUMMARY

The procurement of new plant and equipment has a profound impact on the capacity, profitability, and productivity of the firm. These procurements require planning, coordination, and the cooperation of all involved. The organization normally lives with plant and equipment procurement decisions for many years.

When purchasing new equipment, competition often is not possible. Since users are inclined to insist that only one make of equipment is acceptable, purchasing must take appropriate action to ensure that the equipment specification provides an explicit statement describing what the item is to do without unduly restricting completion.

Purchasing's contribution to the procurement of equipment requires responsiveness and the application of professional purchasing skills. Purchasing has much to offer in this area. In proactive procurement, purchasing can make a significant contribution to the equipment procurement process.

When two or more items of equipment satisfy a firm's needs, the total cost of ownership should be determined. This cost, also known as the life-cycle cost, is computed by aggregating the initial cost of the item together with installation and start-up costs and the present value of likely operating costs and deducting the present value of the item's salvage value. This is the only rational approach to determining a true basis for comparing the cost of owning and operating different equipment. This approach also allows the firm to increase competition, because products that have higher initial prices but lower subsequent ownership costs may be considered.

The most common problem encountered when purchasing new plant construction is selection of the wrong method of contracting. Research conducted on the subject shows that the most commonly employed method of purchasing construction is not only the most costly but requires the most time for completion of a building. Selection of the most appropriate method of purchasing new plant facilities can save both time and money.

Most governments generally utilize competitive bidding and, therefore, conventional methods of purchasing construction. This chapter outlined a two-step approach that allows government units to take advantage of the design and build fixed-agreed-price method of purchasing construction when it is appropriate.

In a production environment, purchasing often lacks sufficient lead time to develop procurement plans and to purchase in a cost-efficient manner. In the area of production materials, such lead time is a function of production planning and of inventory control. The next chapter discusses these challenging areas.

chapter six

TWO KEY INTERFACES: PRODUCTION PLANNING AND INVENTORY CONTROL

Bob Meckline, president and general manager of the Lone Star Manufacturing Company, is addressing his first- and second-line managers: "Ladies and gentlemen, we are confronted with a most fascinating and frightening situation. Don Mann tells me that sales are better than ever. But according to Everet Solomon, we are in a situation of near cash starvation. According to some projections Ev discussed with me yesterday, we are in a situation of profitless prosperity. Ev and I are convinced that the most important thing we can do to get back on track is to reduce our inventory of purchased materials. Money bags, how about sharing your thoughts."

Everet replies, "Thanks, Bob. Well, as Mr. Meckline was saying, and as most of you know, sales are looking pretty good so far this year. But our investment in inventories is eating up most of our profits. Purchased material inventory turnover has fallen from 4 to 1 just 18 months ago to 2 to 1! We now have $9 million tied up in inventories. Our inventory carrying costs are about 33% of the value of the inventory, on an annual basis. My latest pro forma shows our net income before taxes is only $1 million. Now, I figure that if we cut our inventory in half to $4.5 million, we will save about one-half of our current inventory carrying costs. This, in turn, would increase profits by $1.5 million to a respectable $2.5 million. Ladies and gentlemen, there is no quicker way to increase profits!"

Don Mann, vice president of marketing, is the first to respond. "Ev, as you know, we in marketing have done an unbelievable job. Not only have sales doubled in the last 18 months, but our market share has risen from 8% to 14%. And we've done this in spite of having virtually no increase in finished goods inventory. When Charlie and Al talked with me on a way to support an increase in sales without an increase in finished goods inventory, I thought that they were nuts. But they claimed that with a decent inventory of purchased materials, fast purchasing action, and a highly responsive production system, we would be able to support our tremendously successful marketing program. They also pointed out that an increase in purchased materials inventory would be less costly than would an increase in finished goods. No labor investment. As I said, I was skeptical, but now, I'm a believer."

Charlie Teplitz, vice president of operations, joins in: "Large inventories of purchased materials have three major advantages, from my point of view. They allow greater flexibility in planning and scheduling, they minimize production disruptions, and they facilitate longer production runs. I'm certain that you are all aware that both labor and management learn more efficient ways of doing things during long runs, resulting in increased productivity and lower unit costs.

Next, Al Englehart, director of purchasing, offers his thoughts. "Frequently, large inventories are necessary to allow us to buy economically. Just yesterday, I signed a P.O. for 500 steel castings. The unit price was 13% lower than if we'd bought only 199 castings.

"As most of you know, the price of most purchased materials is based on changing supply and demand patterns. Temporary favorable buying situations and the likelihood of future adverse supply situations are good grounds for hedging or laying in inventory in advance of requirements. In effect, an expected higher cost of goods is avoided.

"Administrative costs in purchasing, inspection, receiving, warehousing, and finance tend to be lower on a unit price basis when high inventory levels allow us to process fewer relatively large orders for materials and supplies. Additionally, larger, less frequent orders allow for more efficient utilization of my staff. My buyers are free to concentrate on the development of new sources and on more extensive and better negotiations. Lower unit prices result. Fewer orders reduce the purchase order-contract management work load, resulting in better monitoring of the remaining work load, better control, and the probability of improved timeliness of delivery and quality of material received.

"Further, maintenance and repair supplies are required to operate and maintain our plant and equipment. Paper, pencils, and similar items are required throughout the organization. We need fuel, lubricants, and replacement parts for our vehicles. The availability of such operating supplies is essential for our successful operation. When supplies are not available, efficiency and productivity are greatly reduced, and we can't perform effectively."

Sue Anderson, traffic manager, then chimed in: "Carload and truckload freight rates are a fraction of smaller, less than truckload rates. Large purchase orders result in considerable savings for my traffic budget."

Mr. Meckline was becoming severely agitated. "Boy, Ev, we really opened a can of worms on this one. How in blazes do we know what the optimal level of inventory is?"

Determining the right time at which to make purchases and the right quantity to buy have major impacts on an organization's success. These decisions affect the firm's responsiveness to its customers, its productivity, the cost of its purchased materials, and its administrative, handling, and storage expenses. Many purchasing managers view inadequate lead time as their number one problem. A second major problem in this area is that of inappropriate or suboptimal purchase quantities resulting from faulty inventory policies. In the case used to open this chapter, we see that Lone Star Manufacturing Company is far in advance of many other manufacturers: at least Lone Star management is aware of some of the many issues underlying sound inventory policies.

In proactive procurement, purchasing must interact with those responsible for forecasting, production planning, and inventory management. For this interaction to result in cost-effective decisions, purchasing managers must have a basic understanding of forecasting, production planning, and inventory management. We now turn our attention to these areas.

PRODUCTION PLANNING

Time is a valuable resource in the procurement process. The more time available, the better or more "optimized" is the design process (assuming that the additional time is employed to develop the most cost-effective design and *not* to "gold plate" a design, as happens all too frequently). More time provides the opportunity for better specifications and better cost estimates.

Adequate time is essential for economic purchasing. The amount of time available will affect the quality of the solicitation request, the number of sources solicited, the quality of the negotiations, and the resulting price. For example, if sufficient time is not available to seek competition, we may be forced to purchase on a sole-source basis. As was mentioned in Chapter 2, sole-source procurements tend to cost 12% more than competitively solicited procurements.

The amount of lead time allowed for purchasing action is usually insufficient, resulting in excessively high prices, lower quality of material received, and late delivery. To avoid such situations, it is essential that personnel in marketing, design engineering, production planning, and inventory management become familiar with purchasing's need for realistic lead times and that these individuals then endeavor to provide such lead times.

Production planning—also referred to as aggregate planning, operations planning, and aggregate scheduling—is concerned with the overall operation of an organization over a specified time horizon. Based on customer orders and forecasts for a period 6 to 18 months into the future, production planning determines the size and training of the work force, inventories, aggregate material purchases, overtime, and subcontracting[1] required. These decisions then can be converted into a production budget, which becomes the source of personnel plans (hiring, training, firing, etc.), warehousing needs, purchasing plans, and cash requirements.

The production plan is the basis of the short-range (1- to 6-month) master schedule. Development of the master schedule involves checking on capacity and the allocation of the resources acquired as a result of the production plan to specific products in specific time periods. The master schedule is the basis of a third activity, dispatching, which involves taking corrective actions required as a result of late receipt of materials, absent workers, inoperable machines, changes in priorities, new or canceled orders, and a host of other events that make the master schedule appear to be a wish or an idle dream. Dispatching ranges from coercing suppliers to expedite deliveries of needed materials, to expediting the production of component parts, to appeasing customers while telling them that their order will be late.

Figure 6.1 shows the relationship among these activities. Customer orders and sales forecasts are the basic input to the production plan. Ideally, the production plan will cover a period of 1 to 5 years. If adequate capacity is available, the production plan becomes the basis of the nearer-term master schedule. The master schedule commonly is for a period of 6 months. The master schedule is the basis for releasing purchase orders for materials and work orders. Dispatching then is required to juggle available and additional resources, customers, and production activities.

Production planning involves the development of a series of interrelated shorter-term plans, including the master schedule, an input or resources plan, and an output plan. The master schedule specifies the amount of production (or subcontracting) to be accomplished over a series of future periods. The input plan specifies the inputs to the master schedule by indicating the size of the work force, the length of the workday,

---

[1]Throughout this chapter, the word "subcontracting" refers to purchase of an end item that normally is manufactured by the firm.

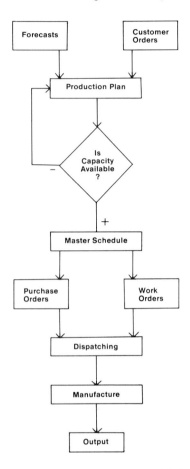

FIGURE 6.1 Production Planning and Scheduling

and the materials that will be required. The output plan details the destination of the manufactured goods to inventory or distribution.

Production planning begins with a forecast of future demand. Normally there are a number of ways that the resources, rates of production, and output rates can be balanced to meet the forecasted demand. Each alternative is likely to have different cost and operating implications. For example, the manufacturer may be able to

- Vary the size of the work force
- Utilize overtime
- Subcontract
- Vary the product mix
- Accept back orders

- Stabilize demand by adding countercyclical products to the product line
- Vary price and promotional efforts to influence demand

Let us now consider a simplified manufacturing process. If forecasted demand is 1,000 units in month 1 and 2,000 units in month 2, how can input, production, and output rates be varied to meet anticipated demand (forecasts)? One approach would be to vary the input, production, and output rates simultaneously as we move from month 1 to month 2. In month 1, sufficient labor and materials would be input to produce exactly 1,000 units. In month 2, these inputs and the rate of production could be doubled to produce exactly 2,000 units of output. A second alternative would be to produce 1,000 units in each of the two months and *subcontract* for 1,000 units for delivery in the second month. A third alternative would be to keep all inputs and production at a constant rate, one equal to the average demand. Under this alternative, 1,500 units would be produced in month 1 with 1,000 going to distribution and 500 to inventory. In month 2, all 1,500 units produced together with 500 units from inventory would go to distribution. Obviously, there are many additional alternatives.

The attractiveness of each alternative depends on the relative costs associated with changing input and production rates and the costs associated with the various ways of disposing of the outputs (i.e., distribution or storage).

As we have seen, the key inputs to the production planning process are customer orders and forecasts. The receipt of customer orders is a straightforward idea requiring no elaboration. Forecasting, on the other hand, frequently appears to be something of a black art. We now will overview commonly employed forecasting techniques in an effort to gain insight into this critical process.

A major manufacturing firm recently learned the importance of accurate sales forecasts. Its sales forecasts for two years were based, in large measure, on bleak economic predictions for the period. These forecasts proved to be approximately 25% below actual demand. This firm operated in an industry where long lead times and allocation of materials by suppliers were common. The firm purchased supplier capacity for its annual materials requirements based on its sales forecasts. Accordingly, it purchased approximately 75% of its actual material requirements from its traditional suppliers. The balance of the material required to meet actual demand was purchased on the open market from middlemen at premium prices.

No single forecasting method gives uniformly accurate results. Accordingly, when, as in the preceding example, forecasting accuracy is of critical importance, it is desirable to use several methods, with each method acting as a check on the others. The two basic approaches to long-term (in excess of one year) forecasting are top-down and buildup. With top-down forecasting, we

- Obtain or develop a forecast of general economic conditions
- Determine the industry's total market potential for the product
- Determine the firm's share of the total industry market
- Identify likely changes in historic activity due to competitive action, pricing and promotional efforts, and so on
- Develop the product's sales forecast

Under the buildup method, we accumulate estimates of future demand from various organizational units in the company. This method may draw on one or more of the following four classes of forecasting techniques: consensus of executive opinion, a sales force composite, users' expectations, and quantitative methods.

Consensus of Executive Opinion

This is the oldest and simplest technique of developing sales forecasts. The opinions of top managers from various departments are obtained and averaged in an effort to develop a sounder forecast than could be developed by a single individual. This technique is quick and relatively simple. But it is based entirely on opinion rather than on facts and analyses. Further, averaging opinions disperses the responsibility for their accuracy.

Sales Force Composite

Under this technique, the opinions of members of the sales department are solicited for their opinions concerning expectations of future sales in their territories. The estimates are reviewed by regional sales managers and then by the general sales manager. This technique also is simple and has the advantage of being based on the specialized knowledge of those closest to the market. But the technique suffers from several disadvantages. Many salespersons tend to be overly optimistic. Others are risk averse and will "play it safe" by underforecasting. Such action ensures that the salesperson's forecast will be met without the individual having to exert himself or herself.

Users' Expectations

Manufacturers in industries with relatively few customers may ask their customers how much they expect to purchase in the forthcoming period. The sales forecasts are based directly on this information. This is a relatively inexpensive method of forecasting; however, the basis of the forecast is expectations, which are subject to change.

Quantitative Techniques

Many organizations rely on one or more quantitative techniques to supplement personal judgment and to increase the accuracy of sales forecasts. These quantitative techniques allow the forecaster to predict the future from past internal data. These techniques, which are beyond the scope of this book, may be obtained from a number of texts on the subject.

The experienced forecaster will develop a forecast and then modify it, if appropriate, by the expected influence of factors that cause deviation from historic trends. Such factors include competition, market demand, economic conditions, proposed legal changes, and the availability of materials. We see that forecasting is both an art and a science!

With the revised forecast in hand, the production planner is now able to plan on an aggregate basis. It is this plan that will be the basis of material input requirements, total work force, total production, the size of inventories, the amount of subcontracting, and the master schedule. While considerable effort is being devoted to operations research approaches to aid the production planner, charting techniques are still the most commonly used approach to carrying out this difficult task.

With charting, once an approved forecast has been developed for the planning period, a table is constructed for the cumulative product requirements. The production planner then investigates alternative strategies calling for different production rates, different work force sizes, different levels of subcontracting, and/or different inventory levels with the objective of maximizing profits. The costs that are investigated include (1) costs due to production rate variation (overtime or excess idle time), (2) costs due to variation in the size of the work force (hiring and training costs, severance, and unemployment pay), (3) incremental costs for materials (quantity discounts, price breaks, etc.), (4) costs resulting from subcontracting for requirements that cannot be produced by the firm under a particular production plan, and (5) carrying costs of different levels of inventory. The most attractive strategy becomes the production plan.

Assuming adequate capacity is available, the adopted production plan becomes the basis for the master schedule. The master schedule provides information both on the total quantity to be produced and variations in quantities by time period. In extremely simple operations, this information can be applied to the bill of materials for the item under study to forecast material requirements. These requirements can be checked against available inventory, ultimately becoming the basis of purchase activity. But, in most manufacturing operations, the number of items produced, the variety and quantities of required purchased materials, and the frequent changes in the master schedule require considerable intermediate-level planning. More and more, we find that this intermediate-level planning is being accomplished through the assistance of a computer-controlled materials requirement planning (MRP) system. Even when a computer-controlled MRP system is not employed, the following logic is useful in understanding the process of converting the production plan to work orders and purchase orders.

MATERIAL REQUIREMENTS PLANNING

Material requirements planning is a new name applied to an established procedure. It is simply a computer program for production scheduling, inventory control, and the scheduling of purchase orders. MRP allows management to time efficiently the ordering and manufacturing of the components and subassemblies that make up completed products. MRP includes a precise scheduling system, an efficient material control system, and a rescheduling system for revising plans as changes occur. The major objectives of the MRP system are simultaneously to

- Ensure the availability of components and subassemblies for planned production of end items for delivery to customers or inventory
- Maintain the lowest possible investment in inventory
- Plan purchasing and manufacturing activities
- Reschedule purchasing and manufacturing activities, as required

The four principal elements in an MRP system are

1. The production schedule
2. The product structure (bill of materials) file
3. The inventory status file
4. The MRP logic

Figure 6.2 depicts an MRP system. We see that the production plan is the basic input and drives the MRP system. But the production plan is constrained by projected production capacity. If projected capacity in the form of facilities, equipment, personnel, and purchased materials (especially long lead components) is not adequate to meet the production plan, resources will have to be increased, excess requirements will have to be obtained from subcontractors, the plan will have to be revised, or

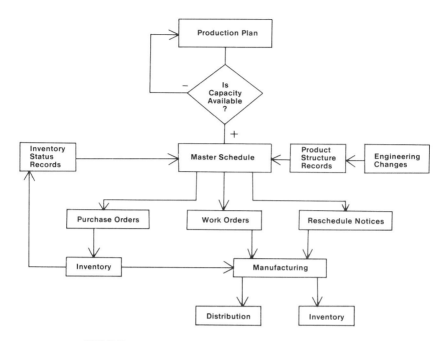

FIGURE 6.2   A Materials Requirement Planning System

marketing will have to be advised that projected demand cannot be met.

Inventory status records indicate the actual inventory level of each item, quantities on order, quantities previously allocated, lead times, and lot sizes. Lead times should be long enough to be feasible without resorting to special efforts by suppliers such as expediting, premium time, and the use of premium transportation. MRP systems which update lead times based on the time the supplier required on the last order can result in production disruptions, premium prices, premium transportation, and extraordinary expediting efforts. There is no guarantee that 10 weeks' lead time will be adequate today, even though 10 weeks were required for delivery on the last order. There are at least three ways of coping with the need for current *and* adequate lead times. (1) One of the approaches to purchasing recurring requirements with guaranteed lead times specified, as discussed in Chapter 9, can be employed. (2) The lead times contained in the inventory records can indicate maximum likely time required. Then when the MRP system issues a requisition for material, the requisition should indicate the required availability date. (3) The timing of purchases can be at the discretion of the buyer based on the production schedule. If this approach is employed, the buyer must be informed when manufacturing activities are rescheduled and then must take appropriate action. The MRP logic takes into consideration lot-sizing techniques based on balancing the costs of ordering and holding inventory. These techniques are discussed later in this chapter.

Product structure files are based on the bill of materials. They show every component or assembly required to produce end items together with the sequencing of manufacturing and assembly operations required to manufacture an item. When an item is designed, an engineering drawing and a bill of materials are created. A process planner then develops route and operation sheets on the actual manufacture of the item. This logic is captured in the item's product structure record.

To understand the logic of an MRP system, suppose that the production plan calls for delivery of a child's wagon in 14 weeks. We know from the wagon's product structure record that the wagon consists of six parts: a steel body, four wheels, two axles, four axle brackets, four axle nuts, and a handle. Additionally, a set of assembly instructions and a printed corrugated shipping box are required. A check of the inventory status records for these items shows that we have only the axle nuts, axle brackets, and the printed instructions in inventory. These records also indicate that the procurement lead times are body, 10 weeks; wheels, 2 weeks; axles, 2 weeks; handles, 4 weeks; printed corrugated boxes, 8 weeks. We also know that it will take a week to assemble the wagon. To ship during the fourteenth week requires that all components be available for assembly in week 13.

We could place orders for all of these items right now, but what would happen if we did? We would have the body in inventory for 3 weeks, wheels in inventory for 11 weeks, and so on. For one wagon, this would not be much about which to worry. But what if we are talking of 100,000 wagons?

Instead of ordering all items now, let's work back from our shipping date of week 14. We will need all the wagon's components in week 13, so we can simply calculate when to place our orders by subtracting lead times. We would order the body in 3 weeks, the printed box in 5 weeks, the wheels and axles in 11 weeks, and the handle in 9 weeks.

Now consider the substitution of a body manufactured in our own facilities for the purchased one. We will simplify by assuming that the body is pressed from purchased sheet steel that requires 6 weeks' lead time. It then is painted with red paint requiring 2 weeks' lead time. Each of the two internal operations (pressing and painting), together with materials handling times, requires one week. Recognizing that the body must be available at the beginning of week 13, our action times would be order steel, week 5; order paint, week 10; press body, week 11; paint body, week 12.

Next, consider a disruption in the production schedule. Suppose that a machine breaks down, throwing a component two weeks off schedule, ultimately affecting end-product delivery by two weeks. As a result of the delayed completion date, there is no reason to hurry the other components along as planned. To do so would merely result in their sitting needlessly in inventory. Instead, the due dates for these items could be delayed by two weeks. Such a revision (slippage) has three important benefits: (1) if the item is produced internally, it frees up production capacity for other jobs; (2) it avoids the "hurry up and wait" syndrome that is so common in manufacturing operations and that is responsible for excessive in-process inventories; and (3) it allows us to reschedule supplier deliveries for purchased components, reducing our inventories of purchased materials.

Now, visualize a manufacturing plant with hundreds of operations and purchased components. While the planning and controlling of the actions required for one wagon can be done by hand, it is not difficult to imagine the complexity of planning for and controlling of a great number of products and parts that interact with one another. Such complexity defies manual control procedures. MRP considers not only the time dimension in planning but also the current and planned quantities of parts and products in inventories. MRP takes into account the dynamics of both time and quantity for interrelated parts and products. With the significant reductions in the cost of high-speed computation we have gained in the recent past, MRP can now rapidly and inexpensively update order priorities weekly or daily if changes in plans and expectations require. Rapid computation is required to explode component requirements from the schedule while simultaneously referencing inventory records to check stock status and lead times and to keep the entire plan sufficiently current to be useful in spite of revised schedules and late material arrivals.

The following benefits result from successful MRP applications:

- *Reduced inventory investment.* Inventories of purchased material and work in process decrease by 10% to 30%.
- *Reduced administrative effort.* Scheduling, inventory control, and purchasing should become more efficient, making the assignment of personnel to more productive tasks possible.
- *Reduced manufacture of obsolete components.* Through the use of product structure records that reflect planned engineering changes, manufacturers are able to coordinate changes with the consumption of dated parts. Such coordination decreases scrap costs substantially.
- *Improved customer relations.* MRP can be used to determine the likelihood of meeting proposed delivery dates before marketing makes delivery quotations. In addition, if an item with a promised

delivery goes off schedule and cannot be brought back on schedule, customers can be notified in a timely manner so that they can revise their plans with minimum inconvenience.

While MRP appears to be highly desirable, there have been many unsuccessful applications. To be implemented successfully, four prerequisites are essential:

1. A commitment by *all* levels of management
2. Stability in employment on the part of those who are to implement and use the system during its initial stages of operation
3. The availability of timely and accurate data
4. The active involvement of those who will use the system in its design and implementation

THE TRADE-OFFS INVOLVED IN DETERMINING THE RIGHT LEVELS OF INVENTORY AND QUANTITIES TO PURCHASE

A high degree of interdependence exists between the inventory level for an item and the optimal quantity to purchase at any point in time. Determining the right inventory level and the right quantity to purchase have very significant impacts on the successful operation and profitability of the organization. As we saw at the Lone Star Manufacturing Company, this determination requires an analysis involving many trade-offs. But the savings potential makes the required effort well worthwhile.

Theoretically, demand for production materials and supplies required for the operation of the organization and the supply of these items could be coordinated to such an extent that inventories would be unnecessary. Such a situation is approximated when an organization employs an MRP system as described earlier in this chapter. (This situation is attained in companies using the Japanese *kanban*—or just in time—system or the definite delivery contract described in Chapter 9.) But for many items and many situations, it may be impossible to know future demand with total certainty. Further, it may be impossible to guarantee availability of all items at a particular moment. Thus, inventories serve as buffers between the demand for and the supply of required materials and supplies. In addition, MRP is *not* appropriate for all organizations. Inventories allow greater flexibility in production. This flexibility has two benefits: (1) the firm can better respond to customer demands for its products, and (2) economies result in the production operation. Inventories also allow a reduction in the overall cost of purchased material and supplies through purchasing, transportation, and administrative economies. And inventories serve as hedges against future price increases and other contingencies such as transportation difficulties, strikes, natural catastrophes, and so on. Large purchase order quantities tend to be associated with large inventories. This relationship is *not* absolutely essential; however, there is such a strong tendency for it to exist that we will say that, based on empirical evidence, large order quantities are associated with large inventories.

Inventory carrying costs currently run between 15% and 45% of the value of the inventory on an annual basis. In today's high cost of capital environment, it is likely that inventory carrying costs are approximately 35% per year. Further, inventories tie up needed working capital and may preclude a firm from being able to take advantage of otherwise attractive investment opportunities.

If we can significantly reduce the amount of inventory required to support a given level of operation without adversely affecting the various costs and impacts in the areas of production, purchasing, and transportation, then we could improve the organization's efficiency and profitability. Such a reduction in inventory requires both effective inventory and purchasing management and a close coordination between the two. The following example illustrates the impact of such improved inventory and purchasing management.

> The Clearwater Company produces farm equipment to order. It relies on a large inventory of purchased material and a responsive production department to meet its customers' needs. Clearwater has an average of $12 million in purchased materials. Its sales are $24 million, for an inventory turnover ratio of

$$\frac{\text{Sales}}{\text{Inventory}} = \frac{24}{12} = 2$$

> Increased emphasis is placed on inventory and purchasing management resulting in a reduction in inventory from $12 million to $8 million. Note that the inventory turnover ratio improves from 2 to $24/8 = 3$. Inventory carrying costs are 35% per year of the value of the average inventory. The $4 million reduction in inventory will lead to a reduction in inventory carrying expenses of $4 million $\times$ .35 = $1.4 million (assuming that the unused capacity in space, equipment, and work force can be released or that this capacity would be absorbed by allowing increased sales with no corresponding increase in inventory).

> If pretax profits for Clearwater were $8 million, this savings of $1.4 million in inventory carrying costs would increase pretax profits by 17.5%! Further, by improving the inventory turnover ratio, Clearwater has freed $4 million that it can invest or use to reduce its current or long-term liabilities.

Several quantitative approaches exist for determining the optimal inventory level and reorder point. These are beyond the scope of this book. But the underlying logic of inventory management can be examined by looking at the tabular approach. We can determine the optimum inventory level for an item by summing the appropriate costs discussed in the earlier part of this chapter and selecting the inventory level associated with the minimum total cost. An example provides further insight into this concept.

The Apex Manufacturing Company purchases blank castings from outside suppliers and machines them to customer orders. Apex uses an average of 2,000 castings per year. Purchase prices and transportation rates for differing quantities are as follows:

UNITS PER ORDER	PURCHASE PRICE FOB ORIGIN	TRANSPORTATION PER UNIT	TOTAL DELIVERED PRICE
0 to 199	$190	$20	$210
200 to 499	175	10	185
500 and over	160	10	170

The administrative costs associated with purchasing, receiving, inspecting, warehousing, and paying the supplier are estimated to be $200 per purchase order. Apex maintains no safety stock of purchased material. Average inventory, then, is one-half the size of each purchase order quantity. Marketing believes that lost sales costs will be a function of the number of orders placed per year, since an out-of-stock condition for the castings will occur between usage of the last casting and receipt of a new shipment. Marketing estimates the lost sales cost (based on expected value analysis) to be $50 each time an order is due in. Production does not begin work on an order until all required blank castings are on hand. Thus, production believes that inventory and ordering policies will have no impact on the productivity of its operation. Hedging is not considered to be feasible by top management. Inventory carrying costs are estimated to be 35% per year.

We now will develop a table to determine the total costs associated with several different order sizes (and inventory levels). Most of the quantities selected are at points of a price break since experience has shown that the optimal order quantity usually is at such a point.

Apex Manufacturing Company

DATA

Order quantity (Q)	50	100	200	500	1000
Average inventory ($Q/2$)	25	50	100	250	500
Number of orders ($2,000/Q$)	40	20	10	4	2

Delivered price per unit	$210	$210	$185	$170	$170
ANNUAL COSTS					
Purchasing and transportation (2,000 units)	$420,000	$420,000	$370,000	$340,000	$340,000
Administrative costs (no. orders × $200)	8,000	4,000	2,000	800	400
Cost of lost sales ($50 × no. orders)	2,000	1,000	500	200	100
Inventory carrying cost (.35 × Q/2 × delivered price per unit)	1,838	3,675	6,475	14,875	29,750
Total costs	$431,838	$428,675	$378,975	$355,875	$370,250

Another way of looking at the optimal level of inventory is to study the relation between the incremental savings and the incremental costs associated with different levels of inventory as shown in Figure 6.3. The incremental savings include: avoided lost sales; improved manufacturing productivity (see Appendix to Chapter 9); lower per unit costs of purchased material due to price breaks, better sourcing, improved negotiations, and hedging; reduced per unit administrative costs due to economies of scale; and lower unit transportation costs. The incremental costs are largely those resulting from carrying additional inventory. We note that since inventory carrying costs are a function of the value of the material in inventory, the incremental cost of additional inventory declines (slopes downward). This phenomenon is based on the fact that larger inventories allow us to purchase in larger quantities. As a result, we enjoy lower delivered unit prices. This, in turn, leads to lower interest and tax liabilities, resulting in lower inventory carrying costs.

As previously indicated, quantitative techniques exist for determining the optimal level of inventory. When demand for an item has a random pattern, a fixed order quantity model normally is employed.

Frequently, we will want to coordinate inventory review and ordering for several items of the same class. Such action reduces inventory management and administrative expenses. Also, it allows the organiza-

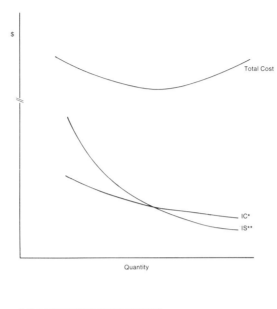

* IC = Incremental Cost of Additional Inventory
**IS = Incremental Savings Associated with Additional Inventory Resulting from:
        Avoided Lost Sales
        Improved Manufacturing Productivity
        Lower Unit Costs of Purchased Goods
        Lower Unit Transportation Costs
        Lower Unit Administrative Costs

FIGURE 6.3   Costs Associated with Various Levels of Inventory

tion to enjoy discounts in purchase prices and transportation as a result of consolidation. In such cases, fixed period order models are appropriate. A useful variation of the fixed period ordering system is appropriate for continuous flow types of manufacturing operations. This procedure calls for the establishment of period contracts (e.g., 6 months) with delivery scheduled on a daily or similar basis throughout the period of the contract. Daily visual review is made of the inventory of such items with any imbalances reported to purchasing and production control. Any changes in production schedules must be furnished to the responsible buyer in purchasing so that delivery schedules may be revised.

CATALOGS: A PROFITABLE INVESTMENT

In most organizations, an inventory catalog will pay for itself many times over. For example, the typical industrial firm stocks between 10,000 and 50,000 items. To control such a large number of items effectively, it is essential to know what the items are, their cost, their usage, and any special considerations. All inventory items should be identified, described, and cross-referenced to the manufacturer's part number and the user's part number. Proper cross-indexing allows users to be aware of the interchangeability of items.

The catalog serves as an important medium of communication. It allows engineers and production personnel to communicate more effectively with purchasing personnel and purchasing with the firm's suppliers. The catalog facilitates the standardization program discussed in Chapter 2. If a designer knows that one of two or three suitable alternatives is a stock item, he or she knows that procurement costs and lead times will tend to be better than for the nonstocked alternatives.

The development and use of an inventory catalog reduces the likelihood of duplicate records and redundant inventories for identical items. Lower inventory levels and a reduced probability of a stock outage result.

Once an inventory catalog has been developed, it then is desirable to analyze the inventory preparatory to controlling it effectively. Each item should be studied in terms of its cost, usage, lead time, and other relevant information. The items then should be arrayed by size of inventory investment. Typically, 10% of the *inventory* items account for approximately 75% of the inventory investment and 25% of the items represent approximately 90% of inventory investment! This same principle is present in virtually all organizations, be they manufacturing firms, hospitals, banks, or governmental agencies. Such an analysis allows management to focus on those areas of greatest savings potential.

PURCHASING AND
MATERIALS MANAGEMENT

In 1956 L. J. DeRose wrote,

> Materials management is the planning, directing, controlling, and coordinating of all those activities concerned with material and inventory requirements, from the point of their inception to their introduction into the manufacturing process. It begins with *the determination of material quality* [emphasis added] and quantity and ends with its issuance to production in time to meet customer demands on schedule and at lowest costs.[2]

Materials management should and does result in improved communications and coordination among production planning, inventory control, purchasing, and those other departments such as traffic, receiving, and warehousing that often are included. This improved communications

---

[2]L. J. DeRose, "The Role of Purchasing in Materials Management," *Purchasing Magazine,* March 1956, p. 115.

and coordination results in significant reductions in inventories, production disruptions and their resulting cost, administrative costs, and the cost of purchased materials.

Unfortunately, *materials management normally does not pay sufficient attention to determining the right item or material to be purchased.* The day-to-day problems confronting the materials manager are so challenging that no time or effort is available to interact with design engineering. As a result, the majority of organizations that have implemented materials management overlook the largest profit potential offered by the integrated procurement system (IPS). They buy the right quantities and buy them effectively. But they frequently are not buying to the right level of quality or the item that best satisfies the requirement.

When determining whether to implement an IPS or a materials management system (MMS) first, it is recommended that the IPS be the choice. Experience indicates that when an MMS is implemented, several years are required to gain control and develop a high degree of coordination among the formerly independent departments of the new organization. During this formative period, the day-to-day problems confronting the materials manager are so challenging that little time is available to pay proper attention to an effective requirements process.

The materials manager of one organization with sales in excess of \$2 billion has addressed this issue by refusing the responsibility for production planning and inventory control. His materials management organization consists of four divisions: material engineering, purchasing, subcontract administration (expediting), and traffic. This executive has convinced top management that the assignment of any additional responsibilities would reduce the savings his organization now makes. Much of the present savings results from the material engineering division's involvement in the appropriate stages of the design process and in value engineering. The IPS is not dependent on any one organizational structure. It can and does work in firms with a materials management organization. And it works in organizations with other approaches to procuring material, equipment, and services.

HOW TO INTEGRATE MARKETING, PRODUCTION PLANNING, AND INVENTORY MANAGEMENT INTO THE PROCUREMENT SYSTEM

Purchasing managers must develop missionary zeal in making marketing, production planning, and inventory managers aware of the cost and productivity implications of inadequate purchasing lead time. Examples showing the results of adequate lead time and results of inadequate lead time should be developed. These examples—some with happy endings and some of them virtual horror stories—should be used in support of this effort. Remember to praise publicly and discuss problems in private.

The brief descriptions of forecasting, production planning, and inventory management provided in this chapter should assist the purchasing manager in this effort. Through an understanding of these topics, the purchasing manager can better communicate with his or her colleagues in these areas. This communication, supported by examples of good and poor purchasing resulting from adequate and inadequate lead time are the keys to obtaining the necessary degree of cooperation. But once this cooperation is achieved, it must be maintained. *This is one of a proactive purchasing manager's most important responsibilities.*

SUMMARY

Determining the right time at which to make purchases and the right quantity to buy has a major impact on an organization's profits and productivity. Many purchasing managers view inadequate lead time as their number one problem. A second major problem is that of inappropriate or suboptimal purchase quantities, resulting from faulty inventory policies.

Because it is concerned with the overall operation of an organization over a specified time horizon, production planning is the key to adequate procurement lead time. Production planning begins with orders and a forecast of future demand. It then determines the size of the work force, overtime, the size of inventories, the size and timing of material purchases, and the amount of subcontracting. Normally, there will be several alternative ways of balancing the rate of production and projected demand. For example, changes can be made in the size of the work force and the amount of overtime. The product mix can be revised. Demand can be stabilized by adding countercyclical products to the product line, or it can be changed by price and promotional actions.

Once the production plan has been developed, it is possible to derive the short-range (1- to 6-month) master schedule. The master schedule, in conjunction with inventory information and the product structure record, is the control mechanism for releasing work orders and purchase orders.

An increasing number of manufacturers are employing an MRP system for intermediate-level planning. MRP is a computer program for production scheduling, inventory control, and the scheduling of purchase orders. MRP facilitates production planning and scheduling, ensures that required materials are available when required, reduces the firm's investment in inventory, and assists in rescheduling purchasing and manufacturing operations. The MRP system has the production plan as its principal input. The MRP system applies its MRP logic to this input and draws needed information from the product structure file and the inventory status file. It schedules the release of purchase orders and work orders and issues any required reschedule notices.

In addition to easier and more efficient scheduling of the firm's production capacity, MRP has the potential to reduce investment in incoming materials and work-in-process inventory, reduce scrap previously associated with the implementation of engineering changes, help to improve customer relations, and aid in long-range planning.

Determining the right quantity of material to maintain in inventory and the right quantity to purchase on a particular purchase order has a significant impact on the operation of any organization. The cost of lost sales, lost productivity due to nonavailability of needed material or supplies, administrative costs associated with purchasing and receiving the items, and inventory carrying costs are all affected by the size of inventory and the size and frequency of purchase orders.

Marketing, operations, purchasing, and materials handling all have arguments favoring large inventories and relatively large quantities on each purchase order. Finance is concerned both with inventory carrying costs and the amount of money invested in inventory. Management's objective is to find the right balance between these conflicting positions.

The typical manufacturing operation requires stockage of from 10,000 to 50,000 items. Nonmanufacturing organizations also stock thousands of items. It is recommended that each organization develop an inventory catalog to aid in the efficient management of its inventory. Ten percent of the inventory items represent 75% of the investment in inventory. These are the items that deserve special managerial attention!

The materials management concept, as originally conceived, calls for the integration of all activities concerned with material and inventory requirements, including *the determination of requirements*. As practiced today, materials management generally results in grouping production planning, inventory control, purchasing, and frequently other departments such as traffic, receiving, and warehousing under one manager. Improved communications and coordination result, leading to significant reductions in inventories, fewer production disruptions, reduced costs of purchased material, and lower administrative expenses.

Unfortunately, materials management, as practiced, normally does not pay sufficient attention to the requirements process. The materials manager generally is so concerned with day-to-day problems that he or she is unable to be involved in the design process. Accordingly, most organizations that have implemented the materials management concept ignore the area of greatest profit potential addressed by the IPS. They buy the right quantities and they buy them effectively, but they frequently are not purchasing the right level of quality or the item that best satisfies the firm's requirement.

We now will look at another area where several departments do or should interact: the make-or-buy decision. Although this is a relatively straightforward area, it is one that continues to be misunderstood and one in which numerous costly mistakes are made. Accordingly, the potential for improving productivity and profits is tremendous.

chapter seven

TO MAKE OR TO BUY: THAT IS THE QUESTION

The Tarheel Tool Company, located in Raleigh, North Carolina, manufactures hydraulic and electric handtools. The company was founded by two veterans of the Korean conflict. Originally, Tarheel purchased all its components. It then began making its gears and, later, its housings and most of its fields and armatures. Sales at Tarheel have grown to $20,000,000 per year.

Three years ago, Jack Thomas, the surviving co-founder and the president of Tarheel, established a make-or-buy committee. The committee consists of Tim Whitney, the chief engineer; Jim McAdams, the vice president of operations; Tom Cervantes, the purchasing manager; John Brooks, the plant engineer; and Judy Jones, the controller. The committee meets at the call of Mr. Thomas, who normally participates in the discussions. A month ago, Mr. Thomas requested that the make-or-buy committee members gather information on the merits of making or buying a new gear fabrication machine. We now observe the make-or-buy committee in action.

Mr. Thomas begins: "Judy and gentlemen, I know that you are all very busy, but we have an important item to discuss today. We have the funds to allow us to upgrade our gear production operation. Basically, we must decide whether to make the machine ourselves or to purchase the new gear fabrication machine."

Jim McAdams comments, "As you may be aware, our gear cutting equipment is 20 years old. It is labor intensive. It is so shopworn that even our senior machinists have trouble holding tolerances. Tom and I have located two machines that will satisfy our projected gear requirements for the next 5 years. I'd be happy with either machine. Tom, how about a few words on the cost implications."

Tom Cervantes contributes his thoughts. "As Jim indicated, we have identified two suppliers. One is the Hamilton Machine Works with a delivered price of $120,000. The other is the Lexington Tool Company with a price of $147,000. I've performed a total cost of ownership analysis on the cost of acquiring and operating both machines for the next 5 years. The Lexington machine's life-cycle cost is a good $100,000 less than Hamilton's."

Jack Thomas then says, "Well, we have a good handle on the cost of purchasing and operating the machine. But based on some reading I've been doing recently, I thought it might be a good idea to look at the implications of making our own gear fabrication machine. Tim, what have you been able to learn?"

Tim Whitney: "As is so often the case, things aren't quite as simple as they initially appear. When Jack asked me to look into this, it seemed pretty far-fetched. But I've gathered data on the cost of designing and assembling our own equipment. Based on costs that Tom's people obtained, the material required to build this machine would cost about $105,000. Jim, John, and I figure that we could pool talent from production, plant engineering, and engineering to assemble and install the machine. Most of the work would be done on an overtime basis since the people we want are already busy. Our best guesstimate is that our out-of-pocket labor costs would be $60,000 to $70,000. Thus, we feel that the machine would cost us about $165,000 or so to make.

"But there is a major, yet subtle, offset. In both Europe and in Japan, we find that manufacturing firms make much more of their own equipment than we do here in America. Everything I've read on the subject indicates that the active involvement of the firm's engineering and production personnel in the design and fabrication of required capital equipment results in a more productive piece of equipment. Based on my research, I'm convinced that we should make the new gear fabrication machine."

John Brooks adds his concurrence to this comment.

Judy Jones interjects, "Gentlemen, I hear what Tim is saying, but I have two questions: Can we be sure that the resulting equipment will be more productive? Are our costs any more realistic than on our last fiasco? As you will all recall, costs grew by some 240% when we built our own chuck assembler!"

"Judy, I'm glad you asked me that," replies Tim. "I've used Tom's life-cycle cost model with two assumptions: first, the initial out-of-pocket cost of making will not exceed $300,000, and, second, our own gear fabrication machine will be 10% more effective than any we purchase. With these assumptions, we still would save well over $500,000 during the next 5 years."

Mr. Thomas interrupts, "I think we've heard enough. I think we should build our own machine. Anyone disagree?" Silence and nods of agreement from all.

The make-or-buy issue confronts most organizations continually. Every job release and every purchase request implies a decision to make or to buy. Most organizations have two basic sources of supply: their own operation and that of outside suppliers. This is as true of requirements for janitorial services as it is for fuel injection pumps.

Many chief executives consider the make-or-buy decision to be among the most critical and most difficult confronting their organizations. Not only are billions of dollars needlessly wasted, but scarce management resources frequently are stretched past the breaking point.

Top management has the ultimate responsibility for make-or-buy decisions. In most cases, this responsibility can be satisfied through operating procedures that develop and pool all relevant information surrounding a make-or-buy issue. Purchasing is a source of much of this information. Also, purchasing frequently should identify candidates for a make-or-buy analysis.

Three major problems are common in the make-or-buy area:

- Make-or-buy decisions are made at too low an organization level.
- Not all factors are considered when conducting a make-or-buy analysis.
- Decisions are not reviewed on a periodic basis. Circumstances change!

Each make-or-buy analysis requires the consideration of many factors. We now focus on some of these factors.

THE ISSUES

The Strategic Issue

What kind of an organization do we want to be? This is the first, and perhaps most critical, issue to be addressed. Pride or purely emotional reasoning plays a major part in many make decisions. Pride in self-sufficiency can become a dominant factor that can lead to many problems. While self-sufficiency in some areas is desirable or even necessary, it is impossible for even a large firm to become entirely self-sufficient. The more a firm strives for self-sufficiency, the larger it becomes, with the management task increasing in complexity and diversity. In such a situation, it is entirely possible that management will be spread too thinly to accomplish effectively the operation of the business. If at all possible, purely emotional reasoning should be omitted from the make-or-buy decision.

Many years ago, a major truck manufacturer had marginal success at a time when one of its objectives required a high degree of self-sufficiency. Today, this firm purchases most of its components and assemblies. The firm is far more successful now that it focuses on design, assembly, and marketing.

Cost

Two key prerequisites are essential to a thorough and sound analysis of the cost considerations of a make-or-buy decision. (1) Costs must be segregated between fixed costs and variable or incremental ones. Such cost figures must include all relevant costs, both direct and indirect, near term and anticipated changes. Realistic estimates of in-house production costs must include expected rejection rates and spoilage. These estimates also should consider the likely effects of learning resulting from long production runs. (2) Accurate and realistic data must be available on the investment required to make or to buy an item. Frequently, the working capital required in the manufacture of an item can equal and even exceed the investment required for facilities and equipment. It is essential to consider both the facilities and the working capital components of an investment.

Table 7.1 provides an example of the cost considerations involved in a typical make-or-buy analysis. Assume that we have an annual requirement for 5,000 units that we may purchase at $213 plus a charge of $7 for material burden per unit. The total unit cost of making these items is $240. There is idle plant capacity adequate to produce the item.

At first glance, it would appear less expensive to buy ($220) than to make ($240). But when we look at variable or out-of-pocket costs, we see that the variable cost of making is $20.50 less per unit ($199.50) than is the cost of buying ($220). The total savings is $102,500 (5,000 × $20.50) per year.

Before concluding that we should make the item, we must consider

TABLE 7.1   **Make-or-Buy Cost Data: An Example**

	MAKE	BUY
Material (incl. freight) (variable)	$ 69.25	$213.00
Direct Labor (variable)	80.00	—
Material Burden (variable)	2.25	7.00
Labor Burden		
fixed	20.00	
variable	48.00	
Tooling (fixed)	20.50	
Total Cost	$240.00	$220.00
Variable Costs	199.50	220.00
Fixed (sunk)	40.50	

the net investment required to manufacture it. Let us assume that the net investment required for equipment and working capital is $430,000 if the item is made and $52,000 if it is purchased. The net investment required to make the item rather than to purchase it then is $378,000 ($430,000 − $52,000). The return on investment becomes 27% ($102,500 ÷ $378,000). While such a return may sound attractive to many executives whose firms struggle to make 20% on investment before taxes, it is only an average return for many operations. Thus, what appeared to be a most attractive candidate for in-house manufacture based on marginal dollar savings ($102,500) may prove to be less attractive as an investment (ROI = 27%) than other alternatives!

Quality

When there is a significant difference in quality between items produced internally and items purchased or when a specified quality cannot be purchased, then management must consider these quality considerations in the make-or-buy decision. One argument for making over buying is the so-called "impossibility" of finding a supplier capable or willing to manufacture the item to the desired specifications. But further investigation should be conducted before this argument can be accepted. Why are these specifications so much more rigid than those of the rest of the industry? The manufacturer should reexamine the specifications and make every effort to secure the cooperation of potential suppliers to ensure that the quality specifications are realistic and that no satisfactory product is available. Frequently, suppliers can suggest alternatives that are just as dependable if they know the intended purpose of the item.

On the other hand, the firm may desire a level of quality below that commercially available. Suppliers may be selling only a quality far above that which would fully satisfy the need in question and may, at the same time, have so satisfactory a volume at the higher level as to have no interest in a lower quality. If this is the case, the user may be justified in manufacturing the item.

Frequently, it is claimed that in-house (make) production may better satisfy manufacturing's quality requirements. The user of an item usually has better understanding of the operational intricacies involved in the use of an item. With a make decision, it is claimed that a better degree of coordination will exist between those responsible for producing the item and those responsible for assembling it into the next higher level of assembly. It is claimed that communications between the two groups are facilitated compared with the situation in which the item is furnished by an outside supplier. If the firm has a weak purchasing department, such claims may be true. But with a professional purchasing operation, the flow of information and coordination between purchaser and supplier should result in no more problems than between two production activities of the same firm.

Since quality must be controlled in either the purchased or manufactured items, a competent quality assurance staff must be employed. The purchase order may state that the purchaser's quality assurance inspectors have access to the supplier's manufacturing, inspection, and shipping departments. In this way, the purchaser can maintain significant control and still not incur the additional cost resulting from manufacturing the item.

Quantity

One of the most frequent reasons for making over buying is that a requirement may be too small to interest suppliers. Small volume requirements of unique, nonstandard items may be difficult to purchase. The firm may feel that it is forced to make such items. However, it may be economically imprudent for the firm to make the item itself. The costs of planning, tooling, setup, and purchase of required raw materials may be exorbitant. It may be far more cost effective to purchase the required item in larger quantities or to identify a suitable substitute.

If a large quantity of an item is required on a repetitive basis, then the analysis described under "Cost" should be made. The company should have a high degree of confidence that its requirements for the item will continue to the point that it receives a satisfactory return on its investment before deciding to make such an item.

Frequently, a firm will follow a conscious policy of making an item at a level of production sufficient to meet its minimum requirements and purchase additional items as required. This policy builds a degree of stability into the firm's production activities. Such a policy should be adopted only after investigating the willingness and ability of suppliers to fill such fluctuating demand.

Service

Service often is defined simply as reliable delivery. In a broader sense, it includes a wide variety of intangible factors that lead to greater satisfaction on the part of the purchasing firm. It is important that this consideration be judged fairly and that the purchasing firm not be given undue credit with respect to service simply for emotional reasons. Merely because the item is produced in house is not proof that service will be superior to that of a supplier.

Assurance of supply is a primary service consideration. When the lack of an item causes serious problems, such as total production stoppage, and totally reliable suppliers are not available, the decision to make rather than buy may be justified.

When a purchaser is faced with a monopolistic environment, the service accompanying the product is generally somewhat poorer than in a highly competitive market. Such a situation may induce the would-be purchaser to make the product. If an item is used as a subcomponent on a product the purchaser is selling and is causing the entire product to be unreliable, the resulting loss of goodwill and sales may be significant enough to justify a make decision, even though the cost analysis does not support such a decision.

Specialized Knowledge

Frequently, a supplier possesses specialized knowledge, abilities, and production know-how that would be very expensive to duplicate. Suppliers may have a large R & D budget leading to improved and/or less expensive products. The cost of attempting to develop such expertise tends to be prohibitive.

Design or Production Process Secrecy

Occasionally, a firm decides to manufacture a certain part because of the additional industrial security that can be provided. This is especially so when the item is a key part for which a patent would not provide adequate protection. This justification must be used with caution, however, as the firm can provide very little protection against design infringement after sale. In short, if a patent will not protect a certain part, then in-house manufacturing may not either. Frequently, a firm may have developed a unique or proprietary production process. Such circumstances may support a decision to make over buying.

Urgent Requirements

The firm usually can purchase a small quantity much more readily than were it to produce the item. If the requirement is urgent, such as to preclude stopping an assembly line, then payment of a higher price to buy the item is justified.

Labor Problems

The production of any new item may require labor skills that the company does not possess. The hiring, cross-training, and upgrading of personnel may be a troublesome and complex process, especially if a union is involved. The company may be entering a field in which it has no experience and no adequately trained personnel. Labor problems are easily shifted to someone else, namely, the supplier, through a decision to buy.

The presence of unions within the company also may be a significant factor. Unions often have clauses in their contracts prohibiting the purchasing of items that can be manufactured within the plant. The history of labor problems in the supplier's company also may influence the make-or-buy decision.

Plant Capacity

Obviously, the more significant the item in question is relative to the company's size, the greater the probability that the item will be purchased rather than produced in house. When the item would require a significant investment, the smaller company has no rational decision other than to buy.

Generally, the more mature company will try to integrate items currently purchased into its production more often than will a new company. The new company understandably concentrates on increasing the output and has very little excess capital or plant capacity to divert to production of components. Quite the opposite is true for the more mature company. Such a firm tends to have extra facilities, capital, and personnel and, therefore, is in a better position to increase profit by producing what was formerly purchased. Excess plant capacity and the likely duration of the excess capacity should always be considered in the make-or-buy decision as should additional expenses such as tooling, setup, and training.

Capital Equipment

Manufacturers sometimes find it necessary to make a needed item, simply because a suitable supplier does not exist. This is most frequently the case with highly specialized manufacturing equipment.

As we saw at the Tarheel Tool Company, there is another potential advantage resulting from a manufacturer developing and fabricating his or her own equipment: integrating the firm's production and engineering experience into the design and fabrication of the equipment may result in greatly increased productivity. The Europeans and Japanese have found this to be the case.

Use of Idle Resources

A make decision can prove profitable to a firm even when suitable suppliers are available. In periods of recession or business slumps, a firm is faced with the problem of idle plant equipment, labor, and management. By making a product that it may have been buying, a firm can put its idle machinery to work and spread its overhead costs over a larger volume of production.

Perhaps the biggest benefits obtained from a make decision during a slump is in the area of labor relations. Employee morale can be maintained and layoff penalty costs can be avoided by timely use of the make decision. Even in times of recession, most firms find it desirable to retain highly skilled production personnel. These personnel can be kept at work and a stable work force maintained by a decision to make. The long-run benefits from good labor relations are obvious.

Great caution must be taken when basing a make decision primarily on temporary idle resources. Make decisions tend to be rather permanent. A decision to make temporarily an item under such circumstances should be reviewed when demand increases.

Make and Buy

Some firms make and buy critical nonstandard items to ensure that a reliable second source is available in case of difficulty with the supplier. Such a policy also serves to provide data that are useful in reviewing internal production and management efficiency.

DISCUSSION

Make-or-buy decisions can have a critical effect on the economic health of a firm, even on its survival. Frequently, these decisions are made at too low a level in the organization. On many occasions, no conscious decision appears to have been made. Things just happen! Obviously, the amount of time and effort and the level of managerial attention appropriate are functions of the amount of money involved and the criticality of the item to the firm's well-being. Normally several departments should be interested and involved in make-or-buy decisions: production, purchasing, engineering, finance, and marketing.

Any of the following situations should precipitate a make-or-buy analysis:

- *New product development and modification programs.* Every major component should be reviewed.
- *Unsatisfactory supplier performance.* If purchasing is unable to develop reliable sources for an item, the item should be reviewed and analyzed to ensure that the specified quality level is essential and to ensure that suitable substitutes are not available. If the item, as specified, passes these reviews, it becomes a candidate for in-house sourcing.
- *Changes in sales.* Sales demand that exceeds capacity calls for a make-or-buy review of those items produced in house that contrib-

ute the lowest ROI. Declines in sales and production should prompt a review of candidates for in-house production.

* *Periodic review of previous decisions.* Changing costs and other considerations can convert a good make-or-buy decision into a bad one very quickly. It is desirable that major make-or-buy decisions be reviewed, preferably as a component of the firm's annual planning process.

SUMMARY

The firm's objective is, or should be, that of optimizing the utilization of its production, managerial, and financial resources. The make-or-buy analysis and resulting decision is a key ingredient in this optimizing process.

As we have seen, there are many considerations influencing a make-or-buy decision. It is far easier to reverse a make-or-buy decision *before* its implementation. Therefore, the make-or-buy analysis should take place during the planning of new product items. This is the right time for such analyses. Due to rapidly changing costs, sales, and conditions of supply, the make-or-buy decision should be reexamined on a periodic basis.

The make-or-buy decision is among the most critical and most challenging confronting an organization. The cost implications of a faulty decision will reduce the firm's profitability. A decision to make items that differ from those currently being produced can so dilute management that no area receives the right level of managerial attention. Profits, productivity, and quality all suffer.

The lasting nature of a make decision causes it to be far more critical than for a buy decision. Once a firm begins making an item or service, all sorts of justifications can be found to support a continuation of the activity, even in the face of evidence supporting a buy decision.

Each make-or-buy analysis is unique. Each requires the consideration of many factors. It is rare, indeed, that all relevant factors will favor a make or a buy decision. The decision must be based on the composite effect of many factors on the firm's operation.

This chapter completes the most critical and least understood part of the procurement process: the determination of requirements. We now will turn our attention to what happens to a requirement that has been soundly developed and determined to be appropriate for purchase from outside sources.

chapter eight

HOW TO SELECT THE RIGHT SUPPLIER

The California Gas & Electric Company (CG&E) was confronted with many problems: increasing costs of diesel oil for its diesel-fired electric generators, delays in planned nuclear plants, a decrease in rainfall leading to reduced hydroelectric generation, reduced net income, and a decrease in bond rating. Many of these issues led to a significant increase in electric rates, which, in turn, led to a storm of consumer protests.

A recently completed study by CG&E engineers and a leading geothermal engineer recommended construction of a geothermal plant in the Mohave Desert. One of the key components of the new generating station was a revolutionary heat exchanger capable of operating in a very hostile environment.

CG&E engineers developed a performance specification for the required heat exchanger. Purchasing identified three firms that were technically and managerially capable of developing and manufacturing the heat exchanger. Each of these firms submitted a preliminary or conceptual solution to the requirement, a fixed price proposal for development, and a target price for manufacture of the machine. Purchasing, with the concurrence of CG&E top management, had decided to enter into a two-phase contract. Phase I was to be a firm fixed price contract for detailed development of the heat exchanger. Phase II, to be covered by an option in the basic contract, would call for a fixed price incentive type of contract for manufacture of the heat exchanger. Appropriate preaward surveys and negotiations had been conducted.

Charlie Holt, purchasing manager for CG&E, was confronted with a predicament. No one supplier was clearly superior. For example, the Akron Manufacturing Company demonstrated the best understanding of the technical requirement and the best delivery schedule, but the worst price. The Bakersfield Scientific Company had the best price, but only second best delivery and technical understanding.

Charlie knew that technical considerations, price, and delivery were all important. He wanted to be in a position to make a recommendation to top management either on who the supplier should be or, at least, on how to select the supplier. But Charlie saw no clear-cut solution to his predicament.

Perhaps the most critical activity for which the purchasing department is responsible is the selection of the right source. The right source is one that can provide the right quality of materials or services, on time, at a reasonable price, and with the services required to create a satisfied customer.

Three problems are common in the source selection process.

- Insufficient attention is given to the screening of prospective suppliers.
- Many purchasers do not take full advantage of foreign sources of supply.
- Competitive bidding, as a source selection process, is underutilized in the private sector and overused in the public sector.

SCREENING POTENTIAL SUPPLIERS

A good procurement rule of thumb is never to request a bid or quotation from a vendor unless knowledge is available on the vendor's qualifications. Buyers should schedule missionary visits to present and prospective vendors in order to become acquainted with the individuals with whom they talk on the telephone. Further, such visits allow the buyer to get to know the vendor's capabilities and equipment. One of the first considerations is a prospective supplier's place in the channel of distribution. Is he or she the manufacturer, a distributor, or a manufacturer's representative? The focus should be on the services required and the prospective supplier's ability to satisfy these requirements. A manufacturer normally provides the right combination of price and service for large quantities. Custom parts made to the purchaser's design specification (and perhaps performance specification) are usually purchased directly from the manufacturer, regardless of quantity. Small lots, requirements for immediate delivery, and credit considerations usually result in purchases from distributors. Normally, distributors carry a wide range of products from several manufacturers. Distributors buy in large quantities, warehouse the items, and resell in smaller quantities to purchasers in their area. If these services are performed both by the manufacturer and his or her distributors, then the purchaser must decide which prospective source provides the more attractive package of price and service.

Many firms object to dealing with manufacturers' agents on the grounds that the commissions received by the agents are excessive. Also, it frequently appears that many manufacturers' representatives are only errand boys between the buyer and supplier, thereby complicating the information flow. While these objections frequently are valid, one must recognize that for many small manufacturing firms, this method of marketing distribution is the most practical and economical available. Again, we must look at the service being provided. In the case of manufacturers' representatives, this service frequently is access to additional sources of supply.

A second concern is the number of suppliers from whom prices should be solicited. The ideal situation is to have sufficient qualified potential suppliers to ensure free and adequate competition. Usually three to five firms will satisfy this criterion. If a significant investment for bid preparation is required, it may be desirable to solicit quotations from only two qualified sources. Two interested and highly motivated firms are apt to provide better competition on such a procurement than are five firms that are only half-interested. Obviously, this is a judgmental issue and one of the reasons that a competent buyer is a prized resource.

A third issue concerns whether to favor local suppliers over those not in the surrounding area. For small quantities, a local supplier frequently will be able to provide the best price and service. Communications generally are simpler. If the material is to come from the local supplier's inventory, delivery will be more certain, since there is less opportunity for delays during transportation. If a local supplier is highly reliable, it may be possible to transfer much of the purchasing firm's inventory carrying function to the supplier. Community relations are strengthened by purchasing locally. This consideration is especially critical for nonprofit organizations that depend on the local community for part of their operating funds.

Buying in regional or national markets tends to be more attractive than local buying in certain circumstances. Large national firms usually can better provide required technical assistance. Economies of scale allow the national firm to sell at lower prices. National companies usually have more production capacity and are more able to cope with fluctuating demand.

Purchasing managers frequently are confronted with the question,

How many suppliers should there be for a particular item? Several issues are involved. Generally, caution must be exercised when purchases by one customer exceed 10% or so of a supplier's sales. If purchases appreciably exceed this amount, the purchaser begins to assume a moral responsibility for the economic well-being of the supplier. The purchasing firm loses needed flexibility in such a situation and may find itself morally committed to a supplier who is no longer competitive or capable of performing the desired services. Thus, it may be desirable to employ two or more suppliers to retain desired freedom of action.

If a significant dollar amount is involved (say, $100,000), then an allocation of the requirement between two suppliers frequently proves to be advantageous. An allocation of 75% to one firm and 25% to a second supplier has many benefits. The firm with the majority of the requirement can enjoy economies of scale that can be passed back to the purchaser in the form of lower prices. Further, this supplier has the incentive and the profit to perform additional services such as maintaining a local warehouse to provide nearly instantaneous delivery. Ideally, the supplier receiving the 25% allocation should be able to provide backup support, if the other source encounters difficulty. Further, the firm with 25% of the requirement will tend to "yap at the heels of the big guy and keep him in line on price, quality, delivery, and service."

If the purchaser is buying a critical item from a new source, dual sourcing should be the rule. A major manufacturer has made this an ironclad rule as a result of previously unsatisfactory sole-source experiences with new suppliers.

When an item critical to a firm's well-being is to be purchased, it is desirable to perform an in-depth analysis or preaward survey[1] of the prospective supplier. Such an analysis also is an essential step in preparing for negotiations. Potential suppliers are not above attempting to expand their business by first securing orders and then worrying about how they are going to fill the orders. They may lack experience, capacity, or adequate sources of supply for their purchased materials and still endeavor to obtain a sales contract. The purchasing firm buys best when it deals with suppliers that have the needed capacity, skills, and sources of supply.

The purchasing department normally is responsible for determining the need for a preaward survey and the breadth of the required investigation. Purchasing calls on other departments (engineering, production, quality assurance, finance, industrial relations, etc.) for assistance in the accomplishment of the preaward survey. The following areas should be included in such investigations:

---

[1]Many terms are used to describe in-depth evaluation of a prospective supplier's capability: evaluation of potential vendors, supplier surveys, vendor capability surveys, plant visits, and so on. The most descriptive term and the one we will use is "preaward survey."

- *Equipment and Facilities.* Does the prospective supplier have modern, up-to-date equipment capable of holding required tolerances suitable for producing the required item? Does he or she have the required space?

- *Production and Quality.* Are the prospective supplier's production and quality control systems efficient? Does material flow smoothly? Will it be possible to rely on the firm's quality control program? Is there a quality control manual? Is there a quality assurance program? How is housekeeping? How are working conditions? What is the status of back orders?

- *Purchasing.* Does the prospective supplier have an adequate source of required raw materials and purchased components? Is adequate and effective competition obtained? Are there special relations with certain companies and affiliates? Does the prospective supplier determine financial, quality assurance, and other capabilities of his or her prospective key suppliers and subcontractors?

- *Financial Resources.* What is the prospective supplier's financial position (current liabilities versus current assets), profit record, net worth, and anticipated sales? If the firm expects to do much subcontracting, it is advisable to check the financial status of prospective subcontractors. How much additional money for working capital or facilities expansion will be needed if the work is to proceed as planned? When must the money be provided? Does the company have the ability to raise the necessary money?

- *Accounting System.* An accounting system review of a prospective contractor is required when other than a firm fixed price or fixed price with escalation contract is to be awarded. The review should determine the adequacy of the prospective supplier's accounting system and its ability to identify and segregate properly costs applicable to each contract.

- *Management.* What is the attitude of middle and top management? Is there a stable, harmonious management team? Is morale good at all levels?

- *Industrial Relations.* What is the history, current, and likely future status of labor relations?

- *Past Performance.* Who are past major customers? Are they satisfied?

FOREIGN SOURCES

Approximately half of all manufacturers purchase some of their materials overseas. Contrary to popular belief, quality and delivery considerations are the primary reasons for purchasing from nondomestic sources. Price also is a consideration, but it is held, by most firms purchasing overseas, to be of lesser importance in the source selection decision than are quality and delivery. Nondomestic manufacturers can be and are excellent sources of supply. But the realistic buyer must be aware of the many additional problems involved when dealing with foreign sources. We now address some of the most common problems.

Culture

Cultural differences pose the largest obstacles to developing mutually profitable business relations with foreign sources. The nature, customs, and ethics of individuals and business organizations from two different cultures can raise a surprising number of obstacles to successful business relations. What is considered ethical in one culture may not be ethical in another. The intention of filling commitments, the implications of gift giving, and even the legal systems differ widely.

Communications

Languages pose significant barriers to successful international business relations. Both parties may think that they know what they have said and what the other party has said. But true agreement and understanding may be missing. Think, for instance, of the confusion the simple word "ton" can create. Is it a short ton (2,000 lb), a long ton (2,240 lb), or a metric ton (2,204.62 lb)?

Financial

Currency exchange rates cause great problems. Some leading firms that buy internationally do business only in their own currency. Others normally conduct their business in the currency of the supplier's home country. And other firms adopt a flexible policy. This variability of approaches demonstrates that no one best way has been discovered.

Many international transactions now contain offset provisions. In effect, we have advanced international commerce to a revolutionary concept known to seventeenth- and eighteenth-century traders as *barter*. Offset provisions complicate such transactions, yet they can be mutually advantageous.

It is the custom in many countries for advanced payments to be made prior to commencing work. Such payments may be necessary to reach agreement on otherwise highly attractive conditions. But this provision ties up the purchaser's capital. Letters of credit also are common in international commerce. Again, the purchaser's funds may be committed for a longer period of time than if a domestic source were involved.

Documentation

Many documents of a unique nature are required for international commerce: export-import licenses, customs documentation, international bills of lading, and certificates of origin. The proper product and use description should be included on all customs documents to eliminate custom duty overcharges.

Ancillary Services

Transportation and insurance procedures and provisions are significantly different from and, generally, more complex than those for domestic material purchases.

Quality

As previously mentioned, foreign suppliers frequently are utilized because they can and do provide the desired level of quality. *But* problems do exist. The United States is the only major nonmetric country in a metric world. This frequently leads to manufacturing tolerance problems. Also, nondomestic suppliers tend to be less responsive to necessary design changes than their domestic counterparts.

Total Costs

The sophisticated purchaser must balance many factors in any sourcing decision. Sourcing from foreign suppliers introduces many issues: higher transportation and insurance costs, additional travel and administrative costs, capital tied up under advanced payments or letters of credit, additional buffer stocks, and political and economic uncertainties. When considering travel costs, for example, the purchaser must take into account the additional cost for overseas travel for the preaward survey team (if required) and for likely expediting or subcontract management trips.

Larger buffer stocks generally are required to accommodate larger variances in delivery time. Such variances arise from variable shipping schedules, documentation and customs problems, and strikes in the suppliers' plants and by stevedores and maritime workers.

In addition, the purchaser must investigate the likely stability of the government and the prospect of nationwide strikes and civil disorder. Obviously, a high degree of certainty of supply is a key consideration for all critical purchased material.

When foreign suppliers are under consideration, the source selection process is little different than were only domestic sources involved. Initially, a purchaser may find it both simpler and more cost effective to deal with sales agents, brokers, import merchants, or trading companies. Many buyers have found that the problems associated with foreign sourcing are best avoided through the use of domestic or foreign trading companies. In most cases, the trading companies offer lower costs, shorter lead times, and more enforceable quality guarantees.

If the dollar value, frequency of purchases, and probability of continuing relations justify the administrative effort, the purchaser should deal directly with potential foreign suppliers.[2] Again, a necessary prerequisite to such transactions is an understanding of the other party's culture and business customs. Also, additional time must be available to develop the business relationship. (These and other nuances of doing business overseas are discussed at greater length in Chapter 10, The Winning Ways of Negotiation). Once a purchaser becomes a significant customer of a foreign supplier, he or she usually is treated as an honorable and valuable member of the supplier's family.

WHEN TO USE COMPETITIVE BIDDING FOR SOURCE SELECTION

Should competitive bidding procedures or negotiation be used to select the source and to arrive at the price to be paid? Under competitive bidding (also referred to as "advertised procurement" in the public sector), the firm prepares a request for bids[3] with the intention of awarding a purchase order or subcontract to the vendor offering the most attractive price *without* further discussions. To employ this procedure successfully, the firm preparing the request for bids must ensure that certain prerequisites have been met:

- The specifications for the item or service to be purchased must be clear and adequate so that prospective suppliers may estimate their costs with a high degree of precision. If this degree of accuracy is not present, suppliers will still submit bids, but they will include contingencies to protect themselves from any uncertainties.

[2]The National Association of Purchasing Management (NAPM) maintains a list of correspondents in 20 foreign nations who have agreed to provide data on suppliers in their countries. The NAPM, in turn, has compiled a guide on purchasing in the United States for members of the International Federation of Purchasing and Materials Management.

[3]A great many terms are used, or misused, in this area. Commonly employed terms include request for quotation, request for bids, invitation to bid, invitation for bids, request for proposal, and inquiries. We will attempt to use the most accurate and most descriptive terms. Accordingly, request for bids will be reserved for situations in which competitive bidding is employed to select the source. The term requests for quotation will be reserved for situations in which formal competitive bidding procedures are not employed.

- The amount of money involved is sufficient to warrant use of competitive bidding. For low-dollar-value requirements, less formal procedures are faster and require less administrative time and effort.
- Adequate competition must be present. Not only must a sufficient number of potential suppliers be available, but a reasonable proportion of these potential suppliers must be willing to price competitively. (As previously indicated, three to five interested and qualified firms generally will furnish adequate competition.)
- There is sufficient time available to employ this technique of source selection. The amount of time and effort involved with this technique is considerable. A formal request for bids, mailing, opening the resulting bids, and evaluating the bids requires more time than might be expected. Additionally, adequate bid preparation time must be afforded to the firms when bids are being solicited.

In addition to satisfying these four prerequisites, four other conditions should *not* be present when employing competitive bidding as the means of source selection:

- Situations in which it is not possible to estimate costs with a high degree of certainty. Such situations frequently are present with high technology requirements, with items requiring a long time to develop and produce, and under conditions of economic uncertainty.
- Situations in which price is not the only variable. For example, quality, schedule, and service may be variables subject to negotiation.
- Situations in which the purchasing firm anticipates a need to make changes in the specification or some other aspect of the purchase order or contract. When unscrupulous vendors anticipate changes, they may buy in with the expectation of getting well and even wealthy on the resulting changes.
- Situations in which special tooling and/or setup costs are major factors. The allocation of such costs and title to the special tooling are issues best resolved through negotiation.

If these conditions are satisfied, then competitive bidding *usually* will result in the lowest price and is the recommended method of source selection. To ensure that the lowest prices are obtained, the competing potential suppliers must be assured that the firm submitting the low bid will receive the award. If the purchasing firm gains a reputation for conducting negotiations subsequent to the opening of bids, then future bidders will tend *not* to offer their best prices initially, believing that they may do better in any subsequent negotiations. They will adopt a strategy of submitting a bid low enough to allow them to be included in any negotiations. But their initial bid will not be as low as when they are confident that award would be made to the low bidder without further negotiation.

When these prerequisites to the use of competitive bidding are not satisfied, negotiated procedures should be employed to select sources and to arrive at a price. The term "negotiated procedures" is applied to low-dollar procurements (frequently using telephone solicitation of proposals) and to larger requirements that involve extensive preparation and skill in face-to-face negotiations with prospective suppliers.

SELECTING THE SOURCE

In most instances, one prospective supplier will be so obviously superior to his or her competitors that selection will be a very simple matter. Unfortunately, the choice is not always so clear. A mathematical rating system can greatly facilitate source selection in such cases. We will look at two examples to see how such a selection process can work.

The mathematical rating system calls for two activities: the identification of the key factors to be considered in the source selection decision and the assignment of weights to each factor.

These factors and weights usually are assigned by a committee of interested members of management. Let us return to the situation described at the beginning of the chapter. CG&E has the necessary information on which to base a source selection decision. Yet, no one supplier is obviously superior.

The ideal way in which to cope with such a situation *is before it arises*! A group consisting, perhaps, of the chief engineer, chief of operations, controller, and buyer should have gathered together and identified the key factors. Then the group should have assigned weights to the factors. We see the results of such an effort under the headings "Factors" and "Maximum Rating" in Table 8.1. The data shown for suppliers A, B, and C are based on field investigations of each supplier's technical understanding, capability in each of several areas, and the outcomes of price negotiations. Assuming that purchasing has a firm fixed price offer from each of the three vendors, the rating for this aspect of the factor "price" is objective. It is based on the relationship between each vendor's proposed price for development of the heat exchanger and CG&E's target price. But when a contract calls for some degree of cost reimbursement (fixed price incentive or a cost-plus type of contract as described in the appendix to the next chapter), the rating for price is subjective. The buyer, purchasing manager, and other involved representatives of the firm rate how well they believe the prospective supplier will do in the area of cost

Factors	Maximum Rating	A	Supplier B	C
Technical				
Understanding of the Problem	10	10	8	7
Technical Approach	20	18	16	15
Production Facilities	5	4	5	4
Operator Requirements	3	2	3	2
Maintenance Requirements	2	1	2	2
Totals	40	35	34	30
Ability to Meet Schedule	20	18	15	12
Price	20	16	20	2
Managerial Financial & Technical Capability	10	10	8	8
Quality Control Standards	10	9 / 88	8 / 85	7 / 67

TABLE 8.1   Source Selection Rating Matrix (Development and Production)

control. Thus, that part of the "price" rating for the production portion of the prospective contract with CG&E is subjective. All the other ratings (understanding of the problem, etc.) are subjective and are arrived at in a similar manner.

In effect, the mathematical rating system takes a complex problem and breaks it down into several components. This approach to source selection, while based on a series of objective and subjective judgments, leads to a fair and reasonably objective result.

A somewhat more mundane, but important, area of source selection concerns selection of a supplier who will furnish Reilly Manufacturing Co. with maintenance, repair, and operating (MRO) supplies under an annual requirements contract. Estimated annual expenditures are $5 million. The Reilly purchasing department has solicited quotations and has conducted inspection of the facilities of the four distributors under consideration (a simplified preaward survey). The findings, together with ratings, are shown in Table 8.2.

In this example, it appears that supplier X is the most attractive source.

SUMMARY

Selection of the right source of supply probably is the most critical activity for which purchasing is responsible. The right supplier is one who

Considered Factor	Maximum Rating	W	Supplier X	Y	Z
Price	25	20	20	22	18
Product Lines Available	20	17	18	15	15
Meantime for Delivery	20	15	18	17	17
Technical Service Capacity	15	13	15	10	10
Management Rating	5	4	5	5	3
Inventory Positions	5	4	5	5	3
Credit Terms	5	5	3	3	3
Housekeeping	5	3	5	4	3
	100	81	89	81	62

TABLE 8.2   Source Selection Rating Matrix (MRO Distributor)

can provide the right quality of materials or services, on time, at a reasonable price, and with the services required to maintain customer satisfaction.

The purchasing firm should know enough about its prospective suppliers to provide a satisfactory level of confidence as to their ability to perform. On small, routine purchases, awareness of the vendor's place in the channel of distribution, the services he or she performs, and his or her financial capability will provide adequate insight.

The degree of competition to solicit is a judgmental matter. Usually three to five interested qualified firms will provide adequate competition. If the requirement necessitates significant investment for bid preparation, two highly interested, highly motivated firms are apt to be more aggressive and provide better prices than are five firms who are only half-interested.

There are several occasions when purchasing in the local market may be attractive. Communications are simpler. Delivery times tend to be less and to be more certain. A local supplier may perform many of the purchasing firm's inventory requirements. On the other hand, regional or national buying tends to result in lower prices and better technical assistance. National firms usually have greater production capacity and are more able to cope with fluctuating demand.

Purchasing from foreign sources has become a way of life for the majority of manufacturing firms. While international purchasing poses certain problems not present with domestic purchasing, a foreign supplier can be a valuable and dependable source of supply.

A preaward survey is an in-depth analysis of a prospective supplier.

Such an investigation should be conducted before award of a purchase order or subcontract for an item that is critical to the well-being of the purchasing firm. The preaward survey normally looks at the prospective supplier's facilities; production and quality systems; purchasing, financial, and managerial capabilities; industrial relations; and past performance.

Competitive bidding is the recommended method of source selection and pricing when several conditions are satisfied. If any of these conditions is not satisfied, negotiation procedures should be employed.

Usually one prospective supplier is obviously superior to his or her competitors. But when several factors play a role in source selection (e.g., price, technical considerations, service, and/or schedule), a mathematical rating system should be utilized to aid in source selection.

Determining a fair and reasonable price to pay for goods or services requires the analysis of many factors and variables. Obtaining such a price affects the firm's financial health and even survival. We will now turn our attention to this critical issue.

chapter nine

HOW TO GET
THE RIGHT PRICE

Morley Amsterdam, senior buyer at QRS Products, was wrapping up another annual purchase order. The order was for an estimated 100,000 molded plastic bases. This was a very tricky seven-cavity mold. The delivered cost was $4.07 per unit. For the third year in a row, Precision Plastics was the low bidder. After preparing an abstract of bids, Morley turned his attention to an informal analysis of the price for which he was about to contract.

Three years ago, QRS had estimated its requirements for the plastic base at 40,000 units. The purchase request cited an estimated unit price of $5.00. Having good specifications and adequate time, and knowing that the molded plastics business was a highly competitive one, Morley had chosen to use competitive bidding to aid in source selection and pricing. He had requested bids from six vendors, four of whom submitted bids. The prices received three years ago (including an allowance for transportation costs) were as follows:

Memphis Molding	$3.75
Precision Plastics	3.65
Injection Processes	3.90
Meadville Plastics	4.00

An estimated requirements order was issued to Precision Plastics. The supplier performed very satisfactorily. The following year QRS's estimated requirements for the base unit increased to 75,000. Again, Morley solicited competitive bids. Again, Precision Plastics was low bidder, with a price of $3.90. Morley knew that the price of plastics was up over 10% on similar items, so he was very pleased with only a 7% increase in Precision's price.

This year, estimated requirements increased to 100,000 units. Once again, Precision submitted the low bid after considering transportation costs:

Ashtabula Molding	$4.15
Precision Plastics	4.07
Injection Processes	4.22
Meadville Plastics	4.27

Having completed his price analysis, Morley began drafting the estimated requirements contract. He was on the verge of turning the order in for typing when Josh Keough, the sales representative from Injection Processes, stopped by to see how his firm had done. On learning that he'd lost once again, Josh said, "Morley, no one is ever going to beat Precision's price. The way you're doing business on a one-year basis, we have no choice but to amortize our special tooling and setup costs over your annual requirements. We figure these costs at $50,000. Not only can we not compete with Precision, but I'd bet you're paying too much to those rascals."

After Josh departed, Morley sat thinking, "Were those sour grapes, or does Josh have something?"

Several prerequisites to good pricing are under the control of purchasing. These prerequisites include

- The right degree of competition
- Adequate price analysis
- Thorough cost analysis when price analysis is inadequate or inappropriate
- Selection of the right method of contract pricing (firm fixed price, fixed price incentive, etc.)
- Use of the right type of contract (requirements contract, indefinite quantity contract, etc.)

Chapters 2 and 8 addressed the importance of obtaining the right degree of competition. Chapter 8 described how to select the right source, being aware that the right source is one that provides, among other things, the right price.

This chapter examines two critical, but frequently misunderstood and misused, purchasing activities: price analysis and cost analysis.

The vast majority of procurement requirements can be satisfied through the use of a firm fixed price purchase order or subcontract. But many high-value requirements can be priced much more successfully through the use of other than the firm fixed price method of contract pricing. A whole family of alternatives exists. Selection of the proper approach can and does save the purchaser significant sums. Since few buyers properly understand and properly utilize these alternate methods of contract pricing, they are examined in the appendix to this chapter.

Cost estimating is the least understood tool of price analysis. Historically, cost estimating has been an engineering responsibility. Based on proven need, several forward-looking purchasing departments have developed their own cost estimating capability. Even when the estimate is developed by engineering, it is important for price analysts and negotiators using engineered cost estimates to understand how the estimate was derived and how reliable the estimate is. Accordingly, the subject of cost estimating, including the role of the learning curve in cost estimating, is examined in the appendix to this chapter.

THE RELATIONSHIP BETWEEN PRICE AND COST ANALYSES

In one way or another, our jobs are all concerned with providing answers to the question, "What's it worth?" The determination of what something is worth is, among other things, a reflection of its availability, quality, and utility. The impact of such factors is translated into dollars or price, usually through the interaction of supply and demand. The asking price attached to an item or service is generally a summation of labor, material, overhead, and profit.

The worth of the item may be the result of many considerations, including the need, the competitive situation, cost comparisons, historical trends, engineering evaluations, actual cost data, and judgment. Our ability as purchasers to assess the proper worth of an item presents as many facets as the criteria used by the supplier to establish his or her concept of worth. The process of arriving at a conclusion of worth in purchasing is called pricing. The process involved in making a sensible decision about the price proposed by the offeror or supplier is known as price analysis.

From a procurement point of view, the objective of pricing is to ensure that the purchaser pays a fair and reasonable price for the timely delivery of the desired quality of a required supply or service. A fair and reasonable price is one that is fair to both parties of the transaction, considering quality, delivery, competition, and the probability of the supplier producing as required by the purchase order or contract. There are several points of view as to what a fair and reasonable price is:

- *Market Price.* One view is that the market price is the fair and reasonable price. Assuming competition among potential buyers for the available material and competition among potential sellers for the available demand, competition determines what quantities will be bought and sold and at what price.
- *Seller's Point of View.* A fair and reasonable price is one that covers the seller's cost of production plus a reasonable profit. This price may change to meet market conditions (e.g., the degree and effect of competition).
- *Buyer's Point of View.* A fair and reasonable price is one that must be paid to obtain a needed item. How much the buyer is willing to pay may be influenced by the intensity of the need, the item's quality, its utility, and the availability of alternatives.

There is no one price that is fair and reasonable from all viewpoints. All three of the dimensions cited must be considered in reaching a conclusion that a price is fair and reasonable. In summary, fair and reasonable describes a conclusion concerning price.

To understand pricing, it is necessary to apply a consistent meaning to the following terms:

> *Cost*—all elements of expense with the exception of profit
> *Price*—all elements of expense plus profit
> *Profit*—the net proceeds obtained by deducting all elements of cost from the price

The buyer, in deciding on the fairness and reasonableness of the price for a product or a service, must determine what kind of information must be used as a basis for the decision. If competition has established the price, the marketplace has in essence established the value or performed a price analysis on the item. Therefore, the buyer can accept that price as a sound basis for the pricing decision. In the absence of effective price competition, or where it is lacking altogether and when the purchase is of a significant size, cost analysis along with price analysis may become necessary for arriving at a pricing decision.

The techniques of price analysis and cost analysis are clearly and distinctly different. Price analysis does not include evaluation of the offeror's detailed cost estimate; that is cost analysis. In the right circumstances, the buyer can make a sound price decision after price analysis without using the technique of cost analysis at all. But, as we shall see, the buyer cannot make a sound price decision on the basis of cost analysis alone.

PRICE ANALYSIS

Price analysis is a broad term that means those actions taken by the buyer to reach a price decision without recourse to cost analysis. Price analysis may be done by comparing different prices or by comparing prices with an engineering estimate.

In competitive bidding, price analysis is used to determine if the price is reasonable. Price analysis may include a look at what suppliers have done on previous contracts, a comparison with prices paid for the same or similar product or service, or a comparison with an independent cost estimate as described in the appendix to this chapter.

Much of modern procurement is founded on the principle that free and open competition is the one sure way to get a fair and reasonable price. The buyer must decide in every case, however, if there is competition for the requirement and if the competition is adequate. As we saw at QRS Products, this decision frequently cannot be made until after an evaluation of the proposals received in response to a request for bid. Adequate competition cannot be guaranteed even though many vendors are asked to submit bids. It is possible that each supplier does not have an equal chance of winning the competition. The fact that several vendors do submit bids does not mean that the price of the low bidder is fair and reasonable. For example, the low bidder already may have amortized significant setup costs that are included in a competitor's costs. The low bidder may be far down the learning curve, resulting in lower labor and material costs. Or the low bidder may be the only source of manufacture for the item with his or her apparent "competitors" being distributors of the product. Good pricing should identify such situations for purchases of a significant value. In such circumstances, cost analysis and negotiations may be necessary to arrive at a fair and reasonable price.

If a comparison of bids does not provide decisive information on the adequacy of competition, the buyer should make a more detailed analysis using past prices, quantities, production and delivery rates, and similar information. When competition is not adequate to support a determination that a price is fair and reasonable, it may be possible to use information from past purchases or cost estimates (prepared in engineering or purchasing) without recourse to cost analysis.

Price analysis is basically a comparative process. Therefore, it is meaningful only if the data being compared are truly comparable. This may not be the case, for example, when prices have been based on different assumptions about technical or performance requirements. The danger of comparing "apples with oranges" becomes particularly great when quotations from earlier purchases are being used for comparative purposes. The reason, of course, is that differences in such factors as specifications, quantities, delivery schedules, buyer-furnished material, improvements in efficiency, and general economic conditions may have an important bearing on price. Frequently, it is possible to make appropriate adjustments in pricing data to reflect the applicable differences by looking at cost behavior patterns.

Cost Behavior Patterns

Costs should also be examined according to their behavior patterns in relation to fluctuations of volume of sales or production. Basically, three types of cost behavior patterns can be distinguished. They are variable, fixed, and semivariable.

Costs that fluctuate directly and proportionately on a total basis with changes in volume of production and business activity are called variable costs. Direct materials and direct labor are fully variable costs. If volume of production is doubled, variable costs are doubled; if volume of production is increased 20%, variable costs increase 20%. Costs that remain relatively constant on a total basis as the volume of production and business activity change are known as fixed costs. Examples are rent, depreciation, insurance, and property taxes. These costs are incurred with the passage of time and are independent of the level of activity within a time period. Costs that vary on a total basis with changes in volume of production or business activity but not in direct proportion are called semivariable. These costs remain relatively fixed between certain production levels and advance when production volume changes from one level to another. Payroll taxes and maintenance are examples.

If the separate cost elements behave according to one of the three described patterns, then the total cost, which is the sum of these elements, must also vary with volume. A graphic picture of these three basic cost behavior patterns is shown in Figure 9.1.

The true behavioral pattern of costs is not necessarily as predictable as the charts portray. Some costs may even decrease with increases in volume. An example is lower material costs resulting from volume discounts. Low sales volume may prompt a company to increase investments in research and development, labor-saving devices, or capital equipment to gain a better competitive position. A sales volume consisting of extensive production of a single item may generate less overhead than the same volume representing a diverse operation devoted to many projects. Despite these volume influences, rules of thumb can be developed with the cost-volume premises that prove useful with further analysis.

Overhead costs normally fall in the semivariable cost patterns. Therefore, it is important to recognize why a semivariable cost varies directly but not proportionately with changes in volume of production. A semivariable cost is actually a composite of a fixed and variable cost. In

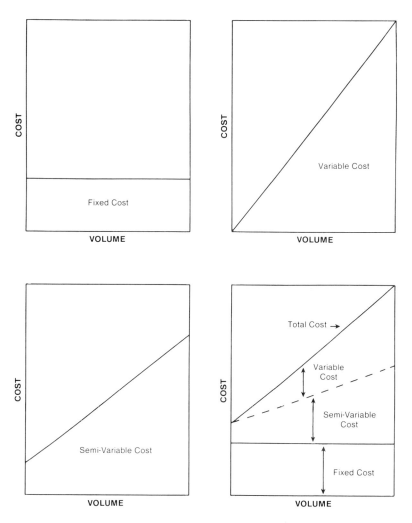

FIGURE 9.1 Cost Behavior Patterns

other words a semivariable cost has a fixed portion and a variable portion as shown in Figure 9.2.

Heat, light, and power are normally viewed as overhead costs. Ordinarily, whether the plant is producing or not, a certain amount of heat, light, and power is required. That portion of this overhead cost would be the fixed cost portion. As production volume changes, the amount of heat, light, and power would change proportionately. The variable cost portion of overhead would be the portion caused by the production volume change.

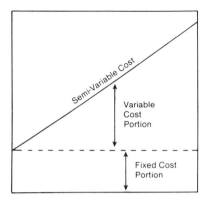

FIGURE 9.2   Semivariable Cost

Cost-Volume Relationships

Keeping in mind the cost behavior patterns, let us discuss cost-volume relationships and the break-even point. The following basic data serve as an example:

Fixed Costs
    Manufacturing overhead (semivariable, fixed cost portion) $250.00
    Start-up costs (all fixed cost)   500.00
    Total fixed cost $750.00

Variable Costs
    Labor and material (per unit) $ 0.50
    Manufacturing overhead (semivariable, variable cost
        portion; per unit)   0.25
    Total variable costs $ 0.75

In Figure 9.3 the total cost line is the sum of the three behavior patterns of fixed, semivariable, and variable. With this information, the following costs could be developed for 5,000 units of production in increments of 1,000:

UNITS	TOTAL FIXED COST	TOTAL VARIABLE COST	TOTAL COST
1,000	$750	$0.75 a unit × 1,000 = $ 750	$1,500
2,000	750	0.75 a unit × 2,000 = 1,500	2,250
3,000	750	0.75 a unit × 3,000 = 2,250	3,000
4,000	750	0.75 a unit × 4,000 = 3,000	3,750
5,000	750	0.75 a unit × 5,000 = 3,750	4,500

Break-Even Point

Using the data that have been developed, let us assume that the manufacturer produces a single product and sells it for $1 per unit. If

1,000 units are sold, the supplier will receive $1,000. If 2,000 units are sold, the supplier will receive $2,000. By plotting these points on the chart and extending them, a total sales dollar or revenue line is developed. When the total sales line is drawn on the chart line, it intersects the cost line at $3,000 and at 3,000 units. This significant intersection is called the break-even point, the point at which sales dollars cover cost dollars. This is how the break-even point is found graphically. Use of the foregoing graphic analysis provides insight into break-even analysis. With this insight, it is possible to use the following formula to determine break-even points in both dollars and volume:

$$BE_u = \frac{FC}{SP - VC} = \frac{\$750}{\$1.00 - \$0.75} = \frac{\$750}{\$0.25} = 3,000 \text{ units}$$

$$BE_\$ = \frac{FC}{1 - VC/SP} = \frac{\$750}{1 - \$0.75/\$1.00} = \frac{\$750}{\$0.25} = \$3,000$$

where

BE_u = break-even (units)
$BE_\$$ = break-even (dollars)
FC = fixed cost
SP = selling price
VC = variable cost

FIGURE 9.3   Cost-Volume Relationships

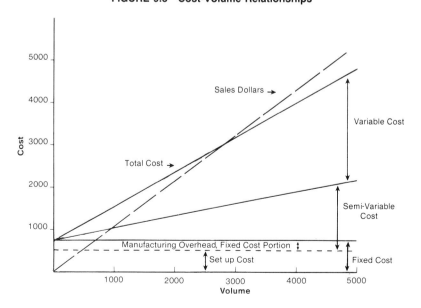

Since much overhead is an indirect cost which cannot be identified specifically with a particular cost objective, it presents problems to the buyer in the areas of manufacturing, engineering, and general and administrative overhead. From a practical standpoint, overhead is based on a flexible budget. As volume increases, overhead costs increase. But in comparison with rising overhead in total dollars, as volume increases the overhead *rate* should come down. In most companies an effort is made to maintain graphs or charts of overhead, on both an historical basis and a projected basis. The buyer should do the same for key suppliers.

It is to the supplier's advantage to project his or her volume of business as conservatively as possible to assure recouping overhead costs even if sales fall short of expectations. Knowing this, purchasing personnel should question the supplier about his or her future business potential in respect to not being as great as current data may indicate.

With these thoughts in mind, let us examine briefly some of the pricing methods that can be used without resorting to cost analysis.

Competition

Competition has been described as rivalry in selling goods. One of the basic principles of good procurement is that *open* competition among sellers is the one sure way to get a fair and reasonable price. It must be decided in every case, however, that there is competition for the requirement and that the competition is adequate. A buyer cannot decide this until evaluating the prices offered and until it has been determined that at least two responsible vendors who can satisfy the requirement have competed independently.

If this condition has been met, the buyer can assume price competition unless it is learned that

- The low bidder has an unusual advantage over the competition. For example, the low bidder may have written off all costs of special tooling and plant rearrangement to previous sales. Another example might be that the low bidder is the manufacturer of a vital component that competitors must buy from him or her.
- The conditions of the solicitation unreasonably denied one or more known and qualified sources the opportunity to compete.
- It was not possible for vendors to estimate costs with a high degree of certainty. (In such situations it is likely that contingency allowances have been included in the bids.)

A price can be based on adequate price competition, even when there is no active rivalry between would-be sellers. Such a conclusion depends on a comparison of current prices for the same or similar items bought in comparable quantities under purchase orders previously awarded after adequate price competition.

To see if competition really exists, a buyer must test past prices, examine the range of prices and experience offered by competing companies, note the exceptions taken to the specifications by a vendor, and compare delivery schedules or other terms of the invitation for bids or request for proposals.

Catalog or Market Price

The prospective supplier may claim that the quoted price is fair and reasonable since the price has been shaped by the "harsh realities" of the marketplace. To test this contention, the vendor's sales record for the recent period should be reviewed on the basis of such information as pricing policies, current prices quoted to others, current catalog price lists, and discount sheets.

Price Comparisons

Comparative price analysis involves comparing a proposed price with another price or other prices. The base price may be another vendor's offer on the same purchase, or it may be a price paid on earlier purchases of the same or similar items. One must be sure that the base price is fair and reasonable and represents a valid standard against which an offered price can be measured. If an original price is being used, it is not enough for the present offer to be lower than the last price paid or even lower than all prices previously paid. Consider the example of an item bought repeatedly from the same supplier:

BUY	QUANTITY	UNIT PRICE
1st	180	$86
2nd	200	79
3rd	172	70
Present	212	58

A steady downward trend in price is often pleasing to the buyer, but it is not proof of reasonableness. Unless one of the previous prices has been established by competition, detailed cost analysis, a cost estimate, or testing of the market for the same or a similar item, there can be no assurance that the present bid is reasonable.

If there is little variation in the quantities in the example for comparability, there should be little difference in price. As a general rule, one expects to pay less per unit as the quantities purchased increase. It is for this reason that consolidation of requirements is urged continually. It does not necessarily follow, however, that a proposed price lower than the last purchase price is reasonable just because the present quantity is greater than on the last buy. Neither does the coupling of a higher price with a smaller quantity prove a price to be reasonable. In either case, the relative price change is a logical one and should be expected, but this does not guarantee that the price is right. Other factors requiring attention are the nature of the item, the number to be purchased in relation to the number sold in a comparable period, and the existence of a price list with quantity breaks that may be used in selling the item to all classes of customers.

Usually price comparison is a starting point that reveals differences to be explained before a price decision can be made. The vendor may be the only source for needed answers, however, and a discussion with him or her may be necessary before a decision can be made. In any event, the buyer must proceed with great caution in analyzing differences, since plausible answers may not be the actual ones.

In a particular situation, the supplier may contend that material and labor costs have gone up in the interval since the last purchase. Therefore, a higher price is justified for the item. A general increase in material and labor costs, however, may not influence the unit cost of a particular item unless the price of the actual material used has gone up, unless the rates actually paid the workers have gone up, and unless there have not been compensating economies in the amounts of material and labor used in manufacturing or in indirect expenses.

A supplier may contend that the last buy of the item was made while the end item of which it was a component was still in production. Now, as an out-of-production part, the item must take full setup costs spread over a smaller quantity. Therefore, the supplier contends, a price increase is justified. In this instance, the last buy may have been made while the end item was being manufactured, but even at that time, the particular part may have been produced in a special, small-quantity run and have carried a full setup charge. Thus, on closer investigation, we find that the cost of manufacture today should not differ appreciably from that previously experienced.

Price comparison requires easy access to price history on an item-by-item basis. Item history cards or machine printouts showing price, quantity, purchase order number, date, supplier, and delivery schedule should be available in any well-run purchasing organization. But care must be taken in using these prices. The mere fact that past prices exist does not make them valid bases for comparison. The buyer also must establish production or delivery rates, the kinds of purchase (competitive, sole source, or similar characterization), and the presence or absence of special considerations before deciding to use a price as a standard.

Cost Estimates as a Basis of Price Analysis

An offered price may be compared with an engineered cost estimate to establish reasonableness when price comparisons are not possible. To be useful, however, the basis for the estimate and its reliability must be established. It is important to determine how the estimate was established, what information and estimating techniques were used, the source of the information, and how earlier estimates compared with resulting contract or purchase order prices.

Figure 9.4 sets out pricing actions in a go/no-go sequence.[1] The purchaser starts with competition as a basis for a decision and goes only as far as necessary to assure himself or herself that the price is right. The buyer starts with an evaluation of the proposals. The buyer decides if effective price competition exists. If it does, the buyer stops; the price is right. If competition is not effective, the buyer may look to catalogs and market prices. If these do not do the job, the buyer moves to price com-

FIGURE 9.4 Pricing—A Decision Chart

Estimated $ Amount	$0 - 500	$501 - 10,000	$10,001- 100,000	$100,000
Basis for Decision				
Competition	If prices considered reasonable, may bypass competition	Generally limited to 3 sources	Maximize to extent consistent with requirement	Maximize to extent consistent with requirement
Catalog or Market Price	Good source	Acceptable	Acceptable	Acceptable
Price Comparisons	Acceptable	Acceptable	Acceptable	Acceptable
Engineering Estimate	Acceptable	Acceptable	Acceptable	No
Cost or Pricing Data	No	No	When Appropriate	Yes
Negotiate	Last Resort	Permissible	Permissible	Yes

[1]Adapted from Richard P. White, "How to Price Contracts Using Price Analysis," *NCMA Journal*, January 1979, p. 25.

parisons and then to engineering estimates. If no price analysis method works, it may be necessary to use cost analysis.

Analysis and decisions probably will not follow this sequence to the letter. Experience frequently will allow one to take shortcuts to reach the decision that an offer should be accepted or negotiated to an acceptable level. *Remember the objective: an acceptable price achieved with minimum effort.*

Cost of Ownership

Altogether too frequently, great emphasis is placed on the initial cost of acquiring an item while ignoring or neglecting the total cost of owning and operating the item. In Chapter 5 we discussed the need for placing attention on the cost of ownership or life-cycle cost of an item. Also, we showed how to develop an item's life-cycle cost. This approach to procurement significantly reduces the purchaser's total cost of owning, operating, and maintaining an item of equipment. Also, by considering all the significant costs over the life of the item instead of merely the initial acquisition cost, we gain an increase in competition since firms whose products have higher initial prices but lower subsequent ownership costs on a total life-cycle cost basis may be able to compete. When the buyer is conducting price analysis on such items, the price to be used is the item's life-cycle cost.

Two-Step Procurement

When a performance specification (see Chapter 3) serves as the basis of a solicitation, a procedure known as two-step procurement may be employed to select the source and determine the price. During the first step of this procedure, interested potential competitors are requested to submit unpriced technical proposals on how they will meet the requirement. Personnel in the requiring organization then review these technical proposals and accept those approaches deemed to be satisfactory. In step 2, firms having submitted acceptable technical proposals are requested to submit a price to perform under a purchase order or contract using the technical approach they previously submitted. On receipt of the price proposals, the purchaser can select a supplier in either of two ways:

1. *Price Competition.* With this approach, award will be made to the bidder submitting the lowest price. With adequate competition, this approach allows price analysis to serve as the basis of a determination that the price is fair and reasonable.

2. *Combination of Technical and Price Considerations.* In this case, a combination of price and technical considerations is the basis of selecting the supplier. A decision must be made as to the adequacy of price analysis alone or

the need to include cost analysis as part of the process leading to a decision that the price is fair and reasonable.

COST ANALYSIS

In the absence of effective competition, or where price analysis alone does not assure a reasonable price, cost analysis may be necessary to establish the basis for negotiation of the purchase order or contract price. When it is anticipated that effective competition will be absent and sufficient dollars will be involved to warrant the cost and effort associated with detailed negotiations, the invitation for bids or request for proposals should require a detailed cost estimate supporting the bid or proposal.

Cost analysis is the review and evaluation, element by element, of the cost estimate underlying the bid. The elements normally included in such a cost estimate are

Engineering effort
Special tooling
Direct and indirect material costs
Direct and indirect labor costs
Overhead

In cost analysis, the costs of the individual elements are analyzed to determine if the overall cost estimate approximates the one that might be expected of a company performing the proposed order with reasonable efficiency. As we have seen, obtaining cost or pricing data from bidders and cost analysis generally are restricted to purchases where it is anticipated that price analysis methods alone cannot be relied on to produce acceptable results. When cost analysis techniques must be used, the starting point is the cost or pricing data furnished by the prospective supplier.

Cost or pricing data are the factual portions of the bid or proposal, or the facts on which the bid is based. They are the parts that can be verified. Usually the data can be supported with accounting records and other documents provided by the prospective supplier. It is this accounting review that fits the popular concept of what cost analysis is. Although there is more than this to cost analysis, the accounting review is one of the three analytical tasks involved in contract pricing, the other two being technical analysis and price analysis.

Accounting analysis requires access to a supplier's books and records. Access to the supplier's accounting system can be difficult to obtain. If such access is anticipated or required, a provision should be included in the invitation for bids or the request for proposals to allow the purchaser to review pertinent records. Access to a supplier's cost data is required for other than firm fixed and fixed price with escalation contracts.

Technical analysis requires the involvement of technical specialists from the purchasing firm. These specialists are experts in such matters as manufacturing techniques, tool design, plant layout, various engineering fields, quality assurance, and packaging. The specialists can give a qualitative evaluation of past and projected costs in their areas of expertise.

The concept of realistic prices ties in closely with the idea that cost analysis is used in the absence of price competition to reach agreement on a fair and reasonable price. The negotiated price should be realistic; that is, it is strongly influenced by the prospect of what it should cost if the supplier operates with reasonable economy and efficiency. Being realistic also means that extremes should be avoided. Because estimates of future events are being dealt with, the buyer cannot expect to attain minimum costs with 100% accuracy. Nor can the buyer expect the price to remain at an optimum level. Pushing too hard on the optimal concept well may result in a price that would spell loss to the supplier unless every single good factor that had to happen did occur.

The buyer must recognize the nature of a price proposal and understand the full implication of what an estimate is. *An estimate is a prediction of what the cost of future actions will or should be.* Some actions can be predicted with a high measure of confidence. The outcome of other possible actions is less certain. If, however, the probability of their occurrence is significant, the estimate must provide for them as well.

In performing a cost analysis, therefore, an attempt is made to isolate these kinds of uncertainties and identify the amounts estimated to cover them. The end objective is to negotiate a realistic price based on all current and correct cost or pricing data available to the buyer at the time of negotiation. Obviously, the method of compensation must fit the situation.

THE ROLE OF PROFIT

There is no set formula for determining what a fair and reasonable profit is. If profit were based on the cost of production, the inefficient supplier would be rewarded. The same result would occur if we followed the European approach of basing profit on the supplier's investment so that he or she can obtain a target return on investment.

Profit is required to induce a supplier to take a purchase order or contract and to motivate that supplier to deliver the quality of product specified on time. Further, profit encourages and assists the supplier to remain in business and become more efficient. Several issues should be considered when deciding on the size of the profit:

- Extraordinary risks justify above-average profits.
- Highly reliable suppliers deserve above-average profits.
- A high degree of technical input and innovation deserves above-average profits.
- Small production runs or small quantities deserve a higher profit than do larger orders.
- Profit tends to be a function of current supply and demand patterns. If supply is tight, the buyer may find it necessary to pay a higher profit. But it is incumbent upon the buyer to oppose suppliers who attempt to maximize their profits based on contrived shortages or on what they think the market will bear. Buyers should resist excessively high profits in every legitimate manner possible. During periods of excess capacity, lower profits will be in order. (It should be remembered that a supplier is better off accepting a price which covers variable costs and makes *some* contribution to fixed costs than rejecting such an order. Thus, in periods of extreme surplus capacity, it is entirely rational for a supplier to accept an order which provides some contribution to fixed costs, even though there is little or no prospect of earning a profit on the order.)

Before leaving the topic of profit, it is desirable to integrate theory and the real world. Is profit the basic motivator in the private sector? Does the practice of giving a supplier an opportunity to maximize profits ensure that we achieve our objectives?

Dr. Raymond Hunt of the State University of New York at Buffalo conducted research on this issue under a NASA grant in the early 1970s. Dr. Hunt found that suppliers are risk averters, not profit maximizers. He concluded that "organizational motivation is a complicated, many-faceted . . . thing, and that contractors (suppliers) are motivated more by general considerations, such as the desire to grow . . . than they are by immediate profit opportunities or by the terms of any given contract."[2]

SUMMARY

The worth of an item may be the result of many considerations: one's need for the item, the competitive situation, cost comparisons, historic trends, and judgment. In purchasing, the process of arriving at a conclu-

[2]Raymond E. Hunt, quoted in Richard White, "Profit Analysis," *NCMA Journal*, July 1979, p. 21.

sion about the worth of an item is called pricing. The purchaser's objective is to pay a price that is fair and reasonable for the timely delivery and desired quality of a required item or service. A fair and reasonable price is one that is fair to both buyer and seller, considering quality, delivery, competition, and the probability of the supplier producing as specified.

Price analysis is a broad term that includes those actions taken by the buyer to reach a decision on the reasonableness of a price without recourse to cost analysis. A basic principle underlying modern procurement is that free and open competition is the one sure way to obtain a fair and reasonable price.

When a comparison of bids does not provide decisive information on the adequacy of competition, the buyer should make a more detailed analysis using past prices, quantities, production and delivery rates, and similar information. It may be possible to make adjustments in pricing data based on past experience by looking at cost behavior patterns.

A hierarchy of preferred pricing methods has been developed. Competition is the preferred method, with catalog or market price analysis second, price comparisons third, the use of the firm's engineering estimates fourth, the analysis of vendor-supplied cost or pricing data fifth, and negotiations being the final (and most costly) basis of reaching a decision on the fairness and reasonableness of a price.

When we are conducting price analysis on an item of capital equipment, the price we should use is based on how much it will cost to own and operate the item: its life-cycle cost.

In the absence of effective competition, or where price analysis alone does not assure a reasonable price, cost analysis may be necessary to establish the basis of negotiation of a fair and reasonable price. Cost analysis is the review and evaluation of the several elements in the vendor's estimate. Any resulting price should be realistic; that is, it should be influenced by the prospect of what the item should cost to manufacture if the supplier operates with reasonable economy and efficiency.

Profit is required to induce a vendor to accept a purchase order and to motivate him or her to perform as specified in the order. The size of the profit should be a function of the amount of risk involved, the amount of technical input and innovation required, the size of the order, the reliability of the supplier in meeting the terms and conditions on past orders, and current supply and demand patterns.

appendix

KEYS TO SUCCESSFUL PRICING

Paul Bierman, a buyer at Ulysses Manufacturing Company, is preparing to negotiate the purchase of 2,000 welded forging assemblies. Immediately on receipt of the request for purchase for the assemblies, Paul reviewed the drawings and specifications and prepared an invitation for bid. This IFB was forwarded to 10 qualified suppliers with the expectation that competition would satisfy all price analysis requirements. Unfortunately, at least for Paul and Ulysses Manufacturing, only one responsive bid was received. Inquiries of all other qualified firms within a reasonable distance indicated that they either were operating at capacity or were unwilling to meet Ulysses' stringent specification.

The one bid that had been received specified delivery over the allotted six months at a unit price of $600, provided that the supplier receive a notice to proceed within seven days. Ulysses Manufacturing Company had no experience purchasing such welded forging assemblies. Therefore, Paul requested an engineered cost estimate of the number of hours required to produce the assemblies and likely material costs. Stan Sharp, estimator at Ulysses, is meeting in response to Paul's request.

STAN: Paul, we don't have experience with any assemblies of this size. However, we have found that the factor method of estimating has been very reliable for units weighing one-fourth to one-half as much as these new assemblies. Based on this approach, I estimate that these big assemblies should require about 10 hours per unit for a lot of 100 units, including all setups. Material cost should be about $50 per unit.

PAUL: Stan, this leaves me a pretty big ballpark in which to play. How applicable is this factor estimate to this size assembly?

STAN: Plus or minus 10% would be my guess.

PAUL: Ouch! I guess this is better than nothing, but not a lot! Your estimate is for 100 units. What rate of learning should we expect?

STAN: The book says about 88%, but our experience is about 92%. Paul, I'm real sorry that I can't be of any more help, but you did not give me any time! I've got to get back to my office. Got a really big one on the front burner.

Paul sits and wonders to himself, "How am I ever going to get ready for negotiations this afternoon with this kind of help?"

APPROACHES TO COST ESTIMATING

Cost estimates are required at several points in the procurement process. There are a number of methods of developing cost estimates. The degree of accuracy of the estimate varies significantly with the approach employed. Those involved in the procurement process must be aware of which estimating approach has been employed so that they know how reliable the estimate is likely to be.

As we saw in Chapter 2, the design process calls for the development of alternative conceptual approaches to manufacturing a product that will meet the needs identified by marketing or the customer. The estimated cost of these alternatives is one of the criteria used to decide which alternatives to pursue. The degree of realism or *likely* accuracy required of the estimate is a function of the stage of the design process, the number of alternatives available, and the likely cost magnitude of the item whose cost is being estimated. Increased accuracy in the estimate is required as the procurement process moves through the make-or-buy analysis on to price analysis, cost analysis, and negotiations. Many faulty make-or-buy analyses, resulting in unnecessary costs, are the result of inaccurate cost estimates. A realistic cost estimate is a key input to the buyer who is conducting a price analysis. If the buyer enters into detailed negotiations, the ability to negotiate a satisfactory price depends, in large part, on an accurate and specific cost estimate and the ability to use learning curve theory, when applicable.

Preliminary Cost Estimating Approaches

A preliminary estimate is one that is made during the formative stages of design, a time when there is a decided lack of verifiable information. Preliminary cost estimates are used to screen designs and to aid in the formation of *a budget*. They assist management in determining which concepts to pursue and which to cull out at an early stage. Mistakes in preliminary estimates can be costly to the firm since they can result in the elimination of potentially attractive designs. We now will look at several preliminary estimating techniques.[3]

The natural estimator. A few individuals are able to combine experience and intuition and predict manufacturing costs with a fair degree of accuracy. Unfortunately, the supply of such individuals is far short of the demand for them. Accordingly, other approaches must be employed when a high degree of accuracy is required.

Conference method. This approach relies on the collective judgment of several individuals from various departments or, possibly, from the cost-estimating department alone. These individuals develop the estimate for a new design by comparing known designs and their associated costs with the new design.

Comparison method. When the estimator has an excessively difficult design and estimating problem—or even an unsolvable one—the principle of analogies can be employed. A simpler design problem for which an estimate is known or can be developed is constructed. The two designs should be as similar as possible. It is then possible to extrapolate from the simpler design and its estimated cost to the more complex one.

Unit method. This is a very popular approach to cost estimating. With this method, the cost estimate is a function of one independent variable. This approach underlies the factor estimating method, described later. Examples of unit estimates are (1) the cost of a factory is a function of the number of square feet of production space ($C = a + 40A$, where C = the cost of the factory, a = a constant, and A = the production area in square feet), and (2) conversion cost is a function of the number of machine shop person-hours ($C = 45T$, where C = cost and T = machine shop hours). The constants and the coefficients may be the result of regression analysis or "feel."

Expected value method. The conference, comparison, and unit methods of estimating all rely on a subtle averaging process. Averaging tends to ignore uncertainty and risk. The expected value method assumes

[3]Much of the material on the various estimating techniques described in this section is based on Phillip F. Ostwald, *Cost Estimating for Engineering and Management* (Englewood Cliffs, N.J.: Prentice-Hall, 1974). The interested reader is referred to this excellent work for additional details.

that the estimator is able to give a probability point estimate for each of several costs over a realistic range of cost outcomes. The cost estimate derived in this manner is the summation of the product of the likely costs and their associated probabilities: $C = \Sigma_i\, p_i c_i$, where C = cost and p_i = the probability of cost outcome c_i occurring. One of the attractions of the expected value method is that the decision maker has an understanding of the range of likely cost outcomes so that areas of risk are more visible.

Assume that a cost estimating group has provided the estimates contained in Table 9.1 for a battery for a power supply under development. Expected sales of the power supply unit are 400,000 units per year at a likely selling price of $30. The most likely cost is $16. The expected cost is $C = 0.1(\$15) + 0.6(\$16) + 0.1(\$17) + 0.1(\$18) + 0.1(\$19) = \$16.50$. Of perhaps equal interest to information on the most likely costs is the range of costs. In this situation, we see that there is 1 chance in 10 that costs will be as low as $16 and 1 in 10 that they will be $19.

Cost estimating relationships.   Cost estimating relationships, generally referred to as CERs, are used to estimate the cost of an item from one or more of its functions or characteristics. For example, the estimated cost of a jet engine may be predicted as a function of its thrust: $C = a + bT$, where C = cost, a = a constant, b = a mathematically derived coefficient, and T = thrust of the engine in pounds. Ostwald cites an example of a CER as

$$C = 0.13937 x_1^{0.74356} x_2^{0.7751}$$

where

C = cost in $10,000,000
x_1 = maximum thrust, in pounds
x_2 = production quantity milestone

TABLE 9.1   Likely Cost Outcomes

Cost Per Unit ($)	Probability of Event Occurring
15	.01
16	.06
17	.01
18	.01
19	.01

Detailed Approaches

The techniques just described are useful for screening and eliminating unsound proposals without incurring extensive engineering and estimating costs. Additional, more accurate methods should be employed on those designs the firm desires to pursue. These methods will be useful in preparing estimates for price analysis and in providing detailed cost estimates to the buyer who is preparing for intensive price negotiations and cost analysis. The following detailed cost estimating methods are more quantitative than those just given. While judgment still plays an important role, emphasis shifts to mathematical models and hard data.

The factor method. We have seen that the unit method of estimating uses only one factor in estimating the cost. This relationship takes the general form of $C = a + bX$, where C = cost, a = a constant, and b = a coefficient of the independent variable or factor, X, which is the number of units in the project whose cost is being estimated. The factor method utilizes the same logic but achieves increased accuracy by incorporating several factors. The cost estimating model takes on the general form of

$$C = a + B_1X_1 + B_2X_2 + \cdots$$

where

C = the dependent variable, cost
a = a constant
B_i = net regression coefficients of the independent variables
X_i = independent variables

Each coefficient measures the change in C (cost) per unit change in the particular independent variable, holding the other variables constant. The values for the various factors (a, B_1, B_2, . . .) allow us to derive a predictive model based on the firm's own experience.

Power law and sizing model. This approach is useful in estimating equipment costs for designs similar in type to items whose costs are known but are of different sizes. The principle underlying the power law and sizing model is that there frequently is a nondirect relationship between the size of two items of equipment that differ only in size. This relationship takes on the general form of

$$C = C_r \left(\frac{Qc}{Qr}\right)m$$

where

C = total value sought for design size Q_c
C_r = known cost for a reference size Q_r
Q_c = design size
Q_r = reference design size
m = correlating exponent, $0 < m < 1$

Bottom-up estimating. The preceding methods have one element in common: they view an item from the top; that is, they look at the item as a whole or a group of subcomponents *without* analyzing the nuts and the bolts and the sheet metal or bar stock and the amount of direct (and indirect) labor required to build the item up into a "thing" to be sold. Bottom-up estimating starts with the lowest level of materials purchased by the firm and traces the information process through which the materials go in the process of becoming an end item. This method of estimating is especially appropriate for material and/or labor-intensive items. The bottom-up approach requires an operation to be broken down into its basic elements. Time factors are then applied to these elements. Although several approaches are available when applying the time factors, the standard time data method is the most useful in estimating labor requirements. Standard time data provide time requirements for standard tasks within the firm. Standard time data are arranged in a systematic order and are used over and over. An accurate bottom-up estimate requires considerable data:

Product specifications
Delivery quantities and rates
A bill of materials
Costs of delivered purchased parts and material
Detailed drawings of parts to be manufactured
Parts routings
Manufacturing equipment requirements
Testing and inspection requirements
Packing and shipping requirements
Time factors (labor standards)
Overhead rates

Modular pricing. This approach to cost estimating requires the development of a data base of information on development and production costs of the modules of a system. A module is defined as a logical work package or subsystem. When estimating the cost of developing and producing a new system, the item is divided into logical modules. Information is obtained from the data base on the cost for developing and producing similar modules. A group of engineering and manufacturing personnel then assigns a judgmental complexity factor to the new module. The item's likely cost then can be estimated by comparing its complexity with that of modules whose cost experience is available. This approach to estimating has proven to be much less time consuming and less costly and more accurate than the other approaches described in this chapter. The modular approach to estimating *does* require forward planning and time and effort to establish the requisite data base.

THE LEARNING CURVE

Many of the estimating methods we have looked at have the ability to consider the implications of the quantity being produced or purchased when developing the cost estimate. However, when the estimate is for a specific unit or units to be produced or purchased, consideration should be given to the phenomenon that labor and management learn . . . that is, they tend to become more efficient as the number of units produced increases.

Learning occurs in virtually all repetitive operations. The learning curve should be employed when developing estimates, when planning and managing manufacturing operations, and when negotiating prices for purchased materials and components. Typically, learning takes place in two general areas: individual learning and organizational learning. Individual learning occurs when an individual repeats a process and gains efficiency from the experience. Organizational learning results from administrative, equipment, process, and related improvements. The learning reflects the collective efforts of many individuals, both in line and staff positions, with the common objective of accomplishing a task progressively more efficiently. One of the first observations of such learning was in aircraft production when it was observed that the hours required to build an aircraft decreased at a constant rate each time the production quantity doubled over a wide range of production.

Learning curves describe an empirical relationship between the number of units produced and the number of hours required to produce them. The direct labor hours required to produce a unit decrease by a constant percentage each time the quantity produced is doubled. This relationship is very useful in production planning, in estimating costs for make-or-buy analyses, and in preparing for and conducting negotiations with prospective suppliers. Table 9.2 portrays the labor required to produce the first four units and the two-thousandth unit of an item with a 90% learning curve.

Frequently, a supplier's production capacity may be a constraint on the purchasing firm's production plans. The learning curve is useful in

Unit Produced	Labor Hours Required for Last Item	Cumulative Labor Hours Required	Average Labor Hours Required Per Unit
1st	10	10	10.0
2nd	9	19	9.5
3rd	8.5	27.5	9.2
4th	8.1	35.6	8.9
2000th	3.1	7423	3.7

TABLE 9.2   Ninety Percent Learning Curve

estimating how many units a supplier can produce per unit of time. If progress payments are to be made to suppliers for extended production runs, the learning curve will assist purchasing in developing a progress payment plan that corresponds with the supplier's incurrence of costs.

Setting aside the effect of inflation, material costs also decrease with experience. Better methods are developed for producing the item, resulting in less scrap and spoilage. Less expensive materials are found to be satisfactory. And purchasing learns; that is, it locates less expensive sources and is able to negotiate lower unit prices. A learning rate of 95% is typical for material expenses.

Different types of manufacturing operations experience different rates of learning. Table 9.3 shows typical basic slopes for representative activities.

In the case at the beginning of the appendix, assume that a detailed bottom-up estimate were available. This estimate indicates that the first welded forging assembly will require 10 hours. During discussions with

TABLE 9.3   Typical Basic Learning Slopes

	%
Job Shop	95
Sheet Metal Stamping	92
Wire Preparation	90
Job Machining	88
Electornics Sheet Metal	87
Electronics Ship Assembly	85
General Subassembly	83
Major Aircraft Assembly	80

the prospective supplier, agreement is reached on this estimate and the expectation that the most likely learning rate will be 90%. It then is possible to estimate the total number of hours required to produce 2,000 units. Using data from the 90% learning rate (Table 9.2), the total hours required to produce 2,000 units will be 742.3 times the time required to produce the first unit (10 hours), for a total of 7,423 hours. If likely material cost for the first unit were $60, then the total likely material costs (setting aside the effect of inflation) would be $60 × 1,230 (from Ostwald), 95% learning rate, 2,000 units, or $7,380. Assume further that delivery of the assemblies paces Ulysses' production schedule. Based on the cumulative hours available in standard learning curve tables, the buyer and prospective seller should be able to agree on a realistic rate of delivery for each month of the contract period.

The learning experience approximates a straight-line pattern when plotted on log-log paper. Figure 9.5 shows an 80% learning curve utilizing the arithmetic plotting format for an item that requires 100 direct labor hours to produce the first unit. Figure 9.6 displays the same information utilizing the conventional log-log format.

When producing a new product or initiating a new production process, the assumption of a constant rate of learning or improvement is reasonable for quantities in excess of 50 units. However, for fewer than

FIGURE 9.5 Eighty Percent Learning Curve (arithmetic)

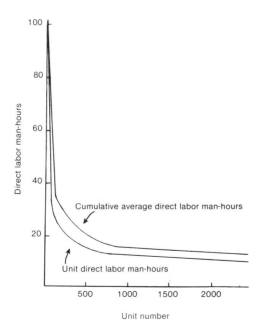

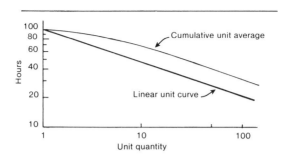

FIGURE 9.6 Eighty Percent Learning Curve (log-log)

50 units, there frequently is a substantial amount of deviation from the linear unit curve portrayed in Figure 9.6. In many situations, costs run considerably higher for the first units of production. The higher costs incurred during the early stages of production result largely from the time compression that normally occurs when introducing a new product.[4] The amount of excess cost (deviations from the costs that would have been incurred were there no time compression) will vary from product to product and by department. Figure 9.7 portrays the effect of such time compression on the rate of learning.

It has not been the intent of this brief discussion on learning curves to develop the reader into an expert on their use. Rather, the concept and limitations of learning curves have been presented to serve as a way of alerting the estimator, the price analyst, the negotiator, and management alike to the implications of learning on production and purchasing

FIGURE 9.7 A New Product Learning Curve

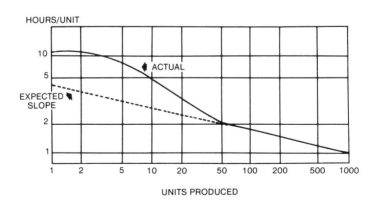

[4]E. B. Cochran, *Planning Production Costs: Using the Improvement Curve* (San Francisco: Chandler, 1968), p. 207.

costs and schedules and of the dangers of extrapolating cost estimates from production lots of one size to another.

ALTERNATE METHODS
OF CONTRACT PRICING

We now direct our attention to a frequently ignored, but crucial, aspect of procurement: selection of the right method of contract pricing. Historically,[5] over 98% of all purchase orders and contracts have specified a firm fixed price for the product or service purchased. But when such an approach is not appropriate, management must have a sound understanding of the attributes and applicability of alternate methods of contract pricing.

Certainly we can find suppliers willing to provide any good or service at a firm fixed price if that price is high enough. But there is, or should be, a relationship between the amount of cost uncertainty in a given situation and the method of contract pricing. By using the correct approach, the buyer can provide appropriate incentives to the supplier to control costs and avoid excessive or contingency pricing. Thus an understanding of the characteristics of alternative approaches to traditional firm fixed price pricing and knowledge of when to use the appropriate alternative will result in significant savings by the purchaser.

In addition to the firm fixed price (FFP) contract, useful alternate contract formats include fixed price redeterminable (FPR) contracts, fixed price incentive fee (FPIF) contracts, cost plus incentive fee (CPIF) contracts, cost plus award fee (CPAF) contracts, and cost plus fixed fee (CPFF) contracts.

Firm fixed price contracts. From the supplier's point of view, the FFP contract offers maximum incentive to perform effectively. It also contains no (or very few) administrative requirements (such as provisions for cost information) imposed by the purchaser.

Assume, for example, that a supplier has agreed to a unit selling price of $110. If the supplier can reduce costs from $100 (point A in Figure 9.8) to $90 (point B), profits increase to $20 per unit because the supplier retains as profit each dollar saved below the initial estimated cost. Conversely, any costs over the initial estimate must be borne by the supplier, even to the extent of a loss (if, in this instance, costs were to exceed $110). Because the supplier receives 100% of all savings below target or incurs 100% of all costs above target, we call this a 0/100 sharing relationship.

[5]This section first appeared as part of the author's article, "The Right Type of Contract for Every Procurement Situation," *Management Review,* May 1976, © 1976 by AMACOM, a division of American Management Associations. All rights reserved, used with permission.

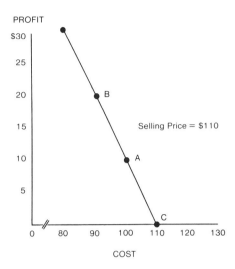

FIGURE 9.8   The Firm Fixed Price Contract

From the purchaser's point of view, two primary benefits accrue: ease of administration and certainty of purchase price. A potential disadvantage to the buyer stems from the supplier's incentive to control cost— every dollar saved represents a dollar's additional profit. Accordingly, a supplier may be tempted to reduce quality to lower production costs. Little danger of this exists if the buyer is purchasing standard, off-the-shelf items. But if the supplier is producing a nonstandard item or is providing a nonstandard service, a desire to maximize profit may conflict with the seller's desire to receive the specified level of quality.

A useful variation of the FFP contract involves the introduction of a provision whereby the customer accepts the risk associated with inflation when it is impossible to predict accurately the degree of potential increase (or decrease) in production costs. To illustrate, let us examine a prospective supplier's pricing strategy when he or she knows, with a high degree of accuracy, the quantity of materials and labor required to provide the product or service, but faces considerable uncertainty as to how much production costs will increase. (The logic for decreasing costs is similar, but will not be carried forward in this discussion.)

In this example, the supplier views the probability of different percentage increases as reflected in Figure 9.9. In effect, the seller believes that costs will rise between 5% and 25%, with an advance of 15% most likely. What value, then, will be used in preparing the price?

If the seller is a rational, risk-averse supplier and believes that the competition is similarly risk-averse, the pricing quote probably will include a contingency sufficient to protect the firm. Thus the seller in this example will tend to use a value of about 22%.

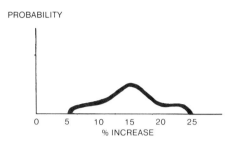

PROBABILITY

% INCREASE

FIGURE 9.9   Fixed Price with Escalation

But if the buyer is willing to assume all risk associated with the uncertainty of the magnitude of cost increases, then the supplier should be able and willing to offer a price containing no contingency for inflation. By assuming this risk, the buyer expects to incur additional costs of about 15%, thereby saving (if expectations prove correct) approximately 7% of the price the supplier would have offered. Obviously, if inflation exceeds 22%, the buyer will pay more than under a firm fixed price containing a 22% contingency for inflation. In most cases, however, the buyer will save money through the use of an escalation provision when the quantity of inputs is known but the effects of inflation are not known.

Fixed price redeterminable contracts.   FPR contracts, which are similar to a letter order or letter contract, should be used with great caution. With this type of contract, the supplier's incentive (assuming him or her to be a rational profit maximizer) is to increase costs to increase profit.

To illustrate, assume a situation in which a buyer who is contracting for a substantial-dollar-value product has located a vendor with adequate resources and managerial ability but no experience producing the desired product. But, because of an urgent need, the buyer is unable or unwilling to take the time to develop a detailed cost estimate. Buyer and seller agree to a ceiling price of $1.10 per item ($1.00 cost plus $0.10 profit), subject to redetermination after the supplier has gained sufficient experience to permit more realistic pricing of the item.

After the seller has gained this experience, the buyer learns that unit costs are running only about half the original estimate of $1.00. What rate of profit should the buyer and seller then negotiate?

Of the several hundred people to whom this question has been posed, only a handful responded that the supplier was entitled to 10 cents or more profit. Most said that, based on a cost of 50 cents, the supplier's profit should be only 4 or 5 cents. But what a strange way to reward a supplier for controlling costs! It does not take a very intelligent supplier long to realize that the greater the production costs (up to the fixed

FIGURE 9.10 **Fixed Price Redeterminable Contract**

ceiling), the greater the profits (see Figure 9.10). When a supplier is able to influence costs, doesn't it make good sense to reward good efforts and to penalize poor performance?

Fixed price incentive fee contracts. FPIF contracts are appropriate in situations where a moderate degree of uncertainty exists about the cost outcome and where the contractor's performance will affect costs. Under this contract, the buyer shares in savings that result when production costs drop below the original target, but also must help to shoulder the added cost if the seller goes above the target cost figure.

An FPIF contract requires buyer-seller agreement on the most likely (target) cost, target fee, ceiling price, and share ratio. Under a share ratio—stated as 75/25, 60/40, 50/50, and so on—the first value indicates the purchaser's share of savings below target cost or of any additional costs above target (but below the point at which the supplier assumes all additional costs—the point of total assumption).

Figure 9.11 illustrates the effect of different cost levels on a supplier's fee. In this example, the target cost is $100,000 (point A) and the target fee is $10,000 (point B), making a target price of $110,000; the ceiling price (point C) is $125,000; the point of total assumption is $121,430 (point D)[6]; and the share ratio is 70/30.

[6]The point of total assumption is determined by solving the following pair of simultaneous linear equations:

y = target profit + share ratio (target cost − x)
y = ceiling price − x

where x = cost, y = profit, and share ratio is the contractor's share stated in decimal form—for example, with a 70/30 share, use .3.

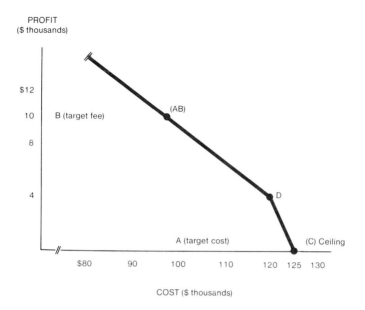

FIGURE 9.11 **Fixed Price Incentive Fee Contract**

Thus, in this example, if actual costs are $1.00 less than the target cost of $100,000, the supplier receives the $10,000 target fee plus $0.30 (30% of $1.00) for a total of $10,000.30. Conversely, if actual costs exceed target costs by $1.00, the supplier must pay 30% of the additional cost, resulting in a net fee of $9,999.70.

Although the customer incurs an exposure equal to the ceiling price under the FPIF contract, his or her most likely expenditure is equal to the target price (target cost plus target fee). Thus, as discussed, the supplier has an incentive to control costs because the supplier shares in any savings and must absorb a significant share of cost overruns.

Cost plus incentive fee contract. The CPIF contract is similar to the fixed price incentive fee contract except that it becomes a cost-plus-fixed-fee (CPFF) contract at two points (A and B in Figure 9.12). Point C in Figure 9.12 represents the target cost ($100,000), and point D represents the target fee ($6,000). Under the contract structure portrayed here, there is considerable uncertainty as to exactly what actual costs will be; however, the most likely cost is $100,000, with small possibility of costs going below $70,000 or exceeding $130,000.

Cost plus award fee contract. The award fee provision of the CPAF contract provides an incentive to the supplier by rewarding superior performance with above-average profits. The award fee is simply a "fee pool"

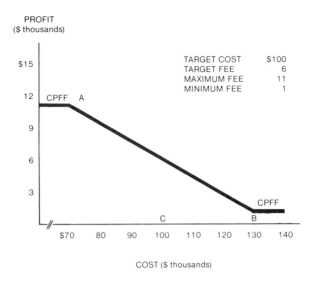

FIGURE 9.12   **Cost Plus Incentive Fee Contract**

(a specific dollar amount) established by the buyer and awarded in portions to the supplier on a periodic basis as earned.

An award fee pool normally ranges from 2% to 10% of estimated costs, and the amount of the pool that the supplier can earn depends on his or her performance—as determined by the buyer—over and above the minimum requirements set down in the contract. The award fee thus gives the buyer's management a flexible tool with which to influence performance. The buyer rewards the supplier in the form of award fee payments based on the buyer's subjective assessment in periodic reviews of how diligently the supplier is applying himself or herself.

This judgmental aspect of supplier performance evaluations provides an inherent flexibility to contracting situations in an uncertain environment, and the supplier, as well as the buyer, can benefit from it.

If progress does not meet initial expectations because of unforeseen circumstances, the supplier still can earn the maximum award fee if performance is judged to be the best possible in the situation. While the buyer reserves the right to make unilateral decisions regarding contractor performance, these decisions should not be made arbitrarily or capriciously; the supplier has certain safeguards.

All performance evaluations, for example, are subject to review at higher management levels within the buying organization, and the supplier is given an opportunity to present his or her case. But the seller's greatest protection is the buyer's self-interest. Unfair treatment of a supplier under any contract destroys the harmonious working relationship that is the key to a successful outcome. Furthermore, a buyer who earns a reputation for unfairness (as opposed to demanding, but fair) will have difficulty obtaining qualified suppliers at reasonable prices for future contracting requirements.

Cost plus fixed fee contract. A CPFF contract requires the purchaser to reimburse the supplier for all allowable costs and to pay a fixed fee regardless of the magnitude of the costs. Such contracts historically have been used to purchase research and development services, exotic defense equipment, and construction when time did not permit the orderly development of plans and specifications. The CPFF contract gives the supplier a set income regardless of performance and how well costs are controlled. In effect, the contractor has no contractual incentive to control costs and turn in a good overall performance.

Under these circumstances, the award fee concept is much more attractive and the CPFF contract should be utilized only where relatively low-dollar-volume purchases are involved or in situations where there is likely to be little correlation between the contractor's dedication and a successful outcome.

Many factors determine what method of contract pricing should be employed in a given buying situation. Of particular importance in this choice are the magnitude of the expenditure, the willingness of the supplier to make records available to the purchaser, and the relative degree of uncertainty as to costs. The last factor—cost uncertainty—assumes special importance when the value of the contract warrants the effort associated with structuring a realistic fee arrangement, when buyer and seller can agree on what cost elements should be allowed (such as overhead), and when the supplier's costs associated with performance under the contract can be audited. More detailed guidance is provided in the author's article "The Right Type of Contract for Every Procurement Situation," appearing in the May 1976 issue of the *Management Review*.

PURCHASING RECURRING REQUIREMENTS

In addition to the various methods of contract pricing just discussed, purchasing has several ways of coping with recurring requirements in an economic and efficient mode. Large quantities required over long periods of time normally are purchased on an annual (or longer-term) basis. Such purchase orders and contracts have many benefits: lower prices, additional services performed by the supplier (e.g., locating inventory points at or near the customer), assured sources of supply, and protection against unjustified price increases. In addition, the buyer's work load is reduced, allowing him or her to devote efforts to other areas. Most recurring requirements for production materials are purchased on an annual basis (frequently with the escalation provision previously described). If substantial start-up costs are involved—whether for equipment, training of personnel, or other reasons—then a multiyear contract may be appropriate. (The situation at QRS Products, described at the beginning of Chapter 9, called for such an approach.) With a multiyear contract, capital investment costs are amortized over the life of the contract with a provision for payment of unamortized costs in the event of early termination by the buying firm. Several of the more commonly employed approaches to different demand patterns (timing) are described next.

Definite delivery (quantity and time) contract.   This is the ideal type of contract, based on maximum certainty on the part of the purchaser and supplier. Prices are negotiated based on definite quantities for delivery on specified dates. Since this type of agreement provides the maximum certainty to the supplier, it should result in the lowest possible unit price. There are several advantages resulting from the use of this type of contract:

- The same or lower unit prices result than when all deliveries are made at one time.
- Less material handling is required. A one-time move is made from the loading dock to the machining area, eliminating the move from the dock to the warehouse.
- Purchased goods inventory is reduced, as are inventory carrying costs.
- Pressure on cash flow is reduced as a result of spreading payments over the contract period.

Definite quantity, indefinite time contract.   When total quantities required for a period of time are known, but production schedules cannot be planned, it is possible to enter into a contract for a known quantity at given unit prices and lead times with a provision that delivery will be scheduled on an "as required" basis.

Systems contract, systems purchasing, or demand contract.   Such contracts call for the purchaser to order all requirements for an item (or class of items) from the supplier, usually at stated prices and lead times. This type of contract frequently is used to purchase MRO and office supplies. When used to buy standard items, the supplier provides either a catalog of all items covered with a price for each item or the firm's standard catalog with a discount applying to the prices shown. This approach has the attractive feature of making it possible for authorized company personnel not in purchasing to obtain supplies immediately and directly from the supplier. Such an approach facilitates obtaining needed low-cost supplies and allows purchasing personnel to concentrate on potentially greater cost-saving procurements. At the end of the contract period, there is no obligation to purchase any remaining inventory since nothing is special.

Indefinite quantity contract. Such contracts provide for the delivery of indefinite quantities between designated low and high quantities at agreed-to prices and lead times. Such contracts tend to result in unit prices somewhat higher than when known quantities are involved, but prices that are significantly more attractive than were the items purchased on several purchase orders as they are required.

Price indexing. Price indexing contracts may be used when purchasing recurring requirements of capital equipment and commodities whose prices are extremely unstable. Delivery lead times are established together with a provision that the price is the price in effect on the date of shipment. The buyer can gain significant savings by negotiating the date of shipment index figure. Price index figures are available on a monthly basis from the U.S. Department of Labor, Bureau of Labor Statistics.

Many firms now are able to employ their MRP system to make calls against these various types of contracts. The daily or weekly MRP printouts are sent directly to the appropriate supplier who treats the printout as a delivery order. This allows purchasing personnel to focus their attention on more profit-saving areas than placing delivery orders.

In a few situations, it now is possible for the requiring firm's computer to "talk" directly with the supplier's computer, eliminating the need for any human interface when ordering against any of the foregoing types of contracts.

SUMMARY

Cost estimates are required at several phases of the procurement process. They are employed in determining which design concepts to drop and which to pursue. The degree of accuracy required is a function of the stage of the design process, with greater accuracy required as the number of alternatives is reduced. Accurate or detailed estimates may be required for the make-or-buy analysis. The buyer in purchasing requires estimates when developing an appropriate procurement strategy. Cost estimates are useful in conducting price analyses. If the buyer is to enter into detailed negotiations and cost analysis, accurate cost estimates are an invaluable input.

It is important for the buyer to know which cost estimating technique has been used. As seen in the incident used to open this section, time limitations and the availability of skilled estimators may result in the use of a less than optimal approach to estimating. The buyer who is aware of the source of the estimate, then, is in a better position to determine how much reliance to place on the estimate during price and cost analyses and negotiations.

Once a realistic cost estimate is available for the first unit of production, the learning curve is a powerful tool. It allows us to estimate the cost and time required for one or more production runs or lots. Any buyer involved in negotiating the price for specialty items must be familiar with the learning curve and be prepared to educate prospective suppliers on its implications.

For critically important contracts (especially those of large value), it is essential that the right method of contract pricing is selected. Several approaches, from firm fixed price to cost plus award fee exist. The considered selection of the right method of contract pricing contributes significant savings and avoids needless customer-supplier problems.

There are several approaches to purchasing materials on a recurring basis. Selection of the right approach to purchasing continuing requirements results in significant dollar savings, additional services being performed by the supplier, guaranteed sources of supply, and simplified internal administrative procedures.

We now turn our attention to the wonderful world of negotiating, the subject of the next chapter.

chapter ten

THE WINNING WAY
OF NEGOTIATING

Larry Smith, purchasing manager for Precision Fabricators of Bridgeport, sat thinking in the board room of the Manchester Screw Press Ltd., in Manchester, England. Larry was due to fly out of Manchester to Heathrow the next afternoon. After two days of conducting first a preaward survey and then discussions that he could not dignify with the term "negotiations," Larry was both frustrated and exhausted. His mind raced a mile a minute, or was it a kilometer per 36 seconds? One thing was for sure: negotiations in the United Kingdom were not the same as negotiations in the United States.

Larry's employer, Precision Fabricators, was a forge shop that employed slightly over 200 employees. The company made turbine blade forgings of titanium, aluminum, steel, and exotic metals. Recently, Precision had entered into discussions with a jet engine producer. The objective of the discussions was Precision's desire to become the supplier of a turbine blade for the new RS-301 jet engine that was under development. After an extensive review and more extensive discussions, the jet engine manufacturer had agreed to make Precision an approved source, provided that Precision purchase a new 7,000-ton screw press capable of exerting twisting power of 150 metric tons. The screw press had to be installed within 10 months. It was estimated to cost $2 million.

Larry contacted all known domestic and foreign firms capable of manufacturing such a screw press. Only one, Manchester Screw Press Ltd., indicated being able to meet the required delivery date. In the interest of time, Larry made arrangements to fly to the United Kingdom. He planned to conduct a site survey and, if appropriate, negotiations with representatives of Manchester Screw. With the possibility of negotiations in mind, Larry forwarded a telex to Manchester Screw Press requesting that the firm prepare a bid for the 150-ton screw press and be prepared to discuss the cost factors supporting the resulting bid.

Larry then contacted several fellow purchasing managers to develop pricing data on similar equipment. No one whom he contacted had purchased this exact-size screw press. But Larry was able to obtain enough data to develop a parametric cost estimating model based on twisting power. The model indicated that Precision's screw press should cost $2.7 million plus or minus 10%.

On arriving in Manchester, Larry was met by Malcolm Bresford-West, O.B.E., managing director of the Manchester Screw Press Ltd. After a pleasant lunch at Mr. Bresford-West's club, the two went on to the screw works. Larry was introduced to the chiefs of sales, manufacturing, and engineering and the controller. Much time then was spent describing the firm's history, World War II and the resulting injustices to Great Britain vis-à-vis the reconstruction aid given to West Germany, and the state of the world economy. The meeting seemed to take forever, but it had lasted only two hours. Then it was time for tea. Following tea, Larry was turned over to Mr. Barney Jones, manufacturing manager, who conducted a tour of the plant. Larry was surprised to see highly sophisticated numeric-controlled equipment standing side by side with pre-World War I machines. When asked if the older equipment could hold necessary tolerances, Mr. Jones stated that the machines might be a problem in the wrong hands. But he had many employees with 30 or more years of experience who "could make those old babies get up and dance any tune they desired!" Larry was reasonably satisfied with the plant and equipment. It was apparent that the plant was operating well below capacity. It was past quitting time when Larry and Mr. Jones completed their tour of the factory.

The next morning, Larry met with Mr. Clarence Gibbons, the sales manager, to discuss Manchester's experience with similar screw presses. Mr. Gibbons had prepared a file containing letters from satisfied customers complimenting Manchester on both its quality and ability to meet delivery terms. By this time, Larry felt that he was indeed fortunate. There was no question in his mind that, provided that no unforeseen work stoppage were to occur, Manchester would meet or beat Precision's delivery requirement.

Larry then asked Mr. Gibbons if he had received Precision's telex requesting a price for the screw press. Mr. Gibbons responded with a courteous smile and rang for his secretary. In response to Mr. Gibbon's request, the secretary brought in a file containing two sheets of paper. Mr. Gibbons proudly presented the document to Mr. Smith. It was a letter, addressed to Precision Fabricators. The letter described the machine in some detail including the fact that it would have a twisting power of 150 metric tons. The press would weigh approximately 190 tons. The screw would be operated by a 350-horsepower reversible short-circuit motor. The price was F.O.B. Manchester, with freight allowed to Bridgeport. Delivery to Precision's factory would be within nine months after receipt of an order. The delivered price would be £2,000,000 with payment as follows: 10% down and 10% at the end of each of the nine months.

Larry sat in a mild state of bewilderment. He had not expected a request for either advance payments, progress payments, or payments in other than dollars. He chose to proceed with discussions with the objective of obtaining cost data in support of Manchester's bid. "There are a few surprises here, but before discussing them, I'd appreciate being able to review the cost data supporting your bid. Could you get them for me, please?"

It was Mr. Gibbons's turn to appear bewildered. He excused himself and returned 15 minutes later with Mr. Angus McFee, the firm's controller. Mr. McFee: "Do ye not find our terms to your liking, Mr. Smith?"

Larry responded that he needed to have all relevant data available before being able to discuss the proposed transaction. "One of the key items of information I require is the cost data in support of your proposal. With this in hand, I'll be in a position to determine if the price is reasonable."

Mr. McFee, "Why, Mr. Smith, we don't do business that way at Manchester Screw! Our price is based on years of experience in the screw press business. Our quality is of the highest order, and our price is totally consistent with our expenses. Ours is not an excessively profitable business."

Larry then spent considerable time attempting to obtain the requisite cost data—to no avail. He began to wonder if Manchester truly did not have any data in support of its bid. He then turned his attention to the price bid by Manchester. In response to Larry's request, Mr. McFee contacted the firm's bankers to obtain the current rate of exchange. The rate quoted was £1 = U.S. $1.7505. This meant that Manchester's delivered price for the screw press would be approximately $3.5 million, some $800,000 over the price Larry had estimated before leaving the United States.

It being lunch time, the three went to a nearby pub for a light meal. On their return, they moved to the firm's oak-paneled board room where they were joined by Mr. Bresford-West, the managing director. Mr. Bresford-West asked if they had had a nice lunch and then asked if his firm's proposal was acceptable. Perspiration broke out on Larry's forehead. He mentally clicked off the areas of differences: price, advanced payments, progress payments, payments in sterling, and liability from Manchester to Bridgeport. His biggest concern was the apparent nonexistence of any cost data. Larry thought to himself, "Are these people as honest and simplistic as they appear, or are they sly as foxes?" Even insight into this issue would be helpful in mapping out his strategy. He also thought of his reservations for departure tomorrow.

Negotiation is the process of arriving at a common understanding through mutual responsiveness, problem solving, or bargaining. Negotiation is not haggling, dickering, or outwitting. Negotiation should be a cooperative process wherein everybody wins or gains something. The first objective of negotiations when such activities are a part of the procurement process is to maximize the total benefit, that is, to enlarge the pie. Then we look at the size of each party's share of the pie.

Negotiation, in the context of the procurement system, is the process of preparing, planning for, and conducting discussions on *all* aspects of a proposed agreement between buyer and seller. Except for low-value procurements, a team usually is developed to prepare, plan for, and conduct the negotiation. The team includes the buyer, who will function as the team captain, engineers, technicians, and cost analysts, as appropriate.

Several problems are common:

- *Inappropriate Application.* Negotiations, as a means of achieving a fair and a reasonable price, are employed all too frequently at inappropriate times. When certain prerequisites are satisfied, competitive bidding usually results in a satisfactory price and with less effort. Conversely, when these prerequisites are not satisfied, negotiations should be employed.
- *Lack of Preparation.* Preparation is the key to successful negotiations. Adequate preparation is the exception rather than the rule. Thorough preparations must be made prior to entering negotiations if the buyer is to achieve his or her planned goals.
- *Failure to Establish Realistic Objectives.* Realistic objectives frequently are not established before entering face-to-face negotiations.
- *Unsound Tactics.* Face-to-face negotiations are a three-phased process. Sound tactics are required to achieve the negotiator's objectives. Again, the application of sound tactics is the exception rather than the rule.
- *Cultural Misunderstandings.* Negotiations with someone from another culture introduce many new obstacles. Few purchasing personnel take the time and effort required for successful cross-cultural negotiations.

WHEN TO NEGOTIATE

As discussed in Chapter 8, competitive bidding usually results in the lowest price and is appropriate when the following conditions have been met:

- The specifications for the item or service to be purchased are clear and adequate so that prospective suppliers may estimate their costs with a high degree of precision. If this degree of accuracy is not present, prospective suppliers will submit bids or quotations that include contingencies to protect themselves from any uncertainties.

- The amount of money involved is sufficient to warrant the administrative expense resulting from the use of competitive bidding.

- Not only are a sufficient number of potential suppliers available, but a reasonable proportion of these potential suppliers will be willing to price competitively. (As previously indicated, three to five firms generally will furnish adequate competition.)

- Enough time must be available to employ competitive bidding as a means of source selection. The amount of time and effort involved with this technique is considerable. A formal request for bids, mailing, opening the resulting bids, and evaluating the bids requires more time than might be expected. Additionally, adequate bid preparation time must be afforded to the firms from whom bids are being solicited.

If any of these criteria is not satisfied, then it usually is desirable to negotiate. In addition, when the procurement involves many variables and/or a high degree of risk, negotiation generally is appropriate. Negotiations should be used to reduce areas of uncertainty (and contingency pricing) such as the following:

- We saw in Chapter 9 that when there is great uncertainty about changes in material prices, the rational risk-averse supplier will include a contingency in the price. This contingency will be large enough to offer protection under most conditions and will be far greater than the most likely effect of inflation or other uncertainty. The use of negotiation allows us to tailor an escalation provision that transfers some of the risk associated with inflation and some of the savings resulting from lower material costs from the seller to the buyer with the prospect of a significant reduction in total expenditure.

- Frequently, the purchasing firm is concerned with several aspects of the proposed procurement, including price, quality, timeliness, and services. Competitive bidding requires that minimum standards be established for all requirements, leaving price alone to vary. In many instances, the buyer may be willing to pay a higher price for earlier delivery or a higher quality, or both. On the other hand, a lower price may be attractive for a somewhat lower quality. Thus we see that a trade-off situation may be present. In such circumstances, negotiation is the way to arrive at a contractual agreement.

- When there is considerable uncertainty about the amount of engineering effort, quantities of purchased materials, or labor, then negotiation is the preferred technique. Discussions between buyer and seller may be able to reduce or eliminate the uncertainty in these areas. If not, and if the dollar amount involved is significant, then one of the methods of contract pricing described in Chapter 9 that ensures that the supplier will be reimbursed for all or a portion of his or her allowable expenses may be appropriate. Such purchase orders or subcontracts can be agreed upon only through the use of negotiation.

- On occasion, a supplier must make or purchase considerable special tooling or test equipment that lends itself only to the production of goods for the purchaser. Questions of cost allocation and ownership frequently arise in such situations. These questions can be resolved best through negotiations.

- In fields of fast-changing technology and other areas where the buyer's requirements may be subject to numerous changes, the use of negotiated procurement is preferred. Competitive bidding *can* be employed to select a source under such circumstances. But if the prospective suppliers recognize the likelihood of numerous changes, there is a good chance that a marginal supplier will "buy in" by submitting an unrealistically low price proposal. This low price proposal is submitted with the expectation of "getting well" on the anticipated changes. In fact, an unscrupulous vendor may take advantage of the situation. The resulting expenditure may greatly exceed that of a well-negotiated purchase order or subcontract. It is far sounder to negotiate with two or three prospective suppliers and develop workable procedures for dealing with anticipated changes. (This situation frequently results in one of the methods of contract pricing described in Chapter 9.)

- One of the prerequisites to employing competitive bidding is that there be adequate competition. The buyer, independently, may choose to purchase the product of only one supplier. Thus, the buyer may create a situation in which effective competition is totally lacking. Under such a condition, negotiation is the best way to prevent the seller from taking unreasonable advantage of the situation.

PREPARATION

Preparation is the key to successful negotiations. We will look at five aspects of preparation: (1) awareness of what is being bought, (2) price and cost analysis, (3) the strengths and weaknesses of the buyer's position, (4) knowledge of the seller, and (5) the need of the buyer to know himself or herself.

Knowing the Item

Even when the buyer is the head of a negotiating team that contains one or more technical experts, it is essential that he or she understand what is being purchased, the production process involved, and its effect on cost. The buyer need not understand all the technical ramifications of the item being procured. The buyer should, however, be aware of its use, limitations, components and purchased materials, and the general production techniques required to produce it. The nature of the item affects the price, methods of contract pricing, terms of the resulting purchase order or subcontract, and the bargaining position of the two parties.

The buyer should be familiar with any plans or specifications for the item. He or she should be aware of the procurement history of the item or similar items and any of the work that can or must be performed by other than the prospective supplier. The buyer should know the language and phraseology used in the particular industry. The buyer should be aware of prospective engineering problems and other areas of uncertainty that the seller is apt to encounter.

Price and Cost Analysis

Once there is an understanding of the item to be purchased, the buyer needs to study available price and cost data, as described in Chapter 9. The ideal situation is one in which there are adequate competition, historic price data, and a detailed cost estimate. Under these circumstances, it is possible to examine and evaluate a prospective price without evaluating the separate cost elements and profit proposed by the prospective supplier. When price analysis is not possible, it generally is necessary to employ cost analysis. Ideally, it should be possible to begin cost analysis by comparing the prospective supplier's cost breakdown with that developed by the buyer's engineering department. Cost analysis includes an analysis of the necessity of all costs, an indication of their reasonableness, identification of areas of contingency pricing, and an understanding and indication of the reasonableness of overhead costs.

Strengths and Weaknesses

Several factors affect the buyer's and seller's respective bargaining positions:

- *Urgency.* How urgently does the seller want an order? The more urgently the seller desires a specific order, the weaker is his or her bargaining position. The buyer can gain insight into the seller's position through a review of published data, Dun & Bradstreet reports, and the judicious use of preaward surveys, as described in Chapter 8.

- *Preferred Source.* Does the seller perceive that he or she has "the inside track" for a particular order? If the seller realizes that he or she is the only or the preferred source, the seller's bargaining position is greatly enhanced. One of the greatest dangers in the use of a negotiating team is that nonpurchasing team members frequently disclose information on the degree of competition to the seller. The seller's gaining of such information can be devastating to the buyer's negotiating position. The existence (or even the appearance) of competition is one of the buyer's major strengths.

- *Lead Time.* Inadequate procurement lead time weakens the buyer's bargaining position and results in an inability to obtain adequate competition (a buyer's best friend). It also results in the seller being able to drag his or her feet during negotiations, secure in the belief that the buyer is under severe pressure to conclude an agreement.

- *Cost or Price Data.* Adequate price or cost data and the time and willingness to analyze them greatly assist the buyer in establishing realistic cost objectives and in obtaining a fair and reasonable price.

- *An Understanding of Your Needs and Those of Your Vendors.* Negotiating skills will help each party to a negotiation. But the buyer who understands his or her needs and those of his or her counterpart and is skilled in the *art* of negotiating is the individual who has the best prospect of achieving success at the negotiating table.

Understanding the Seller

The buyer can never know too much about the people with whom he or she is going to negotiate. The buyer should examine an opponent's past history and study the records of previous transactions with which the opponent was connected (both successful and unsuccessful). Frequently more insight into people can be gained from their failures than from their successes. In the process of this research, the buyer is coming to understand the opponent's needs and behavioral patterns. This insight will be invaluable during the course of negotiations.

The buyer also should understand the nature, character, and needs of the firm with whom he or she is to negotiate. Much public data may be available, including financial statements, published reports, press releases, advertising, governmental reports, Dun & Bradstreet reports, and speeches of officials of the firm. In addition, the preaward survey affords the buyer an opportunity to gain great insight into the prospective supplier's organization, capabilities, executives, and *needs*.

Know Yourself

Preparation for negotiation should begin with a self-evaluation. What are your needs as a human being? Where are you coming from?

Such is the ideal preparation for a negotiation. Before discussing the development of objectives and the tactics of negotiation, let us look at the characteristics of the *ideal* negotiator. Successful negotiators know themselves and their opponents; they understand the items to be purchased, and they are versed in the areas of accounting, business law, economics, human behavior, and quantitative methods. They are skilled in the techniques of negotiation and conference leadership. They are skilled planners, master strategists, and expert tacticians. They view issues and problems from the vantage point of the firm's well-being and not that of their department or their own individual needs. They excel in good judgment. They have high expectations. They are among a firm's most valued employees and should be one of the most highly paid professionals.[1]

DEVELOPMENT OF REALISTIC OBJECTIVES

The next step in preparing for negotiations after the background work has been accomplished is to establish a set of specific objectives.

Several basic objectives are common to most negotiations:

- Agreement on the quality to be provided and procedures for ensuring this level of quality
- Agreement on timely delivery (including production schedules)
- A fair and reasonable price
- Obtaining adequate control over the manner in which the purchase order or subcontract is performed (especially in the areas of quality, quantity, and service)
- A commitment for necessary cooperation
- A continuing relationship with competent suppliers

Specific negotiation objectives should be established for all items to be discussed during the negotiation including, as applicable,

- All technical aspects
- Types of materials and substitutes
- Purchaser-furnished material or equipment
- The mode of transportation and liability for claims and damage

---

[1]Based on Donald W. Dobler, Lamar Lee, Jr., and David N. Burt, *Purchasing and Materials Management,* 4th ed. (New York: McGraw-Hill, 1984).

- F.O.B. point
- General terms and conditions
- Progress reports
- Production control plans
- Labor content and prices
- Overhead
- General and administrative expenses
- Profit
- Incentive arrangements (if other than fixed price contract)
- Patent infringement protection
- Packaging
- Warranty terms and conditions
- Escalation provisions (if fixed price with escalation)
- Payment terms (including discount provisions)
- Patents

As appropriate, an acceptable range and target should be established for each item subject to negotiation. The range should be bracketed by a minimum and maximum position. The minimum position should be based on the outcome if everything during production were to work out favorably. The maximum position is based on the premise that virtually every action required by the supplier will work out unsatisfactorily. The target position is the negotiator's estimate of the most likely outcome for any element being negotiated. It should be the point at which the prospects for overrunning the estimate are substantially the same as for underrunning it.

On critical procurements, the buyer also should establish what he or she believes to be the seller's range and target for any item of discussion. Understanding one's counterparts' needs and objectives can greatly facilitate the ensuing discussions!

TACTICS

Face-to-face negotiations are a three-phased process. During the first phase, the buyer investigates any inconsistency between the vendor's proposal and the buyer's position. During the second phase, the buyer attempts to narrow or close the difference between the seller's and his or her own position. This is done by logic and persuasion. During the third phase, agreement is reached through compromise and hard bargaining.

Phase 1: Fact Finding

Prior to face-to-face negotiations, the buyer will have analyzed all available information in an effort to determine the reasonableness of the proposal. When meeting with the vendor, the buyer should investigate any inconsistencies between the proposal and the buyer's information. Detailed questions of a *who, when, how, what,* and *why* nature should be employed to pursue specific points. Any issues or disagreements should be defined precisely. The fact-finding should continue until the buyer has a complete understanding of the vendor's proposal. Not only does the buyer come to understand the vendor's position, but also the vendor's strengths and weaknesses. On completing the first or fact-finding phase, the buyer should call a recess.

During the recess, the buying team should analyze the strengths and weaknesses of each party on each important issue. Target objectives and maximum and minimum positions should be revised, as appropriate. An agenda should be developed. Strong and weak points should be identified. Any items or topics that should be avoided during the next phases should be noted. Items whose targets *must* be achieved during the negotiation should be identified. A list of items or objectives that would be nice to have but that can be traded in return for something of more importance should be established.

Next, anticipate the vendor's likely strategy and tactics. Identify likely responses to the buyer's points and develop rebuttals. A good negotiator will anticipate all moves and countermoves. A good negotiator becomes intimately familiar with all points likely to be discussed during the ensuing negotiations. Experienced negotiators have had success with two finishing touches when preparing for the second and third phases of critically important negotiations: "murder boards" and mock negotiations.

A murder board consists of senior purchasing, manufacturing, engineering, and quality assurance personnel. The buying team presents to the board its agenda and tactics for the forthcoming discussions. The murder board discusses, analyzes, and dissects the negotiating plan in an effort to uncover weaknesses.

Mock negotiations allow the negotiating team members to prepare for face-to-face discussions with the vendor by simulating the forthcoming negotiations. Senior members of purchasing and other suitably qualified members of top management play the roles of the vendor's negotiating team members. A mock negotiation is conducted prior to entering actual negotiations.

Both murder boards and mock negotiations result in upper management becoming aware of the buying team's objectives and tactics. Negotiations have a way of escalating. Through the use of murder boards and mock negotiations, senior personnel are prepared, should they become involved in the negotiations.

Before entering face-to-face negotiations, the buyer should remind team members that they are to make input only in their own fields and only when called upon. The team members should be reminded that there can be only one captain and that the buyer is *the* captain!

Phase 2: Narrow Differences

The buyer now takes the offensive. He or she defines each issue; states facts, conditions, and assumptions; and attempts to convince the vendor that the buyer's reasoning is sound. If agreement can not be reached on an issue, the buyer may choose to state his or her objective and ask the vendor how to meet the objective. If agreement cannot be reached on one issue, it usually is best to move on to another. Frequently, discussions on a subsequent issue will unblock an earlier impasse.

During this phase of negotiations, mutual responsiveness frequently is employed. Mutual responsiveness calls for the buyer and seller to adjust their concessions to the other party's needs. Mutual responsiveness avoids many of the problems of pure bargaining. It encourages the creation of new solutions, requires less time, creates less friction, and results in more congenial relations at both the personal and institutional levels than does bargaining. In many negotiations, it is possible to reach a mutually satisfactory agreement at this point. However, if such an agreement is not yet possible, it is necessary to employ hard bargaining.

Phase 3: Bargaining

Bargaining employs persuasion in moving an opponent toward one's position. If persuasion fails, threats may be employed. For example, either party may threaten to break off negotiations. The buyer may threaten to take all his or her business elsewhere if the seller does not yield on a point. Or the buyer may threaten to develop alternative sources of supply or even to incorporate alternative materials if the seller does not capitulate. Before employing threats, one should consider their effect and the credibility of the person issuing the threat if the bluff is called. The experienced negotiator does not bluff unless prepared to be called. Unsupportable positions should not be taken unless the buyer is willing to give them up if challenged.

Even when bargaining, the buyer and his or her team should conduct themselves in an ethical manner. Distortions and misrepresentations serve no useful purpose. If detected, they can disrupt or terminate the negotiation. Negotiation is not haggling or chiseling. It is an honest effort to arrive at a mutually acceptable agreement. The result of a negotiation should be an agreement that benefits both parties. If either side leaves the negotiating table feeling that it has been unnecessarily abused, the stage has been set for future confrontations. An agreement reached in such a manner generally leads to future arguments, unsatisfactory performance, and the possibility of claims.

SOME TECHNIQUES OF NEGOTIATING

Control and Progress

Avoid any attempts to sidetrack the meeting onto nonessential issues. Show progress. Use summaries to clarify understanding and to demonstrate progress.

Recesses

Recesses should be used as a tactical tool. They should be planned and executed carefully. Recesses may be used to get the members of the buying team back functioning as a team. Do *not* call a recess when the vendor has made a strong point that cannot be refuted. Avoid revealing your weakness by proceeding tactfully to the next issue.

Sequential or Package Agreement

Sequential negotiations call for negotiation and agreement on all issues *in turn*. This approach will be much more likely to result in deadlocks than will the package approach.

The package approach calls for discussing individual issues with the objective of reaching agreement on each issue, *if possible*. If agreement on an issue is not feasible *while discussing it in isolation,* the needs of each party become recognized. These needs then can be dealt with in the context of an overall agreement with compromises on one issue receiving offsetting compromises on other issues. When all unresolved issues are negotiated together, such offsetting compromises or concessions are relatively easy to achieve. When a sequential agenda is followed, quid pro quo agreements are not practical.

Tacit Agreements

The process of working through to an overall agreement acceptable to both parties is greatly facilitated through the use of tacit agreements. Such tacit agreements are ones that are not expressed or openly disclosed. Rather, they are implied. They are far easier to reach than explicit agreements. While neither party makes a *formal* commitment, the terms of the tacit agreement are quite clear to each. A tacit agreement is easier to reach than is an explicit one since both parties realize that the "agreement" may be broken without an interpretation or change of "bad faith." Tacit agreements become binding only in the context of the entire agreement where they are formalized in writing.

Negotiations with a New Supplier

When buyer and seller are entering into negotiations for the first time, it may be desirable to develop an agenda that calls for discussions on the least important issues *first*. This approach allows each party to feel out the opponent and make minor concessions in the hope of developing mutual trust. As mutual respect and trust develop, it will be possible to make progress on the more challenging items.

Informal Negotiations

Many agreements are concluded away from the bargaining table. Informal communications conducted over lunch or cocktails may move a negotiation that appears headed for an impasse on to a successful conclusion. While considerable benefit may be gained from such discussions, the team members *must* recognize the social occasion for what it is: an extension of the bargaining table. The team members must conduct themselves accordingly!

No Agreement Better Than a Bad Agreement

There are instances where one or both parties are so stubborn or so evenly matched that no amount of persuasion or logic will result in an agreement. If the seller is being totally unreasonable, the buyer should consider terminating the negotiation. Such action may be in the face of demands from the requiring activity in the purchasing firm that an agreement be concluded on any terms. Such demands often are the result of failure, on the part of the requestor, to allow adequate and realistic purchasing lead time and failure to consider the incorporation of competitively procurable materials into the item to be produced. The buyer should *not* enter into an unrealistic agreement in such circumstances.

Several benefits can result from the termination of negotiations. First, the open confrontation between buyer and the requestor may be essential for the development of realistic discipline within the buying firm and adequate planning for future procurements. Thus, although discomfort may be experienced on the initial procurement, future procurements will enjoy the benefit of proper planning (lower prices, better services, more timely deliveries, etc.). Second, the break off of negotiations may cause the seller to revise his or her estimate of the buyer's bargaining position and result in greater willingness to enter into the give and take of true negotiations. Third, such action will move the negotiations to a higher (and, it is hoped, more reasonable) level in the seller's management. Frequently, the seller's representatives become emotionally involved in *winning*. Higher levels of management will tend to be less emotional and more aware of the implication of the loss of the order on the overall well-being of their firm.

Closure

A seasoned and skilled negotiator knows when to close a negotiation. Premature efforts to close a negotiation are as bad as efforts to close too late. Once a point of agreement has been reached, close; don't keep talking! A timely summary will aid in determining if closure is possible. Nothing should be said that might confuse agreements already made. The agreement reached should be outlined in broad terms. The introduction of new issues or any further discussions that might result in reopening issues that have been settled should be avoided.

SUGGESTIONS FOR NEGOTIATING WITH SOMEONE FROM ANOTHER CULTURE

As noted in Chapter 8, purchasing from nondomestic sources is increasingly common. The negotiating principles that we have discussed apply in virtually all settings, but there are many nuances involved when dealing with people from cultures other than our own. The following suggestions are based on the author's own experiences doing business in other cultures and the experiences of several purchasing and marketing professionals.[2]

- Be sensitive to your opposites' culture. Read about their culture during the preparation phase. Ask questions of others who have experience negotiating with individuals of your opposites' culture. Obtain information on local circumstances in the country. The ability to understand your negotiating opposites' cultural background is of great advantage. It puts the other party off guard. You gain a definite advantage in being able to understand where the other person is coming from.

[2]Much of the material contained in this section was developed by the author under contract F 33 615-80-C-5188 which was sponsored by the Air Force Business Research Management Center, Wright-Patterson Air Force Base, Ohio, 45433.

- Find out who your opposites are, who their families are, what their education is, their income, and what makes them tick.

- Attempt to develop a personal rapport, a base of understanding, and a bank of goodwill.

- In Europe, be prepared for negotiations to take two or three times as long as in the United States. In Japan, negotiations may take six times as long as in America.

- Be well prepared on all issues, especially technical ones.

- Conduct extensive cost and price analyses before the formal negotiation meeting. Do *not* expect your European counterpart to have a well-developed cost breakdown. (Remember Larry Smith's situation at the beginning of the chapter?)

- Become familiar with applicable tax laws. Such knowledge can lead to significant price reductions.

- ROI and dividends tend to be lower in many countries than in America. Consider this information during the objective-setting process.

- Obtain guidance from your controller on the issue of exchange rates and the likely costs or advantages of using a particular currency. Then negotiate the exchange rate as you would any other issue.

- Arrange issues in such a manner that your opposite can win his or her share of issues—possibly while you are winning the *big ones*.

- If possible, ensure that the head of the other team has the authority to reach agreement on behalf of his or her firm. (This is not possible in Japan.)

- The position of recorder is a powerful one. Be the recorder or appoint one from your team.

- Use the package approach of discussing each issue in turn, reaching agreement when possible and finally developing an acceptable package addressing all issues.

- Be extremely cautious in being frank and open during discussions. Most non-Americans are not accustomed to such an approach. It may be misunderstood and disruptive.

- Breaks in the negotiation may be required to allow the other team to gain approval of some proposal. But before such a break, an agreement must be reached on the topic to be discussed immediately following the break. Otherwise, negotiations will become protracted.

- A short working lunch is an effective means of getting your opponent's attention. Such a lunch is not consistent with the normal routine in many countries. The period just after lunch is the best time to introduce important issues. Friday afternoons also are extremely productive times since many people desire to clear things up before leaving for the weekend.

- When negotiating with Europeans, be prepared for a level of conflict that differs from that experienced when dealing with Americans. Many Europeans, partly because they live in a more closed society with relatively little social mobility, are used to conflict. They do not mind conflict, and sometimes they enjoy it. Such people are not greatly concerned about negative reactions from those with whom they are in conflict. Because most Americans are pragmatic, they think of conflict as a hindrance to achieving goals. It is important for both parties to recognize this as a cultural difference and not to allow the difference to block successful negotiations.

- Negotiating in Japan is a wondrous experience. When negotiating, it is necessary to convince the whole group whose activities will be influenced by the proposed transaction.

- Americans tend to be uncomfortable with extended silences; the Japanese are not. They feel no compulsion to break a silence. An American's impatience or desire to "hammer out an agreement" results in breaking such extended silences, frequently yielding or compromising on the point being discussed. A good negotiator will recognize that such silences indicate doubt or uncertainty and will be content to allow the silence to run its course.

SUMMARY

Negotiations should be a cooperative undertaking in which common interests are sought. Negotiation is a cooperative process in which everybody wins or gains something. Negotiating, in the context of the procurement process, is a process of preparing, planning for, and conducting discussions on *all* aspects of a proposed agreement. The key ingredients of a successful negotiation are preparation, development of realistic objectives, and compliance with sound tactics.

Preparation is the key to successful negotiations. Preparation includes gaining an understanding of what is being bought, conducting price (and possibly cost) analyses, understanding the strengths and weaknesses of the buyer's position, understanding the seller, and the buyer's analysis and understanding of himself or herself.

After completing these preparatory steps, the buyer must develop specific objectives for each variable subject to negotiation (price, schedule, service, quality, etc.).

Face-to-face negotiations normally consist of three phases. During the first phase, the buyer investigates any inconsistency between the vendor's proposal and the buyer's position. During the second phase, the buyer attempts to narrow the difference between his or her and the vendor's position through the use of logic. Agreement frequently is reached during this phase. During the third phase, agreement is reached through compromise and bargaining.

There are instances when it is better to terminate negotiations than to enter into an unsatisfactory agreement. If the vendor's representative is so stubborn that no amount of reason or logic will move him or her to an acceptable position, it may be best to break off negotiations. The buyer will be under considerable pressure from the requestor in his or her firm to consummate a deal at any price. However, several benefits can result from breaking off negotiations. The ensuing confrontation between the buyer and the requestor may be essential to the development of realistic discipline and adequate planning for future procurements. Such action has the potential of significant savings. The break off in negotiations may result in the vendor's representative revising his or her estimate of the buyer's bargaining position and thus result in greater willingness to negotiate. Further, such action will move the negotiations to a higher and, it is hoped, more reasonable level of management at the selling firm.

A seasoned and skillful negotiator knows when to close a negotiation. Once a point of agreement has been reached, close; don't keep talking! The agreement reached should be outlined in broad terms. Any further discussions that might result in reopening issues that have been settled and the introduction of new issues should be avoided.

Purchasing from nondomestic sources is increasingly common. There are many nuances involved in negotiations with people from other cultures. An awareness of these nuances will greatly aid the negotiator.

The next chapter addresses the cost-saving area of value analysis and value engineering.

chapter eleven

ONE LAST CHANCE TO BUY THE RIGHT QUALITY: VALUE ANALYSIS AND VALUE ENGINEERING

Two days ago, Irv Applebaum, president of the Marysville Manufacturing Company, held a special meeting of line and staff managers. The meeting was a short one. Mr. Applebaum said, in effect, that if costs were not reduced by 15%, there would be no Marysville Manufacturing Company this time next year. Mr. Applebaum stated that in 10 days, he would devote a full day to suggestions from all present on how to reduce costs by 15%.

On returning to his office, Alan McDowell, the purchasing manager, called his four buyers together. Alan described the severity of the situation and asked for ideas on how to reduce purchasing expenditures by 15% to 20%. Several ideas were discussed and Alan planned to introduce the better ones at the general meeting in 10 days. Sue Shaffer, the new MRO buyer, suggested that Marysville should implement a value analysis (VA) program.

Alan and his buyers were so enthusiastic about the VA program that they agreed to take two actions immediately. (Alan felt that such aggressive action would not go unnoticed. He planned to present an implemented action, not a plan, at the forthcoming meeting.) The first action called for each buyer to contact his or her major suppliers to seek suggestions for reducing material expenditures. The suppliers would be requested to make suggestions in any of the following areas: substitutions, changes in materials, order quantities, tests, tolerances, finishes, and simplifications. The second action was for purchasing to develop a checklist covering these areas of possible savings. The checklist became available the next day and was included as a part of all requests for quotations and purchase orders with values in excess of $10,000.

The following Monday, four days before Mr. Applebaum's meeting, Jon Hobbs, director of research and development, stormed into Alan's office.

"Who gave you the right to second-guess my staff?" he bellowed. "It's my job to design products and your job to buy the materials we specify!"

Before Alan could respond, Jon Hobbs left. Alan's blood pressure was up. He felt anger and resentment. He also realized that his "surprise" was backfiring. Maybe a good idea would not get a fair chance.

During World War II, many essential materials used in production processes became scarce. The war effort drained many resources to the point that material substitutions were the order of the day. Mr. H. L. Erlicher, then vice president of purchasing and transportation at General Electric, noticed that creative people in the design and planning functions at General Electric were able to suggest or accept alternative materials that performed satisfactorily. Indeed, many of these substitutions turned out to be improvements. Either they were more reliable at the same price, or they were of adequate quality at a lower price. In 1947, Mr. L. D. Miles, who was then working as a purchasing agent for the company, was assigned the task of developing a systematic approach to the investigation of the function-cost aspect of existing materials specifications. Mr. Miles and his associates not only accomplished this task successfully but subsequently pioneered the scientific procurement concept General Electric called "value analysis."

According to Mr. Miles, value analysis is "an organized creative approach which has for its purpose the efficient identification of unnecessary cost."[1] The term "value engineering" is sometimes used to describe the application of value studies before designs reach the hardware stage. Typically, however, the two terms "value analysis" and "value engineering" are used synonymously. Here, the term "value analysis" is all inclusive.

Perhaps the most attractive feature of value analysis is that it works. The VA technique involves a rigorous analysis of cost versus function. The function of the item is defined in its simplest terms and determinations are made as to which of the design characteristics are really required. Alternative materials, designs, and procedures then are considered along with their respective costs. The alternative finally selected must meet the item's performance criteria at a lower cost, without compromising quality. Most of the difficulties encountered by its advocates stem from the fact that there is nothing really new in the technique. It is a collection of nonoriginal ideas organized into a system. Neither does it have the fascination of critical path analysis nor does it display

---

[1]Lawrence D. Miles, *Techniques of Value Analysis and Value Engineering*, 2nd ed. (New York: McGraw-Hill, 1972).

information with the elegance of many other present-day techniques. Nevertheless, when applied in the proper manner with proper emphasis, the benefits can be substantial.

Purchasing is one of the departments most concerned with the costs of purchased material. The firm's suppliers can, when properly motivated, be a major source of cost-saving suggestions. It is, therefore, very desirable that purchasing personnel understand and employ value analysis.

Aljian's Purchasing Handbook defines value analysis as

> the organized and systematic study of every element of cost in a part, material, or service to make certain it fulfills its function at the lowest possible cost; it employs techniques which identify the functions the user wants from a product or service; it establishes by comparison the appropriate cost for each function; then it causes the required knowledge, creativity, and initiative to be used to provide each function for that cost.[2]

Value analysis is concerned with the elimination or modification of anything that contributes to the cost of an item or task but is not necessary for required performance, quality, maintainability, reliability, or interchangeability. It is important to note that value analysis is not intended to reduce the quality or performance characteristics of an item or task.

Value has a very specific meaning in the context of value analysis. The following definition of value is used:

> The lowest end cost at which the function may be accomplished at the time and place and with the quality required. Value has no direct relationship to cost. . . . The value of any service, material, or product is established by the minimum cost of other available alternatives, materials, products, or services that will perform the same function.[3]

Three major problems are commonly found in the area of value analysis:

- Personnel in top management, purchasing, engineering, operations, marketing, and finance do not understand what value analysis is and what it can do for the organization's profitability and productivity.
- The two aspects of value analysis—in-house programs and vendor programs—do not receive equal attention.

[2]Paul V. Farrell, ed., *Aljian's Purchasing Handbook,* 4th ed. (New York: McGraw-Hill, 1982), p. 8-3.
[3]Ibid., p. 8-4.

- The development and implementation of VA programs frequently is done in a haphazard and, therefore, unsuccessful manner.

PRINCIPLES AND TECHNIQUES

The fundamental approach of value analysis is that it takes nothing for granted and attacks everything about a product including the necessity for the item itself. The techniques employed are usually described in terms of a checklist. Although there are as many different checklists as there are writers, checklists usually can be simplified into five basic questions that require valid and complete answers:

1. *What is the item or service?* The answer to this question is usually quite readily determined from objective information on the item and from functional analysis.
2. *What does it cost?* Costs are often obtainable from recent procurement data. However, accurate costs are sometimes difficult to obtain, especially for a system or item in development. It may be necessary to estimate the cost, using the best available cost data and cost estimating techniques.
3. *What does it do?* This question can best be answered by identifying the function in its simplest terms. By defining the function, the value analyst learns precisely which design characteristics are really required. In value analysis, an attempt is made to express the function in two words—a verb and a noun object. The use of two words avoids the possibility of combining functions or attempting to define more than one simple function at a time, for example, the item "conducts current," "supports weight," "saws wood," or "makes toast." When looking at what the item does, several questions should be asked:

   Can it be eliminated?
   Does the item contribute value?
   To what uses is it put?
   How reliable is the item?
   How does it perform?
   What features does the customer want?
   How strong should the part be?
   How should the part look?

4. *What else would do the job?* This is perhaps the most difficult phase of the analysis. The comprehensiveness of the answer determines, to a large degree, the success of the entire VA effort. No matter how thorough the search, there will always remain other alternatives, some of which may be effective. Alternatives can be obtained by various means. Many have advocated the use of "brainstorming" sessions. In any event, the search for alternatives must be an exhaustive one. A checklist similar to the following should be used:

Can a standard item be substituted?
Are all the features required?
Does the item have excess capacity?
Can the item's weight be reduced?
Are specified tolerances and/or finishes realistic?
Is unnecessary machining performed on the item?
Is the item made on the proper equipment?
Can less expensive materials be used?
Is a commercial quality specified?
Can the item be made (bought) more cheaply?

5. *What would be the alternate cost?* Costs of alternates are derived by cost analysis and study. At this stage, perfection in cost data for each alternative is not necessary. Cost estimates within a range of ±5% are considered sufficient, and costs within a range of ±10% will help to determine whether particular alternates are worthy of additional consideration.

VALUE ANALYSIS
AND PRODUCTIVITY

Many of the questions asked under the heading, "What else would do the job?" lead to simplified and less costly production methods. This analysis not only leads to lower costs but frequently also to increased productivity. Heinritz and Farrell report the three following examples of increased productivity resulting from General Electric's VA program.

- Stainless steel disks used in a dispensing machine were chamfered on one side. Value analysis revealed that the chamfer did not add to the value of the machine. Its elimination significantly increased productivity.
- A hub had been made as a two-part riveted assembly. Value analysis showed that a one-piece casting would be equally suitable. The assembly operation was eliminated, resulting in increased productivity.
- A stainless fitting had been purchased and then machined to provide the desired weld embossing. Value analysis led to a different production procedure utilizing an automatic screw machine. Again, productivity increased significantly.[4]

Other recent VA savings include

- A user of 60-pound weld wire saved 4 hours of downtime per 1,000

[4]Stewart F. Heinritz and Paul V. Farrell, *Purchasing: Principles and Applications,* 6th ed. (Englewood Cliffs, N.J.: Prentice-Hall, 1981), pp. 213–214.

pounds of wire through the substitution of copperless welding wire for the previously employed weld wire.

- A manufacturer of forgings was able to substitute cold forgings for the previous process that called for the machining of parts from bar stock. Productivity more than doubled.

THE TWO FACES OF VALUE ANALYSIS

Value analysis may be conducted either as an in-house activity or as a vendor program under the responsibility of purchasing. As might be expected, the greatest benefits result when the two activities are pursued simultaneously.

In-House Activity

Many savings result through the identification of items that are promising candidates for value analysis. The selection of candidate items should be based on maximizing returns on VA investment (returns of 20 to 1 are common). Generally, potential savings are greatest on those components representing the largest annual outlay. Complexity also provides a clue. Usually the more complex an item, the greater the potential for improved value. An item that was developed in an accelerated time frame frequently will be overdesigned and may be a good candidate for VA study. Nonstandard industrial items have more potential for savings than do standard ones. Items with high scrap or rework costs and those requiring many operations also are good candidates for the VA program. Once a candidate has been identified, the VA procedures described should be applied with the objective of improving marketability or reducing cost, or both.

Three approaches to in-house VA programs are common: (1) dedicated value analysts assigned to the purchasing office, (2) the committee approach, and (3) the integrated approach. The employment of dedicated value analysts is common in large manufacturing firms. The ideal value analyst has a background in design engineering, industrial engineering, and purchasing. He or she possesses knowledge of basic physics, strength of materials, and manufacturing processes and is familiar with the firm's product lines, suppliers, and principal customers. Of even greater importance, a good value analyst possesses an open, inquisitive mind and develops close relations with top management. Thus, a good value analyst has considerable informal authority and is able to overcome resistance to his or her proposals. The most obvious disadvantage of this approach is its cost. Such experienced personnel are not inexpensive. But savings of 5 to 20 times their salary expenses are common.

The committee approach calls for the assignment of experienced personnel from engineering, production, purchasing, quality assurance, industrial engineering, and marketing. Each operating participant develops a better awareness of the techniques and potential contribution of value analysis. Ideally, this carries over to the individual's day-to-day activities. The VA committee reviews proposals submitted by employees under a VA or cost reduction program. Promising proposals are reviewed by a working subcommittee that asks the questions listed earlier in the chapter. The committee coordinates implementation of recommendations based upon its studies. The committee approach employs teamwork at overcoming resistance to change. However, it has the two inherent weaknesses of most committees: an inability to gain support and cooperation and conflicting demands on committee members' time.

The integrated approach requires the exposure of operating engineering, purchasing, and other selected personnel to VA training *on a repetitive basis*. The objectives of this training program are to develop an awareness of the importance of value analysis, an understanding of how to conduct a VA study, and a dedication to the use of value analysis. This approach serves to reduce the resistance to changes in product design and specifications that frequently is encountered. The training program does, however, require time and money.

Vendor Program

Vendors are a gold mine of ideas for the VA program. Usually a vendor knows more about products and their capabilities than does the customer. Once an item has gone into production, it is possible that vendors supplying the required components will be able to make suggestions that lead to significant savings. Frequently, they will be aware of suitable lower-cost substitute items than those being purchased. A vendor's assistance may be obtained in two ways: informally and contractually.

With the informal approach, the purchasing firm may include a supplier checklist with requests for quotations and/or with purchase orders. Figure 11.1 contains such a checklist. The firm may conduct value engineering clinics or post VA project candidates in an effort to obtain VA suggestions. If a vendor submits a suggestion that is implemented, he or she usually is rewarded with additional business.

A formal vendor VA program calls for the inclusion of a VA provision in the purchase order or subcontract. In this VA provision, the purchasing firm agrees to share in the savings resulting from an implemented proposal. One major purchaser includes such a clause in all purchase orders of over $100,000. This purchaser agrees to share net savings resulting from implemented proposals on a 50/50 basis. He also agrees to share savings on future buys for a period not to extend beyond

Part name and number _____

Estimated annual usage _____

Buyer _____

Questions	Yes	No	Recommendations
Do you understand the part function?			
Could costs be reduced by relaxing requirements:			
o Tolerances?			
o Finishes?			
o Testing?			
o By how much?			
Could costs be reduced through changes in?			
o Material?			
o Ordering quantities?			
o The use of castings, stampings, etc.?			
o By how much?			
Could you suggest other changes that would:			
o Reduce weight?			
o Simplify the part?			
o Reduce overall costs?			
Do you feel that any of the specifications are too stringent?			
How can we help alleviate your greatest element of cost in supplying this part?			
Do you have a standard item that could be substituted for this part?			

Other suggestions? _____

_____

Supplier _____   Date _____

Address _____

Signature _____ Title _____

Please add additional comments

FIGURE 11.1   Supplier Checklist for Value Analysis Study

three years, but at a reduced rate. Many firms have had good success with informal programs. But more positive motivation in the form of a sharing of the savings results in wider and more active participation by suppliers and even greater savings.

THE KEYS TO SUCCESSFUL IMPLEMENTATION

If the principles of an integrated procurement system described earlier in the book have already been implemented, the establishment of a VA program will meet little resistance. The cooperative attitude will carry over to this very logical approach to improving profits and productivity. If, on the other hand, purchasing is moving from a reactive to a proactive profit-making status, care and effort must go into the development and implementation of a VA program.

The key prerequisite to a successful VA program is a cooperative attitude on the part of all involved departments and their personnel, especially those in design engineering. It is essential that those responsible for developing, implementing, and managing the VA program recognize people's inherent tendency to identify with that which they create or initiate. Care must be taken to ensure that designers realize that they are not being second-guessed. Those participating in the VA program should have the benefit of different points of view, experience, and knowledge. The initial design serves as an essential first step. Its subsequent review and possible revision must be seen as a necessary and normal process of product development.

Purchasing is the logical department to initiate, promote, and sponsor the VA program for these reasons:

- Every requirement and specification for material passes through purchasing. Accordingly, purchasing is the logical organization to review and identify candidates for value analysis.
- Purchasing personnel have the responsibility of obtaining maximum value for all materials to be purchased. They also have the responsibility of challenging any requirement that appears to be questionable.
- Purchasing personnel have many of the skills and perform many of the tasks required in a formal VA program.
- Through daily exposure to sales representatives and their product offerings, and literature for new products, purchasing personnel are in an excellent position to identify suitable substitutes.

- Purchasing personnel tend to be more objective than the designer who may take excessive pride in the design.
- Under a VA program, purchasing serves as a solicitor and a conduit for the flow of suggestions from vendors.

A VA program will be easier to develop and implement and will be more successful if it is seen by purchasing and design engineering as a collaborative effort. (Remember what happened to Alan McDowell at the beginning of the chapter?) The managers of these two activities have the same end objectives: the survival and profitability of the organization.

Assuming that a cooperative atmosphere exists, several approaches to initiating the program are possible.

- The purchasing manager and the chief engineer together attend a VA seminar.
- The purchasing manager provides the chief engineer relevant and succinct literature on the subject.
- A buyer who has especially good relations with a design engineer plants the seed so that the idea for a VA program emerges in engineering.
- The purchasing manager discusses several recent *friendly* examples of informal value analysis (involving purchasing and engineering) and suggests that the program be formalized.

When relations with engineering are somewhat more formal, purchasing has two logical allies in its efforts to develop and implement a VA program: finance and marketing. The chief financial officer is acutely concerned with anything that will make the firm more profitable. The manager of marketing is equally concerned with anything that will result in goods of a higher quality at the same cost or goods of the same quality at lower cost. If resistance on the part of the design engineering is experienced, purchasing should obtain the cooperation and support of these two departments in an effort to enlist engineering's cooperation.

A VA program can be implemented as a result of a directive from top management. But such an approach frequently encounters informal resistance from some of those involved. This resistance severely limits the success and profit contribution of the program.

Frequently, spectacular success will be experienced during the first year or two of the VA program's life. But after these initial successes, enthusiasm may begin to wane. Since significant savings still are possible and likely, it is important that action be taken to foster a positive attitude toward value analysis. Possible actions include

- If dedicated value analysts are employed, management should avoid the temptation to assign non-VA work to VA personnel.
- If the VA committee approach is employed, the committee should meet on a periodic basis and ensure that a sufficient number of projects are undertaken. (Value analysts, by their nature, will take similar action.)
- The company newspaper, bulletin boards, and other media should be utilized to report on successful projects.
- Lobby displays and contractual VA clauses should be utilized to encourage vendor participation.
- VA workshops should be conducted to bring engineering designers, purchasing personnel, and vendors together.

SUMMARY

Value analysis and value engineering concepts have found widespread application and have resulted in great savings since their inception in the 1940s. Value analysis does not sacrifice quality or performance. Rather, it is a systematic approach to ensuring that every part fulfills its function at the lowest possible cost. Value analysis requires answers to the five following questions:

- What is the item or service?
- What does it cost?
- What does it do?
- What else would do the job?
- What would be the alternative cost?

Promising items for VA analysis are those with large annual outlays, complex items, ones developed in a compressed time frame, nonstandard industrial items, ones with high scrap or rework costs, and items requiring many operations.

Value analysis should be conducted under both in-house and vendor programs. Three in-house approaches are the employment of dedicated value analysts, the committee approach, and the integration approach, which calls for frequent VA training.

Purchasing is the logical organization to initiate, promote, and sponsor the VA program. The VA program is easier to develop and implement and is more successful when it is a collaborative effort. Ideally, a cooperative attitude should exist on the part of all those involved in the VA effort.

Under the vendor program, suppliers are requested to submit VA proposals with their bids and under the resulting purchase orders. Vendors also are invited to participate in VA clinics. It is recommended that VA provisions calling for a sharing of net savings resulting from adoption of VA proposals be included in major purchase orders and contracts.

We now turn our attention to one of the least efficiently performed purchasing functions: expediting and subcontract administration.

chapter twelve

HOW TO ENSURE TIMELY DELIVERY OF THE RIGHT QUALITY

Rolland Hall, purchasing manager at Goliath Enterprises, sat reviewing data from his chief of subcontract administration. "It's always a pleasure," he thought, "to be an agent of *successful* change." Rolland's mind took him back to a point a little over three years before when he had made a major organizational change. The objective of the change was to reduce quality problems and late deliveries. The rejection rate on production material had reached 20%, 1,100 lots awaited inspection, 500 lots of rejected material awaited action, and late deliveries represented 17% of all shipments. The incoming inspection and quality control staffs had grown at twice the rate of the increase in purchase orders. The purchasing department was working overtime in an effort to expedite late purchase orders.

In response to these and related problems, Rolland reorganized his staff of 150 into three principal groups: material engineers, buyers, and subcontract administrators. The material engineers were assigned three responsibilities: coordination with design engineering, value analysis, and the development of new *qualified* sources. The buyers were responsible for planning for and executing successful procurements. The subcontract administrators were charged with the responsibility of ensuring the timely delivery of materials and services of the specified quality.

There had been many problems and many frustrations. Rolland chuckled to himself as he recalled one coup he had pulled off: he had obtained the support of the finance manager and the executive vice president for a partially self-supporting subcontract administration program. All requestors had to identify critical items requiring "extraordinary" subcontract administration and *furnish the funds to administer* the resulting purchase orders and subcontracts.

Rolland brought himself back to the present and again reviewed the status of the department's subcontract administration effort: late deliveries were down to 3%, the production material rejection rate was down to 4%, and rejected material was disposed of in an average of four days. A smile crossed Rolland's face as he thought of the impact of his program on personnel: incoming inspection and quality control were both down 50%, and purchasing was handling a 20% increase in purchase actions with no increase in personnel. Rolland felt very good.

The most important functions for which purchasing has primary responsibility are (1) obtaining the specified level of quality, (2) on time, and (3) at the right price. Most purchasing activities do a good job at getting the right price. They should, for this is where they concentrate their efforts! Few purchasing managers are comfortable or satisfied with the jobs that their organizations do in the area of subcontract administration. The term "subcontract administration" (frequently referred to as expediting) includes all actions *after award of a purchase order or contract* to ensure timely delivery of the specified quality of material. Subcontract administration can and should be as carefully planned as are source selection and negotiations.

The situation that existed at Goliath Enterprises three years ago is altogether too common. Inadequate subcontract administration results from

- Failure to properly organize and staff for subcontract administration
- Failure to plan and prepare for subcontract administration
- Failure to manage for timely delivery
- Failure to manage supplier production quality

and causes

- Production disruptions and late deliveries
- Excessive inventories containing large buffer stocks
- Excessive test and rework cost
- Unacceptably high rates of field failures

ORGANIZING AND STAFFING FOR SUBCONTRACT ADMINISTRATION

The key to successful subcontract administration is a recognition of the critical contribution this activity makes. Once an organization recognizes the critical role of subcontract administration, it should carefully select, train, and organize personnel to carry out subcontract administration responsibilities.

Organization

Two basic organizational approaches are common: (1) assignment of all responsibilities for sourcing, pricing, negotiation, and subcontract administration to buyers and (2) departmental specialization into three functions: material engineering, buying, and subcontract administration expediting.

The assignment of all responsibilities to the buyer has the following advantages: (1) one individual is responsible for all aspects of the procurement, (2) economies of scale, (3) increased familiarity with both customers and suppliers, and (4) increased leverage—the buyer can better extract timely delivery of the right quality since the buyer controls future awards to the supplier.

While these arguments contain much merit, the advantages of specialization more than offset the benefits resulting from the total responsibility approach. Buying and subcontract administration each requires specialized skills and expertise. The highest degree of efficiency results when the purchasing office is organized into three divisions or branches, with close coordination with quality assurance:

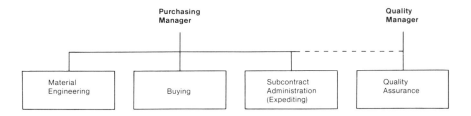

Each of these divisions has a key role to play in the successful administration of the firm's purchase orders and subcontracts:

- Material engineering prequalifies potential new sources of supply with emphasis on vendor capability and process control.
- Buying plans for subcontract administration and includes necessary language in bid invitations and purchase orders or contracts to allow successful subcontract administration. In addition, buying prices with the realization that, if the recipient of an order has little prospect of making a profit, quality may be slighted.
- Subcontract administration takes action to ensure the timely delivery of the goods or services in the specified quality.

- Quality assurance is responsible for three critical activities. It
  - Reviews potential suppliers passing the initial materials engineering review to ensure that they can meet the firm's quality standards
  - Approves or monitors suppliers' in-plant quality performance when required by the nature of the product or contract
  - Monitors the quality of incoming purchased materials

Staffing Considerations

A successful subcontract administrator should possess the following attributes and skills:

- Initiative—it may be necessary to contact officials up to and including the president of the supplier company
- A native ability to relate to personnel in the supplier's and the purchasing firms
- An awareness of statistical quality control methods and the knowledge of when to call on the quality staff for detailed assistance
- An investigative nature
- Tact and diplomacy
- Tenacity

In many industries, subcontract administrators (expediters) receive compensation commensurate with buyers. Their contributions to the success of the organization are equally important!

PLANNING AND PREPARING FOR SUBCONTRACT ADMINISTRATION

When preparing the invitation to bid or request for quotation and the resulting purchase order or contract, the buyer must know the criticality of the purchase. This knowledge is the basis of preparation for successful administration on the resulting purchase order (subcontract). The purchasing firm may require unrestricted access to monitor—or even control—the supplier's production process and quality control. The purchasing firm may require some or all of the following data from its suppliers:

- *A Program Organization Chart*—This should designate the program manager and show the key members of the organization by name and function. The program manager's functional authority should be clearly defined.

- *Milestone Plan*—This should identify all major milestones on a time-phased basis including those of the seller's major subcontractors.
- *Funds Commitment Plan*—This should show estimated commitments on a dollar versus month basis and on a cumulative dollar versus month basis (required on cost reimbursement contracts).
- *Labor Commitment Plan*—This should show estimated labor loading on a labor-hour versus labor-month basis.
- *Monthly Progress Information*—This report should be submitted 10 days after the close of each month. The report should contain as a minimum:
  - A narrative summary of work accomplished during the reporting period, including a technical progress update, a summary of work planned for the next reporting period, problems encountered or anticipated, corrective action taken or to be taken, and a summary of buyer-seller discussions
  - A list of all action items, if any, required of the buyer
  - An update of the milestone plan showing actual progress against planned progress
  - An update of the funds commitment plan showing actual funds committed against the planned funds by time
  - A report on any significant changes in seller's program personnel or in the financial or general management structure, or any other factors that might affect the seller's performance.
- *Missed Milestone Notification and Recovery Plan*—The seller should notify the buyer by phone within 24 hours after discovery of a missed major milestone or the discovery of an anticipated major milestone slip. The seller should provide the buyer with a missed milestone recovery plan within seven working days after notification.

Such data can be costly and should be requested only when it has been determined that their cost and the cost associated with using them to manage a purchase order or subcontract will result in a net savings. Such savings result from avoided production disruptions, reduced inventories, avoided quality problems, fewer late deliveries, and fewer lost sales.

MANAGING FOR TIMELY DELIVERY

Suppliers are responsible for the timely and satisfactory performance of their purchase orders and subcontracts. Unfortunately, the purchaser cannot rely entirely on the supplier to ensure that work is progressing as scheduled and that deliveries will be made as specified. Accordingly, purchasing must monitor supplier performance closely. The method of monitoring depends on lead time or period of performance and the complexity and urgency of the purchase order or subcontract.

At the time a purchase order or subcontract is awarded, the buyer should decide if routine or special attention is appropriate. On many orders for noncritical supplies, monitoring timely receipt of an inspection and receiving report may be adequate. On others, telephone confirmation that delivery will be as specified may be sufficient. But on orders for items critical to the firm's well-being, more detailed procedures are in order.

When evaluating a supplier's progress, the purchaser is interested in *actual* progress toward completing the work. Progress data may be obtained from many sources: ongoing information from the supplier's process control system, production progress conferences, visits to the supplier's plant, or periodic progress reports from the supplier.

When appropriate, the supplier may be required by the terms of the purchase order or subcontract to submit a phased production schedule. Such a requirement should be made a part of the invitation to bid or request for quotation and the resulting purchase order or subcontract. A phased production schedule shows the time required for the production cycle: planning, design, purchasing, plant rearrangements, tooling, component manufacture, subassembly, final assembly, testing, and shipping.

The purchaser may include a requirement for production progress information in the invitation to bid or request for quotation and the resulting purchase order or subcontract. Such reports show the supplier's actual and forecasted deliveries compared with the contract schedule, delay factors if any, and the status of preproduction work (design and engineering facilities, tooling, construction of prototypes, etc.). The report also should contain narrative sections in which the supplier explains any difficulties and action taken or proposed to overcome them.

Production progress reports do not alleviate the requirement of conducting visits to the supplier's plant on crucial contracts. The right to conduct such visits should be established in the invitation to bid or request for quotation and the resulting purchase order or contract. On major critical subcontracts, it may be desirable to establish a resident plant monitor at the supplier's facility.

The buyer should be present when engineers or quality control personnel discuss possible changes in the original specifications with the supplier. When such changes are necessary, the new price should be negotiated and agreed to prior to an agreement to implement the necessary changes. The buyer negotiates from a position of weakness rather than one of strength if changes are agreed to before agreement is reached on the change in price.

Successful management for timely delivery cannot be confined to the purchasing office. *The subcontract administrator must get into the field and check actual progress.* Visits to factory floors and discussions with first-line supervisors and workers will identify present and potential problems long before they appear in status reports. The successful subcontract administrator manages to avoid problems—or to "nip them in the bud."

Two somewhat different situations are encountered when managing for timely delivery. The first is that of flow process, where all or a portion of the supplier's production flows into the purchaser's ongoing manufacturing operation. The second involves unique items for special projects.

As the supplier's operations become more closely intertwined with our own activities, we *must* integrate the supplier's and our communication systems. With such integration, we can notify our suppliers *immediately* of changes in our rate of demand. The suppliers, in turn, can inform us immediately of any (or potential) problems or delays. Control and communications systems must be tailored in such situations.

When dealing with special projects—including construction, defense projects, and other situations of short production runs—one or more of the standard control techniques widely in use, including Gantt charts, line of balance, and PERT, can be employed.

ENSURING RECEIPT OF THE RIGHT QUALITY

There are two key prerequisites to obtaining the required level of quality in purchased materials: (1) a determination of the desired level of quality and (2) ensuring that the specified level of quality is obtained. Marketing should determine the desired level of quality. Design engineering then develops the design logic including the quality of purchased materials and required manufacturing processes. This function should be performed with the cooperation and involvement of marketing, production, and purchasing. The latter's involvement should help to ensure that the material to be specified is economically available.

The second aspect of quality—that of ensuring that the specified level of quality is obtained—is the primary responsibility of purchasing with the cooperation and involvement of quality assurance. To ensure that the specified level of quality is obtained, purchasing must perform four vital functions:

- Select sources of supply that can produce the specified level of quality.

- Develop a realistic understanding with the supplier on all aspects of quality requirements.
- Monitor quality of the material produced by the supplier. This function may be accomplished at the producer's facilities, the purchasing firm's receiving point, or both.
- Motivate the supplier to produce at the specified quality level.

Perhaps the most challenging aspect of obtaining the specified quality level is the monitoring function. Historically, this task was performed at the purchaser's facility. As producers' quality control programs improved, it became possible to satisfy the monitoring function by relying on the producer's quality control program, reducing or eliminating the purchaser's incoming materials inspection. This transfer of responsibility avoids duplication of effort and results in significant savings in quality monitoring.

When a purchase order or subcontract is awarded, the supplier assumes responsibility for timely delivery and satisfactory performance. Protection is afforded under provisions of the Uniform Commercial Code and by the inspection and warranty provisions in the contract. Uniform legal provisions, called the Uniform Commercial Code (UCC), have been enacted by all states except Louisiana. Pertinent provisions of the UCC dealing with services are included next.

The Uniform Commercial Code and Quality Merchantability, Usage of Trade (UCC 2-314 (1977))

Unless excluded or modified, a warranty that the goods shall be merchantable is implied if the seller is a merchant with respect to goods of that kind.

Goods to be merchantable must be at least such as:
(a) pass without objection in the trade under the contract description; and in the case of fungible goods [fungible goods are those where all units are identical, e.g., grains of corn] are of fair average quality within the description; and
(b) are fit for the ordinary purposes for which such goods are used; and
(c) run, within the variations permitted by the agreement, of even kind, quality and quantity within each unit and among all units involved; and
(d) are adequately contained, packaged, and labeled as the agreement may require; and
(e) conform to the promises or affirmations of fact made on the container or label, if any.

Fitness for Purpose (UCC 2-315 (1977))

Where the seller at the time of contracting has reason to know any particular purpose for which the goods are required and that the buyer is relying on the seller's skill or judgment to select or furnish suitable goods, there is, unless excluded or modified under the next section, an implied warranty that the good shall be fit for such purpose.

Although implied warranties provide protection to buyers, an implied warranty may be specifically excluded by calling the buyer's attention, in understandable language, to the fact that warranties are excluded and that there is no implied warranty. In addition, an implied warranty is excluded when a buyer has examined the goods, sample, or model as fully as he or she wanted to (prior to entering into the contract) or has refused to examine the goods. Also by agreement of seller and buyer, the extent of remedies can be restricted or limited.

Once a buyer accepts the goods, they must be paid for. Once accepted, the goods may not be rejected, however, the buyer may still seek other remedies. To seek remedy for an alleged breach, the buyer must notify the seller within a reasonable time after the "breach" is discovered or should have been discovered. The burden of proof, of course, is on the buyer.

Express Warranties

Express warranties by the seller are created as follows:

- Any affirmation of fact or promise made by the seller to the buyer that relates to the goods and becomes part of the basis of the bargain creates an express warranty that the goods shall conform to the affirmation or promise.
- Any description of the goods that is made part of the basis of the bargain creates an express warranty that the goods shall conform to the description.

The purpose of using a warranty clause is to increase the purchaser's latitude in exercising (within a specified period of time after acceptance) the right to have the supplier correct a deficiency in an item, or accept a reduction in price, or provide other remedies. This additional period of time may begin at the time of delivery or at the occurrence of a particular event and may run for a number of days or months until the occurrence of another specified event.

Warranties are not free; therefore, cost must be weighed against risk. Specific factors must be considered in deciding whether to use a warranty clause. These factors include

- The nature of the item and its end use
- The cost of the warranty and degree of price competition as it may affect this cost
- The criticality of achieving specified performance capabilities and design specifications
- The cost of correction or replacement, either by the supplier or another source, in the absence of a warranty
- The administrative cost and difficulty of enforcing the warranty
- The ability to take advantage of the warranty, as conditioned by storage time, distance of the using activity from the source of repairs, or other factors
- Operation of the warranty as a deterrent against furnishing of defective or nonconforming supplies
- The extent to which acceptance is to be based upon supplier inspection or quality control
- Whether or not the inspection system would be likely to provide adequate protection without a warranty
- Whether the supplier's present quality program is sufficiently reliable to provide adequate protection without a warranty, or if not, whether a warranty would cause the supplier to institute an effective quality program
- Reliance on "brand-name" integrity
- Criticality of item for protection of personnel
- The stage of development of the item and the state of the art
- Customary trade practices

Although protection ceases after a specified date contained in a warranty clause, the supplier's liability for latent defects under the standard inspection clause continues after the expiration of a warranty clause period.

SCOPE OF WARRANTIES

Failure-Free Warranty

This is sometimes referred to as a hardware guarantee. Under this agreement, the supplier agrees to correct any failure or defect that occurs during a specific time or measured amount of operation. Extreme care should be exercised before this warranty is used because its cost may be high—high in both contract price and in the administrative cost of maintaining records and controls over these items.

Correction of Deficiencies

Under this type of warranty, the supplier agrees to correct any design, material, or workmanship deficiencies that become apparent during test or early operation and that result in the item performing below specification and contractual requirements.

Supply Warranty

Under this warranty, the supplier is responsible for replacement or rework on contract items if defects in material or workmanship existed at the time of acceptance of the item. This clause usually gives the purchaser a specified period of time in which to discover defects. Normally, there is very little increase in item price for this kind of warranty. It should be quite easy to make a positive determination that a defect existed at the time of acceptance if it is found when the item is drawn from stores for initial use. It will be much more difficult to determine that the defect existed at time of original acceptance if the item has been installed and operating for some appreciable period of service and is then found defective.

Service Warranty

Under such a warranty, the supplier agrees to reperform defective services, providing that defects in workmanship existed at time of acceptance and are discovered within a specified time period. Here again, little is paid for this warranty because, unless the purchaser spots defective workmanship soon after return of overhauled or repaired items, it will be extremely difficult to conclude that the defect existed at the time of acceptance. It may also be difficult to prove that the supplier performed the defective work.

Construction Warranty

This warranty is used in construction contracts and requires the contractor to remedy, at his or her own expense, any nonconforming work and any defect of material, workmanship, and contractor design.

INSPECTION[1]

The purpose of inspection is to determine whether the item or service conforms exactly to what has been ordered. The extent of inspection var-

[1]This material is based on the author's article, "Understanding Quality Control," *Journal of Purchasing and Materials Management,* May 1973, pp. 12–24, and is used with permission.

ies with the dollar value of the purchase order and the type of product. For example, a purchase order for off-the-shelf items may require minimum inspection after the items are received. Such inspection may be limited to counting items, determining damage in transit, and verifying that the items are what was ordered. On the other hand, an order for electronic components or sophisticated machinery costing millions of dollars may require a detailed inspection system that starts at the raw materials, continues through production, and ends with the completed item.Table 12.1 relates inspection requirements to the types of items and their applications.

The two approaches to inspection are based on the inclusiveness of the population being inspected. The first approach calls for the inspection of all items. The second approach relies on sampling. Both methods may be used at the origin and destination.

Screening, or 100% inspection, is the process of inspecting every unit. At first glance, this should result in acceptance of all conforming units and rejection of all defective ones. In practice, however, such accuracy rarely is achieved. Inadequate facilities and the monotony of screening lower the effectiveness of inspectors and defects are overlooked. Experience has shown that when humans are involved in the inspection process, at least 200% inspection is required to approach 100% defect-free products.

Screening has limited application in most types of high-volume production. It is expensive and time consuming and cannot be employed when destructive testing is required. However, when inspection can be performed mechanically in an economical manner, or when the items to be 100% inspected are extremely critical, then screening is appropriate.

Sampling, or lot-by-lot inspection based on statistical techniques, is the alternative to screening. Two assumptions underlie the use of sampling: (1) 100% conformance with specifications is not required, and (2) the production lots to be sampled will be homogeneous. Several benefits may be gained through the use of sampling inspection:

- It is less costly to inspect only a portion of a lot of material.
- The amount of damage inflicted on the lot being inspected is reduced when sampling is employed.
- The use of sampling requires the purchaser to examine his or her quality requirements.
- Decisions on the acceptability of the lot are made more quickly, allowing time to obtain satisfactory replacement material or reschedule production.

Item Technical Description	*Kind of Item	*Application	Type of Inspection Requirement
Commercial	Noncomplex	Noncritical Common and Peculiar	(A)*
Commercial	Noncomplex	Critical	(B)
Commercial	Complex	Noncritical Common	(A)
Commercial	Complex	Noncritical Peculiar	(B)
Commercial	Complex	Critical	(C)
Design/Performance Specification (D/PS)	Noncomplex	Noncritical Common and Peculiar	(B)
D/PS	Noncomplex	Critical	(C)
D/PS	Complex	Noncritical Common	(B)
D/PS	Complex	Noncritical Peculiar	(C)
D/PS	Complex	Critical	(D)

*Explanations are contained below.

Complex Items have quality characteristics, not wholly visible in the end item, for which contractual conformance must progressively be established through precise measurements, tests and controls accomplished during purchasing, manufacturing, assembly, and functional operations either as an individual item or in conjunction with other items.

Noncomplex Items have quality characteristics for which simple measurement and test of the end item is sufficient to determine conformance to contract requirements.

Critical. A critical application of an item is one in which the failure of the item could injure personnel or jeopardize the wellbeing of the organization.

Noncritical. A noncritical application is any application which is not critical.

Peculiar. Meaning items which have only one application.

Common. Meaning items which have multiple applications.

The four letters indicate a hierarchy of inspection demands placed on the contractor. This hierarchy, from least to most stringent is:

(A) No Specific Quality Requirement in the Contract: In this situation, the purchaser does not perform any inspection or quality assurance at the supplier's facility system. No specific obligation is placed on the contractor for the performance of quality control.

TABLE 12.1 Inspection Requirements

(B) Standard Inspection Requirement: With this approach, the contractor is required to maintain an inspection system acceptable to the purchaser. Normally, the contract will allow the purchaser to visit the contractor's plant to monitor the inspection process.

(C) Inspection System Requirement: Under this approach, the contractor must establish and maintain an inspection system in accordance with a contract specification. The purchaser will have access to the production plant. This requirement is included in contracts when technical requirements are such as to require quality control by in-process as well as final end item inspection. In-process inspection includes control of such elements of the manufacturing process as measuring and testing equipment, drawings and changes, inspection, documentation and records.

(D) Quality Program Requirement: When the technical requirements of the contract are such as to require control of work operations, in process controls, inspection, organization, planning, work instructions, and documentation control; the contractor is required to develop a quality program in accordance with the contract specification. The purchaser will have access to the contractor's plant.

TABLE 12.1 (Cont.)

The first step in developing a sampling plan is to determine the characteristics to be inspected. If two or more characteristics are critical, it may be appropriate to develop a separate sampling plan for each single characteristic or group of characteristics of similar criticality.

The second step is to determine what constitutes a lot for inspection purposes. Here there is a trade-off between the desire to make the lot as large as possible due to the benefit from the economies of scale for inspection and handling and the realization that all items contained in a lot should be produced under identical or nearly identical conditions. For example, material produced by the same equipment from identical raw material but by two different production shifts may be considered as comprising two lots.

Next, choose between lot quality (frequently referred to as lot tolerance percent defective, or LTPD) and average outgoing quality level (AOQL) protection. LTPD provides much more stringent control of quality. (Remember, the customer pays for the level of quality demanded.) AOQL protection ensures that the average quality accepted will not be poorer than some agreed-upon level.

Additional insight into the details of quality assurance may be gained by reading the author's article "Understanding Quality Control," which appeared in the May 1973 issue of the *Journal of Purchasing*.

THE ECONOMICS
OF INSPECTION
AND QUALITY CONTROL

Except under abnormal economic conditions, the purchaser ultimately pays for the producer's quality control. Thus, the purchaser is confronted with two conflicting forces: a desire to minimize the number of defective items and the knowledge that using a quality control approach that is very demanding results in extremely high costs that are passed on to the purchaser.

If the purchaser conducts an economic analysis, the optimal approach to quality control that should be demanded of the supplier can be determined. Such an analysis may be performed as follows. With the supplier's assistance, determine the additional or marginal cost, MC, of implementing more stringent or demanding control programs. Then, with the purchaser's production and marketing departments, determine the marginal savings, MS, of different levels of defects entering into production. These savings will include rework and reject costs avoided in production. They also should include marketing's estimate of savings for costs avoided in replacement shipments, field warranty expense, and the loss of customer goodwill. The optimal level of quality control is the point at which $MC = MS!$

SUMMARY

Subcontract administration (frequently referred to as expediting) includes all actions required to ensure timely delivery of the specified quality of materials or services. Subcontract administration should be planned for and executed with the same degree of rigor as source selection or negotiations. Inadequate subcontract administration is one of the most common weaknesses of modern procurement. Inadequate subcontract administration results in (1) production disruptions, (2) excessive inventory, (3) excess test and rework costs resulting from low-quality material entering the system, (4) an unacceptable high rate of field failures, and (5) needlessly large expenditures for inspection and purchasing personnel.

Four major failures in the area of subcontract administration are common: inadequate organizational staffing, inadequate planning and preparation, inadequate management for timely delivery, and inadequate management of supplier quality.

Personnel in material engineering, buying, and subcontract administration require specialized skills and expertise. The greatest degree of efficiency results from specialization in these areas. Personnel in each of these functions and in the area of quality assurance have key roles to play in achieving timely delivery of the specified quality of material.

Successful subcontract administration begins with a determination of the level of monitoring and control required. Then the buyer must include provisions for subcontract administration in the invitation to bid or request for quotation and the resulting purchase order or subcontract. These provisions provide for the required level of control, data requirements, and access to the supplier's production activities.

Managing for timely delivery requires judgment and initiative. Orders for noncritical supplies usually require passive monitoring or management by exception. Orders for items critical to the firm's well-being require more detailed control. Two somewhat different situations are common when managing for timely delivery: flow process, where a portion of the supplier's production flows into the purchaser's continuing manufacturing operations, and unique items for special projects. With the first situation, the supplier's and purchaser's communications systems must be integrated. Then we can notify our suppliers immediately of changes in our demand rate. Suppliers can inform us immediately of any problems or delays on their side. In the second situation (that of special projects), we can employ one or more of the standard control techniques widely in use, including Gantt charts, line of balance, and PERT.

Successful administration of purchase orders and subcontracts requires field visits. Such visits help to identify present and potential problems long before they appear in status reports. The successful subcontract administrator manages to avoid problems. Purchasing has four vital functions to perform to ensure that the specified level of quality is obtained:

- Select sources of supply that are capable of producing the specified level of quality.
- Develop a realistic understanding with the supplier on all aspects of quality requirements.
- Monitor the quality of the material produced by the supplier (with the active involvement of quality assurance).
- Create motivation on the supplier's part to produce at the specified level of quality.

Normally, the purchaser ultimately pays for the supplier's quality control. The purchaser is confronted with two conflicting forces: a desire to have the producer's quality control system minimize the number of defective items and the knowledge that excessively tight quality control standards will be extremely expensive. The solution is to find the point at which the total cost of quality control (including resulting rejects) and the cost of defects entering into the purchaser's supply system are at a minimum.

Purchasing *should be* concerned with the external supply environment of the firm. All too frequently, this external awareness is lacking—causing many avoidable problems. We now turn our attention to this challenging area.

chapter thirteen

PURCHASING AND THE EXTERNAL ENVIRONMENT

Paul Krebs, purchasing manager at the Ada Manufacturing Company, was sitting in a crowded meeting of the local Purchasing Management Association. The speaker, Dr. Gayton Davis, dean of American purchasing consultants, had been addressing the group on the topic of "strategic purchasing."

Dr. Davis stated that the most common shortcoming he had found in purchasing management during the past 10 years was the failure of purchasing managers to assume their responsibilities as strategic purchasers.

Dr. Davis proceeded to describe what he saw happening, or about to happen, in the supply environment:

- There will be frequent short-term shortages of raw materials and components.
- There will be fewer experienced sources of supply. But new, inexperienced sources will partially offset this loss.
- There will be a reduction in the availability of quality material. At the same time, purchasers will attempt to impose tighter specifications.
- Purchasers will have to buy what is available rather than be able to motivate vendors to provide what the customer desires.
- Buyers and sellers will become more efficient in dealing with inflation. Suppliers will offer cash discounts pegged to the rate of inflation together with penalties for late payments.
- International trade will become increasingly complex, especially in the areas of taxes, exchange, and offsets (barter).
- There will be an increase in the barter of goods and services.

- Reciprocity and trade relations will find increasing application in obtaining raw materials for the manufacturer and his or her suppliers.
- More, not fewer, government regulations and controls will limit the purchaser's freedom of operation.
- Development costs will increase, with customers providing financial assistance.
- There will be an increase in the rate of growth of technology.
- There will be an increasing emphasis on buyer and corporate ethics.

Dr. Davis proceeded to describe purchasing's role in the firm's strategic planning process. Finally, he discussed some of the actions that were involved in strategic purchasing.

At the conclusion of the address, there was the customary courteous round of applause. Obviously, many of the order placers could care less about strategic purchasing.

Paul Krebs was deep in thought. He was oblivious to his table companions. The points Dr. Davis had made hit Paul directly between the eyes. He realized that he had been so busy supervising his staff of 27 and worrying about an endless stream of problems that he had not paid any attention to securing his firm's sources of supply. He recognized that he had much to do!

Purchasing and marketing are the two departments that are concerned with the external environment on a daily basis. Marketing focuses on the external environment in its efforts to identify and satisfy potential customers' wants and needs. Purchasing, by contrast, appears to be determined to minimize the attention it pays to the external environment. As a result, a number of problems exist in the area of the interface between purchasing and its supply environment:

- Many purchasing managers myopically define their role and do not view themselves as strategic purchasers operating in a rapidly changing environment. Purchasing should be a key member of the corporate planning function. Input from the corporate planning process is an essential prerequisite for strategic purchasing. Purchasing has critical input for the planning process both in the areas of new opportunities arising from new materials, products, and technology and constraints due to anticipated shortages and price increases.
- The purchasing-supplier interface too often is conducted in an adversarial atmosphere. Many benefits result from collaboration and long-term relations.

- The development and management of suppliers frequently is left to chance. Dedicated and competent suppliers are valued resources. But once such suppliers have been developed, they must be properly managed.
- The firm has two ethical responsibilities: personal (buyer) ethics and the responsibility to treat its vendors with respect and consideration. Not only are the firm's reputation and image at stake, but also its ability to purchase effectively.
- The temptation to employ trade relations or reciprocity can be a powerful one. Yet several hidden problems detract from this approach to increasing sales.
- Many firms are not prepared to purchase effectively in an era of shortages. Wise purchasing managers are familiar with the tools that will minimize the impact of shortages on their firms.

STRATEGIC PURCHASING

Strategic purchasing links the firm to its environment, especially as the environment affects future procurement requirements. Decisions on such future requirements necessitate a sharing of information between buyer and supplier on the nature of the requirements. Strategic purchasing objectives and the resulting plans and actions are an outgrowth of the firm's long-range planning process. At the same time, input from purchasing may affect the establishment of the corporate goals and objectives. For example, purchasing may have information on new products and new technology. Also, purchasing may have information on the likely future availability of materials and changes that will have an impact on the establishment of corporate or divisional goals and objectives.

At a macro level, strategic purchasing requires purchasing managers to

- Monitor their environment
- Forecast and anticipate changes in the environment
- Share purchasing-related information with suppliers and managers within their own firm
- Identify the firm's competitive advantages and disadvantages relative to its suppliers

At a micro level, strategic purchasing requires the identification of critical materials, an evaluation of possible supply disruptions for each critical material, and the development of plans for all identifiable problems. These plans must be well thought out and developed in advance of all foreseeable shortages.

Success in this area hinges on improved vendor relations, including a sharing of planning data. Both customer and supplier must work toward common technical objectives and form long-term continuous relationships.

In addition to the previously discussed responsibilities, purchasing must, on a periodic basis, analyze its suppliers' abilities to meet the firm's long-term needs. Areas that deserve particular attention include the supplier's general growth plans, future design capability in relevant areas, the role of purchasing or materials management in the supplier's strategic planning, potential for future production capacity, and financial ability to support such growth.

If present suppliers appear to be unlikely to be able to meet future requirements, the firm has three options: it may assist the appropriate supplier(s) with financing and technological assistance, it may develop new sources having the desired growth potential, or it may have to develop the required capability internally.

THE ADVANTAGES OF COLLABORATION

The era of the one-night stand, the cheap, spot buy is over—or fading fast. Reason: What is expensive and risky to buy is also usually expensive and risky to sell. Thus, both buyers and sellers need the security and stability of long-term relationships. Buyer-seller guessing games have become too expensive in terms of brute costs, opportunities lost, and unnecessary risks for all concerned. Upshot: Smart purchasing pros are working to construct long-term relationships based on cooperation, candor, coordination, and concessions on both sides. None of this means that the purchasing department is going to be transformed into a corporate doormat. But it does mean that both sides of the negotiating table are going to have to work to end the often adversary relationship between buyer and seller.[1]

A good supplier is an invaluable resource to the organization requiring his or her product or service. Such suppliers make a direct contribution to a firm's success. They assist their customers with product development, value analysis, and timely delivery of the desired level of quality. Good buyer-seller relations facilitate the buyer's efforts in gaining superior performance, extra service, cooperation on cost reduction programs, and a willingness to share in new processes and procedures. Farmer and MacMillan introduce several arguments for what they call "voluntary collaboration"[2] or continuing relations:

- Every time a new set of partners comes together, a learning process

---

[1]"Why the Old Buying Game Has Ended," *Purchasing*, May 29, 1980, p. 52.

[2]David H. Farmer and Keith MacMillan, "Voluntary Collaboration vs. 'Disloyalty' to Suppliers," *Journal of Purchasing and Materials Management*, Winter 1976, pp. 3–8.

is required. The potential for communication difficulties is much greater during early transactions than during later ones.

- Changing market conditions and changing technology that affect the buying process require adaptation on the part of buyers and sellers. Such adaptation can be much less painful under conditions of an ongoing and mutually beneficial relationship where the parties have teamed to adapt together.

- The likelihood of quality problems and late deliveries is greatly reduced in a continuing relationship.

- Open relationships can help to cushion bad times. Customers and suppliers who value each other based on long-term relations and respect are more likely to come to each others' aid during times of adversity.

- Suppliers learn from the behavior of an aggressive, price-optimizing purchaser. Such buyers will find it more difficult to obtain delivery of the required goods on time than will buyers who have developed continuing relations with their suppliers.

- Opportunistic buyers are more subject to shocks resulting from capacity or supply problems encountered by the vendor than are buyers who maintain continuing relations with their suppliers.

- Opportunistic buyers should expect less effective performance from suppliers who believe that they have little to lose in the way of follow-on business.

Alfred Chandler, in his book, *Strategy and Structure,* conducted intensive studies of General Motors, DuPont, Standard Oil of New Jersey, and Sears, Roebuck. He observed the importance of collaborative dealing with suppliers in the growth of these organizations. Marks and Spencer, the highly successful U.K. retailer, benefited from "close and intimate cooperation with their suppliers."[3] It is interesting to note that Sears experienced great difficulties in the late 1970s when it shifted to a more adversarial relationship with its suppliers.[4]

The Japanese motorcycle industry has come to dominate world competition. A 1975 study reports,

> Overall, a clear picture emerges of a closely integrated parts supply system . . . it does not seem to be the case of the motorcycle manufacturers earning their profits at the expense of the parts suppliers—and the relationship between them and the motorcycle manufacturers is such that they simply profit from the intimate cooperation.[5]

[3]Goronwy Rees St. Michael, *A History of Marks and Spencer* (London: Weidenfield & Nicolson, 1969), p. 101, quoted in Farmer and MacMillan, "Voluntary Collaboration."

[4]*Business Week,* February 16, 1981, p. 53.

[5]*Strategy Alternatives for the British Motor Cycle Industry* (London: Her Majesty's Stationery Office, 1975), quoted in Farmer and MacMillan, "Voluntary Collaboration."

We see that continuing relations between buyer and supplier—based on good prices, service and quality, respect, and an awareness of the benefits of the relationship—are significant assets to both parties.

During the material shortages of 1973 and 1974, many firms moved marketing personnel into their purchasing department for the express purpose of marketing the firm as a desirable customer to potential suppliers. Out of experiences with purchasing under conditions of scarcity has come a realization that suppliers cannot be taken for granted. Also, we have become aware that both parties to an exchange receive benefits, frequently in areas in addition to the item being exchanged. We now recognize that the buyer has much more to offer the supplier than just money.

The buyer's product offering consists of those elements that satisfy various supplier needs. Included are technical know-how, volume of purchases, loyalty, credit rating, other business that can be done, and the prestige of supplying the customer. A buyer can modify a product offering toward the needs of target suppliers or modify the suppliers' perceptions of his or her product offering to be more favorably evaluated by suppliers.

Brokaw and Davisson point out that suppliers can and do allocate several resources to their customers based on their preferences for doing business with various customers. These resources include

- The quality and quantity of products
- Technical and sales services
- Financial assistance
- Distribution services
- Assumption of various inventory functions
- Provision of market information[6]

Although collaboration and continuing relations have many advantages, both buyer and supplier must be careful that complacency does not enter the picture. The purchase cost should be justified at least annually. At this time, the buyer should ask, "What can this supplier do that will result in a cost reduction for my firm?" Some degree of turnover (e.g., 5–10%) may be necessary to keep suppliers alert, competitive, and willing to provide better service and quality.

The buyer-seller interaction is the dyad that frequently is the appropriate unit of analysis. The idea of exchange to mutual advantage and the interactive buyer-seller relationship needs the attention of all purchasing managers.

[6]Alan J. Brokaw and Charles N. Davisson, "Positioning a Company as a Preferred Supplier," *Journal of Purchasing and Materials Management*, Spring 1977, pp. 9–11.

THE DEVELOPMENT AND
MANAGEMENT OF VENDORS

In Chapter 2 we saw the benefits of competition. An adequate vendor base is essential to the economic well-being of the firm. Such a base is as much a resource as are research scientists or skilled production personnel. This vendor base is especially critical in high-technology industries and in industries where scarcity of materials is a present or potential occurrence.

Efficient vendor development programs have one or more full-time specialists assigned to the processing of the applications of companies offering new techniques, equipment, and materials. These specialists are the first point of contact for the potential new supplier. The specialists describe the corporate organizational structure as it relates to the vendor. They provide the vendor with a current list of all purchasing agents and buyers, their specialties, and their phone numbers. The vendor relations (VR) specialists then obtain information on the vendor's capability, resources, and product lines. If the vendor is dealing with fairly standard items required by the firm, he or she is turned over to the appropriate buyer.

If the vendor has a new product or technology of possible interest to the company, the VR specialist assumes even more responsibility. He or she arranges for conferences between the vendor and company technical personnel. For an item or process of potential interest to many company employees, the VR specialist may arrange for a full technical presentation. The VR specialist provides advice and even coaching to ensure the success of such technical presentations. Advance data and a sample of the product are obtained from the vendor and are distributed to interested company personnel. This allows the preparation of questions and helps to overcome the native tendency to resist change and new ideas. Adequate time must be allowed between receipt of the advance data and samples and the full technical presentation.

The VR specialist ensures that all interested personnel are invited to the technical presentation. After the presentation, the specialist becomes a conduit of communications between the vendor and company personnel. Finally, if the new product or process is accepted, whether as a result of informal conferences or full technical presentations, the vendor is turned over to the appropriate purchasing agent or buyer.

The VR specialist also investigates complaints from suppliers who feel that they have been treated unfairly. The VR specialist does everything possible to bolster supplier goodwill.

While such a program requires an expenditure in the form of salaries for the VR specialist(s), it is far more efficient and less costly than the more common hit-or-miss approach that results in wasted time and effort on the part of purchasing, manufacturing, engineering, and the vendor's personnel. Of even greater importance, new ideas, products, and sources are gained. Such action can give the firm a great edge over its competition.

It is essential that all purchasing personnel recognize the importance of being available to vendors. If buyers are not available, vendors will circumvent purchasing and go to the originator of requirements for his or her product line. Such vendors will receive advanced information and may be successful in having their products specified as "sole source."

The management of vendors requires the collection of vendor performance information. This information is an essential tool for subsequent negotiations and source selections. Several different approaches to rating vendor performance are in use today. Some are very subjective, but adequate for their intended purpose. Other rating schemes are more quantitative. Figure 13.1 portrays such a rating scheme. Many organizations consider only quality or quality and timeliness when rating their vendors. Others include the factors of quality and delivery plus price and lead time. Weights may be assigned to each element, indicating purchasing's judgment of the relative importance of the factors included. If vendors are truly to be managed, it is important that they receive periodic feedback on how well they are doing and where they rank in relation to their competitors.

Vendor quality performance is an especially crucial item. It is a measure of a vendor's ability to provide material that complies with the purchasing firm's specifications and quality standards. Poor-quality performance raises the operating costs associated with the inspection and discovery of rejected material while increasing the costs associated with financing rejected inventory. Many firms recognize the effect of poor-quality performance on cost during the source selection process. These firms add an increment onto price quotations from a vendor based on past experience with the vendor. Such firms are concerned with the total cost of purchased items, not just the price that appears on the invoice.

Another approach to dealing with poor vendor quality is based on a major manufacturer's experience. This firm found significant quality problems in vendor supplied parts in one of its divisions several years ago. Prior to introducing a vendor evaluation system, this division was experiencing an unacceptably high rejection rate on incoming materials.

The division established a rating program for its vendors based on the volume or dollar value of material supplied and the type and frequency of quality discrepancies noted on the products received. Each vendor was presented with an acceptable product quality level that he or she would have to maintain or face the loss of the firm as an account. Each vendor was advised of his or her known shortcomings and was permitted to discuss them.

A VENDOR EVALUATION CHECK LIST

Vendor_____ P. O. #_____

Item(s)_____ Date_____

A.   Delivery completed - all items

[50] [ ] On Schedule

[50] [ ] Late - insufficient lead time allowed

[30] [ ] Late - less than 30 days - vendor responsibility

[0] [ ] Late - more than 30 days - vendor responsibility

B.   Quality

[50] [ ] Accepted 100%

         Defects in vendor material:

[40] [ ] Minor - in quantity and/or severity, accepted as is

[20] [ ] Major - in quantity and/or severity, schedule not jeopardized

[0] [ ] Very Serious - schedule jeopardized

C.   Vendor rating

      Accumulated points   _____

      Buyer's further evaluation of deficiencies:

[10] [ ] Isolated case

[0] [ ] Chronic case
                            TOTAL SCORE   _____

FIGURE 13.1   A Vendor Evaluation Check List

Within three years, 900 of the original 1,700 suppliers had been dropped. The remaining 800 firms picked up over $29 million during this period. In addition to improving total product reliability and performance, the program produced the following cost benefits:

- A 50% reduction in personnel at receiving locations

- A reduction of the rate of vendor lot rejections from 22% to 6%
- A 75% reduction in storage space requirements for rejected materials
- An acceptance rate of 96% defect-free material during the last year of the effort[7]

We see, then, that an effective vendor rating system can have a significant impact on the quality of incoming material. It can reduce the likelihood of production disruptions due to the unavailability of material of a specified quality level. And such a program can reduce work force and inspection space requirements.

PERSONAL AND ORGANIZATIONAL ETHICS

The purchasing department, to a large extent, is responsible for the firm's reputation for honesty, ethics, and considerate business relations. Not only should the firm's buyers conduct themselves ethically, but their actions should be above question or suspicion. Several actions should be taken by management in this area:

- Buyers' salaries must provide for an adequate standard of living.
- Definite standards of conduct should be established and communicated to all personnel in the firm having a role in procurement (this includes not only purchasing personnel but also designers, production, and inspection personnel).
- Violations of the foregoing standards of conduct should result in appropriate disciplinary action.
- Buyers should have an expense account. Many occasions arise where business will be discussed over lunch. Such discussions are as much in the purchasing firm's interest as that of the supplier. When circumstances call for such an event, the buyer's firm should treat such costs as a legitimate business expense.
- The acceptance of gifts or entertainment *may* place the purchasing agent under ethical pressure that conflicts with the goals of dealing with all vendors fairly and equitably. Such action should be seen for what it is: bribery. In the United States, such action should be rejected out of hand. (Much more discretion is required in dealing with foreign suppliers, where the buyer must be sensitive to different cultural practices. In such situations, reciprocity of gift giving

[7]L. R. Lamberson, D. Diederich, and J. Wuori, "Quantitative Vendor Evaluation," *Journal of Purchasing and Materials Management,* Spring 1976, pp. 19–28.

and entertaining may be a prerequisite to success and the most practical solution.)

- The practices of the director of purchasing and of top management must set an example in the area of ethics to be embraced by all personnel involved in procurement.

In addition to establishing and maintaining a viable set of ethical standards, the purchasing department has a responsibility for considerate business relations. The buyer should promptly inform all firms that have submitted bids when an award is made. Many small companies cannot afford to have a large number of bids outstanding. Each bid represents a tentative commitment of capacity. Thus, vendors having submitted bids should be relieved of these tentative commitments promptly. Information on where the bid fell short of the purchaser's requirements will provide essential feedback to allow the vendor to be more responsive and competitive on future requirements, leading to the development of a future useful source of supply. Further, such action will temper the unsuccessful supplier's disappointment in not receiving the award.

When awards are to be made as a result of the competitive bidding process, care must be taken to protect the integrity of the bid process. Only bids received on or before the indicated bid opening hour and date should be considered. If clarifying information of a substantive nature is provided to one bidder, it should be provided to all. If revisions are permitted, all bidders should be afforded the opportunity of revising their bids. If specifications are changed as the result of submission of an attractive alternative by one bidder, then all firms should be invited to bid on the new specifications.

If a bid appears to be excessively low compared with other proposals, the buyer must request a recalculation and confirmation of the bid. Such action is both ethically sound and in the best business interest of the purchasing firm. The law does not allow a buyer to take advantage of a palpable error. Further, purchase orders and contracts that are based on miscalculation and that virtually guarantee that the supplier will incur a loss are difficult or impossible to administer. Not only is great effort required on the part of the purchasing activity in managing the resulting contract, but the probabilities of low quality, late delivery, and even default are very high.

This is not to say that the purchasing personnel are under any obligation to ensure that a supplier makes a profit. As we have seen, a supplier's price frequently is based on an estimate of likely costs plus a margin of profit. If experience proves these estimates to be too low to allow a profit, this is the supplier's problem. Suppliers may appeal for relief when events turn out contrary to their expectations. In such circumstances, the purchaser is under no obligation to modify or relinquish his or her contractual rights, assuming that the agreement has been made in good faith. However, recognizing the difficulty in administering such contracts, the buyer may choose to make an adjustment that does not adversely affect the well-being of the company.

The ideal purchasing department, from a vendor's point of view, is one that treats sales representatives with respect, makes them feel welcome, respects their knowledge and experience, and regards them as allies in the effort for greater value. The majority of well-run purchasing departments solicit, either on a continuing or periodic basis, input from their suppliers indicating how the purchasing department is doing in its effort to deal efficiently and effectively with its vendors.

TRADE RELATIONS
AND RECIPROCITY

The process of giving preference to suppliers who also are customers is known as "reciprocity" or "trade relations." Purchasing and marketing must blend their interests in this delicate area. The courts and Justice Department take a very critical view of trade relations that *appear* to restrict competition or that are the result of economic threats ("if you don't buy from me, I won't buy from you"). On the other hand, it is entirely legal to purchase from one's customers at *fair market prices.* Buyers should be made aware that reciprocity purchasing for the sake of reciprocity is extremely dangerous. Such action may subject the purchasing firm to prosecution under the Sherman and Clayton Acts for antitrust action.

Most purchasing executives and theoreticians are opposed to reciprocity. Even when it is legal, reciprocity tends to restrict purchasing's efforts to obtain the right quality of material at the lowest total cost to the firm. Marketing, on the other hand, tends to be much more supportive of the practice. It must be remembered, however, that it takes many dollars of additional sales to contribute the same amount of profits as results from a dollar's reduction in material expenditures!

Several problems can arise from the use of reciprocity:

- The companies that enter into such trade relations may be subject to examination by government agencies and prosecution.
- The purchasing, marketing, engineering, and production departments of both firms may become complacent and not perform their respective responsibilities with appropriate diligence. Eventually, both firms may suffer.
- Vendors who normally would compete are dissuaded from attempting to sell their products since they feel "locked out." Purchasing

loses the benefits of competition cited in Chapter 2. Further, the firm may not be able to enjoy the benefits of technological advances made by other potential suppliers.

Reciprocity, in all actuality, is neither a purchasing nor a marketing problem. It is an issue to be decided by top management. If a careful appraisal of the situation indicates that reciprocity will legally add to the profitability of the enterprise, then management may embrace a program of reciprocity or trade relations.

RELATIONS WITH VENDORS DURING PERIODS OF SHORTAGES

In spite of the best of plans and sound procurement actions, shortages will occur. A well-run procurement system has many tools at its disposal to deal with such shortages. The firm should take many defensive actions to avoid the impact of potential shortages:

- A good value analysis program may be able to identify satisfactory substitute materials.
- A recycling program may be able to reduce requirements of critical materials significantly.
- The firm can build up inventories of critical materials when the benefits outweigh the costs.
- The firm should become a preferred customer by ensuring that suppliers receive prompt payment.
- Management, engineering, and technical assistance can be provided to suppliers to help increase their capacity.
- Financing in the form of prepayment and loans can be advanced.
- Purchasing can help to obtain scarce raw materials for its suppliers.
- Suppliers can be provided access to the firm's transportation service.
- New suppliers should be developed.
- Consideration should be given to providing incentives to suppliers for fair prices and timely delivery.
- It may be necessary to resort to the "gray market." But buyers should remember that gray markets tend to keep shortages alive in order to produce excessive prices and profits. Buyers should avoid buying in gray or black markets as much as possible, in part, to discourage the continued existence of such markets.

- The firm should establish an allocation program that decides which finished products get which raw materials in short supply.

SUMMARY

Purchasing should be a key member of the corporate planning function. Corporate goals and objectives are the key input to purchasing's strategic plans and actions. Purchasing has information on the likely future availability of and potential price changes for material required by the firm. This information will impact on the firm's goals and objectives. Successful purchasing managers monitor their environments and prepare in advance for anticipated changes in their environments.

Purchasing managers, together with the rest of top management, must identify critical materials and take positive action to ensure the availability of such material in an uncertain future. Success in this area requires improved vendor relations, including a sharing of planning data.

A good supplier is an invaluable resource. Such suppliers assist their customers with product developments, value analysis, and timely delivery of the desired level of quality. Many benefits accrue from continuing buyer-supplier relations. These benefits flow to both parties. At the same time, care must be taken to ensure that neither party becomes complacent. Some degree of supplier turnover may be necessary to keep suppliers alert, competitive, and willing to provide better quality and service.

A program to develop and qualify new vendors is far more efficient and less costly than is the common hit-or-miss approach. The management of vendors also requires attention. Vendor performance information is an essential tool for timely delivery of the right quality. This performance information also is useful during subsequent source selections and negotiations.

The purchasing department has a significant responsibility for the firm's reputation for honesty, ethics, and sound business relations. This responsibility calls for the development and management of standards of conduct applicable to all involved in the procurement process.

The firm has the responsibility for promptly informing all firms that have submitted bids when an award is made. Also, the purchasing department must take responsibility for the integrity of the competitive bidding process.

Trade relations or reciprocity may *appear* to be attractive ways to increase sales. Both legal and economic considerations must be carefully investigated before entering into trade relations. Reciprocity is neither a purchasing nor a marketing problem: it is an issue to be decided by top management.

A well-run purchasing department has a number of tools at its disposal for dealing with shortages. Many defensive actions should be taken to avoid or minimize the impact of potential shortages. These actions range from a good value analysis effort, to supplying assistance to the firm's suppliers, to the establishment of an allocation program.

Periodically, we should review how well we are doing things with an emphasis on progress achieved and new challenges to be met. In the next and concluding chapter, we look at the elements of an audit of the integrated procurement system.

chapter fourteen

THE PROCUREMENT AUDIT

It is Monday morning, April 1. Ted Jones, newly appointed vice president of operations, enters his corner office at Eagle Towers. He greets his secretary who congratulates him on his promotion. Ted strides to his desk, sits down, and turns to look out at the city and the lake beyond. His mind takes him back to a time four years ago. Things were not so satisfying then. After two years as purchasing manager of the Eagle Manufacturing Company, Ted had felt more like a firefighter than an executive. He thought of that fateful day in September when he had lunch with Rolland Hall, purchasing manager at Goliath Enterprises. During lunch, Ted had described some of his problems and frustrations at Eagle. Rolland had suggested that Ted sell his management on the need for a procurement audit. Rolland gave Ted the name of a consultant who specialized in procurement.

Ted met with the consultant, Dr. Eric E. Erickson, one of the nation's leading procurement authorities, to discuss the scope and cost of such an audit. Next, Ted met with Ian Montgomery, president of Eagle, to outline his thoughts on the desirability of a procurement audit. Mr. Montgomery was most enthusiastic. In fact, he said, "I've had a feeling that something needs to be done in this area. Let's get on with it."

A few days later, Dr. Erickson met with Mr. Montgomery. The two discussed the scope of a procurement audit. Then they talked about the need for top management's support both in conducting the audit and in implementing the recommendations. The following day, Mr. Montgomery called a special staff meeting of his department heads in which he described his concern over the cost of material expenditures, the need for improved product quality, and his belief that productivity both in manufacturing and the rest of the organization could be improved. Mr. Montgomery then introduced Dr. Erickson and requested that he be given total cooperation with the forthcoming procurement audit.

During the ensuing six weeks, Dr. Erickson conducted his audit. He found a good level of competence and dedication in most areas under review. But it soon became apparent that the majority of departments appeared to be optimizing their own efficiency, with little awareness of the effect of their actions on other departments or on Eagle as a whole.

On the completion of his audit, Dr. Erickson met first with Mr. Montgomery and then jointly with the president and his department heads. Dr. Erickson described and discussed his findings and recommendations. Two of the key recommendations were (1) the establishment of a project team to develop and implement an integrated procurement system tailored to Eagle's situation and (2) the establishment of challenging, but attainable, objectives. These objectives were to be in the areas of material expenditures, improved product quality, and increased productivity. After considerable discussion, Mr. Montgomery established a task force consisting of the directors of marketing, engineering, manufacturing, and purchasing, with Ted Jones as chairman. Ted was to report weekly to Mr. Montgomery on the task force's progress.

As Ted had anticipated, the biggest difficulty encountered was in the area of the engineering-purchasing interface. Once Grant Richards, the director of engineering, was aware of the need for improved coordination and greater purchasing involvement in the design process, he became a dedicated member of the task force. Several actions were taken to overcome the previously existing situation. Purchasing received approval to hire four materials engineers. Two engineers were "promoted" to two of these positions, and two experienced materials engineers were recruited from outside. Two experienced buyers were co-located in the engineering department. The buyers assisted design engineers by advising them on the procurement implications of different materials under consideration. A system of formal reviews was established. During the reviews, representatives of engineering, marketing, manufacturing, quality assurance, and purchasing reviewed all designs prior to manufacture or purchase.

The task group oversaw establishment of a make-or-buy committee. A value analysis (VA) committee was established and active in-house and vendor VA programs were instituted. Cooperation with marketing and production planning resulted in better purchasing lead time.

Ted had much to do in his own department. In addition to the four new material engineers, three expeditors were hired. Increased and improved training was implemented. Better sourcing, usually the result of an increased level of competition, took place. Professional price analysis and negotiations became the norm. Late deliveries became the exception. A strategic material plan was developed in cooperation with marketing, engineering, and manufacturing. Purchasing became a member of the long-range planning process.

Engineering, manufacturing, quality assurance, and purchasing collaborated to improve the quality of incoming materials. Productivity, sales, and profits all increased handsomely.

Dr. Erickson had been invited back for a follow-up audit two years after his first visit. Areas requiring further attention were identified. A much shorter list of recommendations was left with top management. It was agreed that, due to changing business conditions and personnel changes, the audits would continue on a semiannual basis.

Ted's secretary coughed discreetly, bringing him back to the present. She indicated that Dick James, director of purchasing at the All American Test Company, had called asking if a luncheon could be arranged with Ted this week. It seems that Mr. James is having firefighting problems at All American and would like to pick Ted's brain.

The procurement audit is a guide to management highlighting problems and opportunities. It determines how well the procurement system is performing and identifies areas requiring managerial attention. Underlying the procurement audit is the belief that the procurement system should be a major contributor to the organization's profitability and survival.

The procurement audit is extremely broad, encompassing all aspects of the procurement system. To ensure objectivity, the audit should be conducted by an outsider, either someone in the firm not involved in the procurement system or a qualified outsider. The procurement audit is a diagnostic device that identifies opportunities for increased profitability. As such, it should be conducted on a periodic basis. The procurement audit must be systematic and comprehensive. The following questions form the basis for such an audit.

ORGANIZATION, POLICIES, AND PROCEDURES

- Is top management aware of the *increase* in *profits* and related benefits resulting from an integrated procurement system (IPS)?
- Does engineering understand its role in the IPS?
- Do production planning and inventory control understand their roles in the IPS?

- Does operations understand its role in the IPS?
- Does quality assurance understand its role in the IPS?
- Are procurement objectives in each part of the procurement system consistent with corporate objectives?
- Is there a systematic program to broadcast examples of the benefits resulting from interdepartmental collaboration on procurement requirements?
- Has engineering been successfully integrated into the procurement system?
- If the firm operates under a materials management concept, are members of the material management organization involved in the appropriate stages of the requirements process?
- Are inventory management policies and procedures realistic?
- Is purchasing *actively* involved in the corporate planning process?
- Does purchasing receive and take timely action on the firm's long-range plans as they affect supply?
- Does purchasing monitor the supply environment?
- Does purchasing provide those responsible for long-range planning input in the areas of strategic opportunities arising from new materials, products, and technology; anticipated shortages; and anticipated price increases?
- Does purchasing notify marketing of changes in the price and availability of materials that would affect quotations, current selling prices, and delivery?
- Do policies exist that adequately cover all important aspects of the procurement process?
- Is purchasing's authority and responsibility clearly defined?
- Do policies, procedures, and managerial checks exist to ensure that purchasing actions conform to corporate objectives and policies?
- Are periodic analyses conducted to ensure the most cost-effective level of centralization of purchasing?
- Are there documented purchasing plans and strategies?
- Is the organization of the purchasing department tailored to balance purchasing objectives and the resources and skills available?
- If investment in additional resources and skills would be cost effective, has the purchasing manager obtained management support?
- Is documentation within purchasing adequate without being excessive?
- Are procedures for small purchases efficient?

- Does an up-to-date purchasing manual exist?
- Has the purchasing manual been distributed throughout the firm with a directive from top management requiring compliance?
- Have necessary procedures been developed and implemented to minimize or eliminate decentralized ("back door") purchasing?

THE REQUIREMENTS PROCESS

- Does purchasing contribute to the process of establishing price, performance, timeliness, quality, and reliability objectives during the design process?
- Does purchasing provide input on the economy and availability implications of the materials and subassemblies to be purchased under alternate design approaches?
- During the design process, is purchasing invited to comment on the probability of obtaining the desired level of quality of purchased material?
- Are the manufacturing productivity implications of different materials considered during the design of new products?
- Does quality assurance review proposed design specifications and manufacturing plans to ensure that the quality called for in the marketplace is the quality that will result if engineering's design is followed?
- Does purchasing participate in engineering design reviews?
- Is there an active engineering change management program?
- Is there an active standardization program?
- When developing or adopting purchase descriptions, are restrictive features that would limit competition avoided?
- Are sound policies used to guide initiators of requirements on selection of the most appropriate purchase description?
- Is procurement research employed to investigate the availability of commercial products before employing unique design specifications?
- Are the productivity implications of different supplies (such as copy paper and floor wax) considered when determining supply requirements?
- Are sales force estimates a reliable basis for production plans?
- Does marketing provide realistic planning lead time for changes in demand?

- Are two or more forecasting techniques employed in an effort to develop realistic forecasts?
- Is purchasing provided with advanced information on new requirements so that it may develop adequate competition?
- During production planning, is consideration given to possible constraints posed by supplier capacity?
- If an MRP system is employed, are the delivery lead times contained in the inventory status records realistic?
- When determining inventory levels, is consideration given to the variable cost of purchase order preparation and related administrative costs, quantity discounts, transportation costs, the cost implications in production and marketing of different inventory levels, as well as inventory carrying costs?
- Does the organization maintain a current inventory catalog?
- Are future anticipated prices and availabilities of required materials considered when determining inventory levels?
- Are adequate statements of work incorporating appropriate inspection procedures developed for service requirements?
- When developing service requirements, does the requestor identify the organization's primary objective(s)?
- Is productivity properly addressed during the determination of plant and equipment requirements?
- When the firm is developing capital equipment requirements, is purchasing responsive to its customers' needs for technical, delivery, and price information on available products?
- When developing requirements for capital equipment, are performance specifications considered and used, when appropriate?
- When developing purchase descriptions for capital equipment, is action taken to ensure that the description is precise enough to satisfy the organization's needs without unduly restricting competition?
- If equipment specifications are developed under contract, does the purchasing firm obtain title to the resulting data?
- Docs it retain the right *and the flexibility* to obtain competition for the fabrication of the required equipment?
- Are purchasing, plant engineering, and plant maintenance involved in the development of detailed facility requirements?
- Are the alternative methods of purchasing building construction all considered before selection of the appropriate method?
- Does purchasing challenge requirements that do not appear to be economical or otherwise not in the firm's best interests?

SELECTING THE RIGHT SOURCE

- Are make-or-buy decisions made by upper management?
- Are all relevant factors considered when conducting a make-or-buy analysis?
- Are make-or-buy analyses conducted on service requirements?
- Are make-or-buy analyses conducted on all new requirements?
- Are make-or-buy analyses reviewed on a periodic basis?
- When participating in make-or-buy analyses, does purchasing ensure that accurate and realistic costs are obtained from prospective suppliers?
- When calculating the firm's cost to "make" an item or service, are *all* relevant costs included?
- Is a make-or-buy analysis conducted on all significant components of new products?
- Are make-or-buy analyses conducted before a decision is made to perform services in house or to obtain them under contract?
- Does a sound vendor development program exist?
- Are suppliers rated on their performance?
- Are suppliers rewarded for good performance and punished for poor performance?
- Do policies exist to ensure that vendors are treated with courtesy and respect?
- If a trade relations program exists, does purchasing provide input to top management on potential disadvantages?
- Are vendors prequalified before being invited to bid?
- When developing a bidders' list, is consideration given to the services required (delivery, maintenance support, technical advice, etc.)?
- Are sufficient vendors invited to bid to ensure free and adequate competition?
- Is dual sourcing employed when appropriate?
- Does purchasing actively avoid or minimize situations in which it assumes a moral responsibility for the economic well-being of its suppliers?
- Are preaward surveys conducted when purchasing items or services critical to the firm's well-being?
- Does purchasing solicit and obtain timely support from other departments for required preaward surveys?

- Are preaward surveys well planned and conducted in a professional manner?
- Are foreign sources invited to bid when appropriate?
- When buying from overseas sources, is professional advice obtained on the issue of currency exchange?
- When considering a purchase from a foreign source, are all potential incremental costs considered (transportation, insurance, travel and administrative, capital tied up under advanced payments or letters of credit, buffer stocks and the implications of political and economic uncertainty)?
- Is competitive bidding the preferred method of source selection when the prerequisites for its use are satisfied?
- When competitive bidding is employed, is award made to the low bidder without further *price* negotiations?
- Is a mathematical rating system employed when several factors must be considered in source selection?
- When selecting a source to perform services, does the buyer focus on the organization's *primary* objective(s)?
- Are purchase orders and contracts for services structured to motivate the supplier to concentrate on the organization's primary objective(s)?
- When selecting the supplier of capital equipment, are factors such as the reliability of the prospective seller, his or her willingness and ability to provide required technical assistance, his or her ability to perform required repairs quickly, the timely availability of spare parts, and the seller's service history considered?
- When purchasing capital equipment, is a strong warranty clause included in the contract?
- When requesting bids for equipment, does the purchasing firm establish that its terms and conditions will govern in any resulting purchase order?
- Are all appropriate standard and nonstandard issues addressed in these terms and conditions?
- Do requests for bids for equipment include (as separate items) prices for periodic and emergency maintenance, repairs, and spare parts?
- When selecting the supplier of capital equipment, is the total cost of ownership considered?
- Does purchasing periodically analyze its suppliers' ability to meet the firm's long-term needs?
- If present suppliers appear to be unlikely to be able to meet future requirements, is timely action taken to develop the required capability?

GETTING THE RIGHT PRICE

- Is *overall* corporate profitability the key factor in purchasing decisions?
- Do buyers attempt to obtain a reasonable degree of competition to establish a fair and reasonable price?
- Are the cost and service implications of alternate shipping methods considered when making awards?
- Is a price analysis conducted on all purchases?
- Is a determination made that the price is fair and reasonable prior to award of all orders?
- Are accurate engineered cost estimates available for price analysis?
- Is cost analysis conducted when price analysis is inadequate?
- When it is anticipated that cost analysis and/or negotiations may be required, does the request for quotations require a detailed cost estimate in support of the bid or proposal?
- Under the foregoing conditions and also when other than a firm fixed price method of compensation will be used, is the right of access to the prospective supplier's records established in the request for quotation and resulting contract?
- Does profit vary with the amount of risk, the supplier's reliability, the amount of technical input and innovation, the size of the order, and current supply and demand patterns?
- Do all negotiators understand and use the principle of the learning curve when appropriate?
- Is the right method of compensation used in all situations?
- Is the right type of contract employed to purchase continuing requirements?
- Are negotiations employed when appropriate?
- When negotiations require a team approach, does the buyer function as team captain?
- Is adequate preparation made for successful negotiations including the gaining of an understanding on the technical and production implications of the item, a study of available cost and price data, and an analysis of the buyer's and the seller's strengths and weaknesses?
- When preparing to negotiate with someone from another culture, does the buyer study his or her opposite's culture and make all of the *extra* preparation required for a successful negotiation?
- Are realistic objectives established prior to face-to-face negotiations?

- Are target objectives and ranges of acceptable outcomes established on all critical issues prior to face-to-face negotiations?
- Are all negotiators adequately trained in the use of negotiating tactics?
- Are sound tactics employed to achieve the negotiator's objectives?
- Is cost analysis conducted when appropriate?
- When cost analysis is employed, is it complemented by price analysis?

SUBCONTRACT ADMINISTRATION

- Is subcontract administration properly planned and prepared for (including necessary language in the request for quotations and resulting orders or contracts)?
- Is the right to data required for subcontract administration established in the request for quotations and resulting orders?
- Does a cooperative attitude exist between purchasing and quality assurance in qualifying new sources, monitoring suppliers' in-plant quality performance, and monitoring the quality of incoming material?
- Are all buyers and subcontract administrators aware of their firms' quality rights under the Uniform Commercial Code?
- When purchase orders or subcontracts are issued, does the buyer determine if routine or special subcontract administration is required?
- Is progress information posted and closely monitored?
- Is such information complemented by appropriate field inspection visits?
- In situations where the supplier's production *flows* into the purchaser's *ongoing* manufacturing operation, does an integrated communications system exist?
- Is a decision on the degree of quality inspection required made on each order or contract?

OTHER IMPORTANT ISSUES

- Does purchasing actively monitor, gather, and analyze relevant environmental information that may affect prices and the availability of present or potential materials?

- Do good communications exist between purchasing and its vendors so that important information (new products, potential price changes, capacity, etc.) that impacts the procurement strategy is obtained in a timely manner?
- Does an active VA program exist?
- Does the VA program have the support of top management?
- Are personnel from purchasing, engineering, operations, and marketing involved in the VA program?
- Is there an active in-house VA program?
- Is there a sound vendor VA program?
- Is there a high sense of cooperation between purchasing and other components of the IPS?
- Is morale of members of the IPS acceptable?
- Have standards of conduct been established and communicated to all personnel in the firm having a role in the procurement system (including purchasing, design, production, and inspection personnel)?
- Is the organization of the purchasing department appropriate for the situation?
- Are assigned material engineers experienced and properly trained?
- Are buyers experienced and properly trained?
- Are subcontract administrators (expediters) experienced and properly trained?
- Are purchasing personnel actively involved in continuing educational programs?
- Are purchasing personnel encouraged to obtain their C.P.M. certificates?
- Do promotional opportunities exist (both within the purchasing department and into and out of purchasing)?
- Are the purchasing manager and his or her staff familiar with the various tools that can be employed to reduce the impact of shortages on the firm?
- Is purchasing department efficiency measured against previously established objectives or standards?
- Are variance reports showing the difference between standard and actual costs used in the purchasing department?
- Is delivery performance monitored and compared with previously established objectives?
- Is quality performance monitored?
- Is there a procurement training and development program for *all* individuals involved in the procurement system?

- Are all purchasing personnel aware of their role in maintaining the firm's reputation for honesty, ethics, and considerate business relations?
- Are the salaries of purchasing personnel adequate to provide a reasonable standard of living without recourse to "free lunches"?
- Are buyers aware of the importance and the contribution of voluntary collaboration or continuing supplier relations?
- Have realistic objectives been established for improvements in the IPS for the next reporting period?

A FEW CLOSING WORDS

The need for a proactive approach to procurement has never been greater. Procurement will become proactive—with or without us. It is our choice to be included or to go the way of the green-eye-shaded bookkeeper.

We have the insight, the tools, and the ability to implement those concepts and principles which apply to our organizations. All that is required is a "can do" attitude, top management's support, and a lot of elbow grease.

Good luck!

INDEX